Subjectivity and Decolonisation in the Post-Independence Novel and Film

Subjectivity and Decolonisation in the Post-Independence Novel and Film

Sarah Jilani

EDINBURGH
University Press

Edinburgh University Press is one of the leading university presses in the UK. We publish academic books and journals in our selected subject areas across the humanities and social sciences, combining cutting-edge scholarship with high editorial and production values to produce academic works of lasting importance. For more information visit our website: edinburghuniversitypress.com

© Sarah Jilani, 2024, 2025

Grateful acknowledgement is made to the sources listed in the List of Illustrations for permission to reproduce material previously published elsewhere. Every effort has been made to trace the copyright holders, but if any have been inadvertently overlooked, the publisher will be pleased to make the necessary arrangements at the first opportunity.

Edinburgh University Press Ltd
13 Infirmary Street
Edinburgh EH1 1LT

First published in hardback by Edinburgh University Press 2024

Typeset in 10.5/13pt Bembo
by Cheshire Typesetting Ltd, Cuddington, Cheshire

A CIP record for this book is available from the British Library

ISBN 978 1 3995 0728 8 (hardback)
ISBN 978 1 3995 0729 5 (paperback)
ISBN 978 1 3995 0730 1 (webready PDF)
ISBN 978 1 3995 0731 8 (epub)

The right of Sarah Jilani to be identified as the author of this work has been asserted in accordance with the Copyright, Designs and Patents Act 1988, and the Copyright and Related Rights Regulations 2003 (SI No. 2498).

Contents

List of Figures	vi
Acknowledgements	vii
Introduction	1
1. Reconciling Us To Ourselves: Decolonisation and the Question of Subjectivity	32
2. Women and Anti-Colonial Nationalisms: Gendering Subjectivity in Satyajit Ray's *Home and the World* and Ngũgĩ wa Thiong'o's *A Grain of Wheat*	51
3. Neocolonialism's Subjects: Complicity and Resistance in Ousmane Sembène's *Xala* and Ayi Kwei Armah's *The Beautyful Ones Are Not Yet Born*	73
4. History From Within: Violence and Subjective Experience in Ritwik Ghatak's *The Cloud-Capped Star* and Buchi Emecheta's *Destination Biafra*	98
5. Emplacing the Self: Environment and Labour in Kamala Markandaya's *Nectar in a Sieve* and Souleymane Cissé's *Work*	121
Conclusion	147
Bibliography	155
Filmography	182
Index	183

Figures

Figure 2.1 Our Struggle. *Ghare Baire [Home and the World]*.
Dir. Satyajit Ray, 1984   65
Figure 2.2 Textiles of the home. *Ghare Baire [Home and the World]*.
Dir. Satyajit Ray, 1984   67
Figure 2.3 Colonial capital. *Ghare Baire [Home and the World]*.
Dir. Satyajit Ray, 1984   67
Figure 2.4 The humanist sahib. *Ghare Baire [Home and the World]*.
Dir. Satyajit Ray, 1984   68
Figure 3.1 Beggars of Dakar. *Xala*. Dir. Ousmane Sembène, 1975   79
Figure 3.2 The Franco-American. *Xala*. Dir. Ousmane Sembène,
1975   82
Figure 3.3 Rama's mobility. *Xala*. Dir. Ousmane Sembène, 1975   85
Figure 4.1 Landscapes of loss. *Meghe Dhaka Tara [The Cloud-Capped Star]*. Dir. Ritwik Ghatak, 1960   102
Figure 4.2 Taran's nostalgia. *Meghe Dhaka Tara [The Cloud-Capped Star]*. Dir. Ritwik Ghatak, 1960   103
Figure 4.3 Neeta's burden. *Meghe Dhaka Tara [The Cloud-Capped Star]*. Dir. Ritwik Ghatak, 1960   107
Figure 5.1 The inspection. *Baara [Work]*. Dir. Souleymane Cissé,
1978   136
Figure 5.2 Bodily labours. *Baara [Work]*. Dir. Souleymane Cissé,
1978   137
Figure 5.3 Architectures of independence. *Baara [Work]*.
Dir. Souleymane Cissé, 1978   140
Figure 5.4 Françafrique. *Baara [Work]*. Dir. Souleymane Cissé,
1978   142

Acknowledgements

I would like to thank the following people who helped make this book possible. For guidance and feedback throughout its earlier iteration as a doctoral thesis, Professor Priyamvada Gopal, Dr Chana Morgenstern, Dr Chris Warnes and Professor Madhu Krishnan. Thank you also to the financial support of the Arts and Humanities Research Council UK, the Isaac Newton Trust, the Faculty of English at the University of Cambridge, and King's College, Cambridge, during those years. Especial thanks to my former colleagues Dr Joe Shaughnessy and Dr Sara Kazmi for their friendship, insight and support throughout the development of this project.

At Edinburgh University Press, my gratitude to Gillian Leslie for guiding the proposal for this book through to a second iteration, peer review, and contract – and to Sam Johnson, then later Kelly O'Brien, Fiona Screen, and Grace Balfour-Harle, for assisting its progress assiduously. Thank you also to the Department of Media, Culture and Creative Industries at City, University of London for funds spent on indexing and the purchase of film stills, helpfully provided by Criterion. My gratitude to Rachel Goodyear for compiling the index.

I am indebted to those whose input over the past three years has enabled the conditions that made writing this book possible. Months of applications and interviews for research fellowships and lectureships coincided with writing its proposal, during which Professor Judith Buchanan, Dr Gerard McCann, Professor Ankhi Mukherjee, Professor Emma Hunter, Professor Claire Chambers, Dr Uzoma Esonwanne and Dr Anna Bernard generously gave of their time and advice. Thank you to Professor Patricia Moran and colleagues at City for bringing those applications to a welcome end. My appreciation also extends to the AHRC/BBC New Generation Thinkers scheme, and Robyn Read, for enabling me to bring some of the research in this book to Radio 3 listeners.

Endless gratitude to my parents, Gia and Gönül Jilani, for the love and support they have set me up with for life. Thank you to my husband Othman Al Bahri for being my port in the storm and my discerning reader, all-in-one. And finally my gratitude to some of the past thinkers and writers noted in the bibliography, whose words and actions reached across time and space, and changed me.

Introduction

In a scene from the 1967 novel *A Grain of Wheat* by the Kenyan writer Ngũgĩ wa Thiong'o, a man thought to be an anti-colonial hero confesses to Independence Day crowds that he betrayed them.

> As soon as the first words were out, Mugo felt light. A load of many years was lifted from his shoulders. So he was responsible for whatever he had done in the past, for whatever he would do in the future. The consciousness frightened him. (232)

The reclusive Mugo's confession, and his subsequent feelings of relief and fear, suggest his turbulent psychic state could not have been resolved internally. He lives under the burden of recent history, which Ngũgĩ suggests renders him no more or less guilty than any other participant in the Kenyan anti-colonial struggle. But he has also been suffering from a self-imposed social isolation. In this climactic scene, Mugo chooses to risk facing the consequences of his actions in order to arrive at a different relationship with himself, and ultimately, with his community. This is 'frightening' in its new responsibilities towards self and others. But Mugo returns to partake of the everyday, and in sharing his shame, a 'load of many years' is lifted. Weaving remembered past events into its present-day narrative, Ngũgĩ's novel is, in great part, about subjectivity – specifically, how it is transformed by the politically, socially and emotionally complex demands of decolonisation.

The self has been an important problem for thinkers and actors of anti-colonial struggle. The unreconciled paradoxes of a self 'living in a world that exists for others' (Young 2003, 1) – a world shaped by colonialism – has given rise to questions of why, and how, to change that world itself. Space and place were the objects of colonial domination, but the reformation of minds was where subjectivities could be and were shaped. From the Christian missions and schools established in African colonies, to the creation of classes 'Indian in blood and colour, but English in tastes, in opinions, in morals and in intellect' (Macaulay 1835, 34), the subjugation of the colonised via the refusal, manipulation and re-constitution of their subjectivities was common to the varied practices of European colonialisms. It was sometimes manifest in the instilling of a sense of inferiority via a colonial education that, in Frantz Fanon's words, would 'hammer into the heads of the indigenous population that if the colonist were to leave they would regress into barbarism, degradation, and bestiality' (1961, 149). Sometimes it would manifest through discursive and material machinations, whereby the oppressor's history became the 'natural order' of things, and the oppressor the normative subject. Racialising sexuality, politics, society and economy where it went, colonial rule also elevated those colonial subjects who could demonstrate they had internalised these teachings well. They would often be put in positions – educational, judicial, medical, administrative – where they could reproduce the colonial practices, knowledge systems, and social hierarchies they had internalised. Re-constituting subjectivities was, as Tejumola Olaniyan observes, a method of 'securing discursive reproduction and stability' (2008, 273) for colonial rule – as such, however, it was also always a site of resistance and refusal.

The mid-twentieth-century period of decolonisation and independence, marked by the birth and consolidation of new nation-states, was a time when the above confrontation took on a new urgency. Historic decolonisation in the mid-twentieth century pursued projects (usually state-led) that – often genuinely, sometimes allegedly – looked for transformations out of the social, political and economic structures of extraction and dependency that European colonialisms had implemented. These projects were primarily nation-building ones, sometimes occurring along lines of capitalist globalisation or socialist internationalisation.[1] But transformations out of colonial structures were largely 'arrested', in Biodun Jeyifo's (1990) words, by a variety of local and global forces. There are many historical culprits of this arrest that are beyond the scope of this book to analyse. Some of the factors widely studied include CIA-led destabilisation in post-independence nation-states (usually with anti-Communist intentions); the implementation of neocolonial dependency via debt and IMF structural adjustment programmes; the failures of postcolonial governments; and the fracturing and pacification of anti-colonial nationalisms, revolutionary militancy and Afro-Asianism in the then so-called Third

---

[1] On nation-statism with internationalisation as a far from contradictory tendency, see also Chris Harman (1991) and Immanuel Wallerstein (1992).

World.² Fundamentally related to these, though harder to define, were setbacks in what Ngũgĩ brings under the umbrella of his evocative phrase 'decolonising the mind' (1986). This problem, which does not exist apart from the material forces above, is this book's guiding concern.

Just as colonialism evolved the material conditions that served it over time, bringing the world into what Kehinde Andrews calls a 'new age of empire' (2021) today, so did it shape and re-shape people's subjectivities. For example, the metropole-educated native elites that British and French colonialisms created in India and West Africa respectively were more often than not cultural Europhiles, and after the independences, frequently turned economic compradors. In positions of leadership after the independences, rare were those who developed a programme of decolonisation rooted in first-hand knowledge of the conditions of the majority of their people. Some who attempted to, like Patrice Lumumba of the Democratic Republic of the Congo and Thomas Sankara of Burkina Faso, were assassinated upon demanding resource sovereignty and debt cancellation, too soon for their policies to bear full fruit.³ Others, like the poet-president Léopold Sédar Senghor of Senegal, never fully positioned himself outside of the colonial framework, 'taking up one trumpet or the other ... A black among blacks or a French-speaking person among francophones' (Kesteloot and Kennedy 1990, 51). While to a considerable degree less influenced than their native bourgeoisies by a European colonial education and worldview, the majority of colonised peoples were also not exempt from the problem of 'decolonising the mind'. As the structure of colonial violence produces its own hegemonic culture with the help of print and audio media, this cultural production 'penetrates the body and the mind of the colonized and the colonizer, shaping their interiorized subjectivities accordingly' (Sharifi and Chabot 2019, 253). In *A Dying Colonialism* (1959), Fanon writes: 'The Algerian people have thus decided that, until independence, French colonialism will be innocent of none of the wounds inflicted upon its body and its consciousness' (118). Although he is speaking in relation to a specific moment and movement, he helpfully names two sites of the effects of colonialism that cross class demarcations: 'body' and 'consciousness'. Colonialism's exploitation of human labour was in a mutually effectual relation with the exercise of power over people's ways of understanding and producing

---

² See also Susan Williams (2021) and Vincent Bevins (2020) on US destabilisation methods in the decolonising world; Rocío Zambrana (2021) on debt as neocolonialism; and Carolien Stolte and Su Lin Lewis, eds. (2022) on Cold War Afro-Asianism.

³ See also Emmanuel Gerard and Bruce Kuklick (2015) on Lumumba and Brian J. Peterson on Sankara (2021).

themselves (this notion of the 'production' of subjectivity will be returned to). If the 'body' of the colonised in Fanon's words, racialised and belaboured, evidences the violence of a colonialism that pretends to innocence, then as does the 'wound-inflicted ... consciousness' of the colonised. The link between them renders 'decolonising the mind' an inseparable component of decolonisation. Whether or not this was understood or pursued in practice by post-independence leaders of new African and Asian nation-states, decolonisation needed to include the means for people to re-constitute their subjectivities.

This problem lends itself to methodologies and frameworks found within many fields of study, especially Sociology, Philosophy and Psychology. However, understanding production in Marx's sense (1844, 1847, 1932) – not just as work, but also 'in terms of the myriad ways in which actions, habits, and language produce effects, including effects on subjectivity, ways of perceiving, understanding, and relating to the world' (Read 2022, 342) – opens up an interdisciplinary vista. This vista must and can include the methods, concerns, theoretical insights and critical possibilities found in Comparative Literature and Film Studies. As Jason Read summarises, the production, shaping, or constitution of subjectivities can be understood as a simultaneous, dual-pronged process: 'the manner in which subjectivity is produced and the manner in which subjectivity is productive, not just in terms of value or wealth, but in terms of its general capacity to produce effects' (343). The simultaneity of this dual process means that 'decolonising the mind' is necessarily about transforming the structures that sustain a (neo)colonial world, and vice versa. This involves understanding the particularities of capitalism in the colonial and postcolonial world, as in Fanon's invitation to 'stretch Marxism' (1961, 40). But it also means understanding the psycho-political effects of these structures as they are lived, understood and narrated by people.[4]

Experiencing the 'End of Empire'

In search of these psycho-political effects, this book examines eight diverse but related narratives from Africa and South Asia. These texts will take us from the 1950s to the 1980s: Kamala Markandaya's *Nectar in a Sieve* (1954), Ritwik Ghatak's *The Cloud-Capped Star* (1960), Ngũgĩ wa Thiong'o's *A Grain of Wheat* (1967), Ayi Kwei Armah's *The Beautyful Ones Are Not Yet Born* (1969), Ousmane Sembène's *Xala* (1975), Souleymane Cissé's *Work* (1978), Buchi Emecheta's *Destination Biafra* (1982) and Satyajit Ray's *Home and the*

---

[4] I use 'psycho-politics' in Derek Hook's (2004) sense throughout his analyses of Fanon's and Steve Biko's writings.

World (1984). There is much literary and cinematic work from Africa and South Asia within these post-independence decades that can be considered with critically rich results vis-à-vis subjectivity, from Chinua Achebe's novel *A Man of the People* (1966), which speaks closely to Chapter 3's discussion of native elites, to Mrinal Sen's cinematic Calcutta trilogy (1970–6), which takes up post-Partition urban experience as Chapter 4's cinematic text does. As Ruth Craggs and Claire Wintle point out in *Cultures of Decolonisation* (2015), 'literary, cinematic and visual texts, as well as material cultures and institutions, have provided a voice for and insight into those experiencing the "end of empire" in the colonies' (7) – and these experiences have been as diverse as their representations in mid-century African and South Asian texts. My selection situates Indian independence in 1945 as a starting point for the first post-independence decade of cultural production, and stretches into the next three decades, which saw independences and nation consolidation proceed across Africa and South Asia. Together, these texts encompass years that can also be understood as a period of fallout from the terms, trajectories and conditions under which independences occurred. They not only encode the complex and often contradictory social, political and economic changes that sought various forms of postcolonial nation-building, capitalist and otherwise, but also tragedies that were directly related to post-independence border-making, such as the devastating 1967–1970 Nigerian Civil War (the setting of Buchi Emecheta's *Destination Biafra*) and the violent events of 1947 in the Subcontinent (what haunts Ritwik Ghatak's *The Cloud-Capped Star*). Markandaya, Ghatak, Ngũgĩ, Armah, Sembène, Cissé, Emecheta and Ray present multi-faceted narratives that capture the sheer range of historical contexts and formal approaches via which these complex experiences of the end of empire, and the birth of the postcolonial nation-state, were interrogated through storytelling. Defining and locating the many ways in which colonialism remains internalised and reproduced after independence becomes, in these eight texts, one of many things they do – and yet it is closely related to, and intersects with, all of the social, political and economic contexts of decolonisation.

Indian decolonisation and its aftermaths, from various standpoints, backdrops Markandaya's novel, and Ghatak's and Ray's films. Markandaya's *Nectar in a Sieve* is set in an unnamed Indian village in the 1950s and follows the protagonist Rukmani, a tenant farmer, from childhood through marriage and into widowhood. Meanwhile, the novel depicts a systemic change in post-independence India, wherein rural industrialisation undertaken by the centralised powers of the new Indian nation-state is complicating, but not entirely displacing, semi-feudal power structures. In this way, the novel also comments on the psychic experience of what Neil Lazarus (2018) calls the 'second moment' of the generalisation of commodity production and wage labour across the globe after the independences. 'Governed by the experience of "globalization" – of capitalist modernization in its phase of consolidation, regularisation, and global dispersal' (Lazarus 2018, 165–73), the global peasantry, far from caught in a clash between the unstable categories of 'traditional' and 'modern', has been very much part of the story of capitalist accumulation. In *Nectar* we see that peasant life in post-independence India is particularly subject to the demands and pressures of this 'second moment'. Markandaya's protagonist is temporally and spatially at the heart of an Indian national project that has chosen to pursue capitalist industrialisation, leaving the redistributive promises of decolonisation on uncertain ground. In addition to commenting on gender, ecology, and the relationship between subjectivities and their environments, that the novel articulates the psycho-political experience of this global mid-century economic shift is part of its enduring achievement.

Ghatak's *Cloud-Capped Star* adds to this picture the fallout from Partition in the urban and semi-urban India of his time. The Partition of the Subcontinent into India, West Pakistan and East Pakistan in 1947 saw civil conflict, mass forced migration and territorial re-configurations. Involved with the Indian Peoples' Theatre Association as an actor, playwright and director until 1954, Ghatak was deeply affected by the Partition of his home region of Bengal into India and East Pakistan, becoming a refugee in the 1940s when he had to leave Dhaka for Kolkata. His own subsequent state of poverty, and his disillusionment with the Communist Party of India (from which he was expelled in 1955), gave forth a cinematic vision that looked beyond nationalist optimism. Indeed, Ghatak's interest in Bengal's refugees like himself made for a cinematic practice that has been said to 'fatally undermine the nation-building project by displaying huge sections of people whose emotional roots are in land and property that are now to be considered a foreign, even an enemy, country' (Raychaudhuri 2009, 477). Emerging from this wider context, wherein the voices of the millions displaced and impoverished on the Subcontinent were often swallowed up by the rhetoric of independence – a 'tryst with destiny', in Nehru's abstract phrase (1947/2023) – Ghatak's use of setting and form in *Star* unearths the psychic suffering that resulted from Partition. The interiorised effects of Partition's intersecting oppressions – economic, gendered and political – encode, for him, the true impact that this seismic event had on his people throughout its subsequent decades.

Satyajit Ray's cinematic adaptation of Rabindranath Tagore's *Home and the World*, meanwhile, emerges in the aftermath of another socially traumatic period known as the Indian Emergency (1975–1977) and takes a longer view on the limits of post-independence nationalist rhetoric in a rapidly changing India.[5] Ray's film lands particularly on a key aporia in Indian anti-colonial nationalism: its failure to incorporate women into its (however flawed) vision of liberation. In this historical drama set in colonial Bengal during the nationalist Swadeshi movement of 1905–1917, the discourses of both colonial class norms and Indian anti-colonial nationalism are used politically and psychologically by the two male characters in order to delimit the impact of Swadeshi on Bimala, the story's female protagonist. Ray's adaptation takes important departures from Tagore's material to critique both the liberal humanism of Bimala's Anglicised husband Nikhil, and the self-serving patriotism of her love interest Sandip, uncovering anxieties around intersecting socio-sexual spheres during this moment in Indian anti-colonial nationalism. Yet this period drama also speaks beyond its pre-independence setting, resonating with the political context of Ray's final years in the early 1980s. These years in India marked the decisive end of a post-1945 period of Nehruvian development under the Congress Party with the assassination of his daughter Indira Gandhi in 1984, the year of the film's release. Sikh separatism and a rural Naxalite–Maoist insurgency had emerged as serious political forces, articulating various demands that intimidated the post-independence state. *Home and the World* illustrates how the post-independence Indian state's continued investment in patriarchy and caste is inextricable from a mutually beneficial relationship between upper-caste Indian leaders and the economy: a relationship that was transformed, not severed, with the coming of independence in 1945.

Culture was an evolving and dynamic terrain in the transition from colonial rule to self-rule in West Africa. The new governments of Mali, Senegal and Ghana looked to harness the arts, as well as architecture, in public displays of nation-building and national cohesion. After their independences in 1957 and in 1960 respectively, Kwame Nkrumah in Ghana and Modibo Keïta in Mali pursued infrastructural and economic regeneration projects, as well as cultural and educational ones. These were intended to consolidate national sovereignty but also to try and foster – often in a top-down manner – a sense of national unity in their populations of diverse ethnicities, languages and religious beliefs. In Nkrumah's Ghana, as George Hagan observes, public cultural display and the establishment of cultural institutions often 'generated a *philosophy* of an African personality' (original emphasis) (2005, 61), but not necessarily sustained and popular policies. Emerging from this landscape were works like Ayi Kwei Armah's novel *The Beautyful Ones Are Not Yet Born*, which marks perhaps

---

[5] See also Raita Merivirta (2019) on the cultural trauma of the Indian Emergency through a reading of five seminal novels.

the harshest of literary responses to post-independence nationhood among this book's case studies. Armah was one of the first African writers to question the meaning of independence from colonial rule and to address the continent's continuing dependence on the West. Born in 1939 to Fante-speaking parents in Takoradi, Ghana, his first novel is laden with the disappointment of the failed socialist promises of anti-colonial struggle. Centring his protagonist's subjective experience to the material conditions that Armah critiques, the novel, as Jarrod Dunham observes, also 'positions individual characters in relation to one another in interactions that mirror and amplify Armah's larger social concerns' (2012, 281). The transformation of Nkrumahism away from its initially revolutionary promise within the space of years weighs heavy on the protagonist, as the plot hurtles towards the moment (itself left unnamed) when Nkrumah was deposed in 1966 by the National Liberation Council in a *coup d'état*. While Armah illustrates how Nkrumahism was already failing the majority of Ghanaian people, the coup brings no sense of resolution or change. Nonetheless, by the end, the novel's protagonist has reached a state that has a certain ontological and existential dynamism, as he is able to see through the political machinations that are hurtling post-independence Ghana into new forms of dependency.

In Senegal, Léopold Sédar Senghor's *Négritude* movement (co-founded with Aimé Césaire) animated cultural activities such as the 1966 World Festival of Negro Arts – which Senghor envisioned as an expression of what he called 'the black soul', to mixed critical acclaim.[6] The Senegalese writer and filmmaker Ousmane Sembène won one of the Festival's literary prizes for his novella, *Le Mandat* (*The Money Order*), but was a vocal critic of *Négritude*. David Murphy argues that Senghor and Sembène were both 'compatriots and arch-enemies' in their mutual belief 'in the significance of culture as central to the development of post-independence Africa' and in their diverging views as to 'the modes of expression appropriate to this process' (2015, 3). Forged both through his own working-class experience as the son of a fisherman from Casamance and a dock worker in post-war Marseille, Sembène's Marxist commitments sat ill-at-ease with a discourse like that of *Négritude*. Its racial essentialism, Sembène felt, 'had no answers for a contemporary Africa emerging from the trauma of colonial rule' (Murphy 3). Adapted by Sembène for a mass audience from his own novel (Gugler and Diop 1998, 147), *Xala* (1975) is a satirical film that allows Sembène to raise some of these unanswered questions. It addresses three key facets to an encroaching neocolonialism in Senegal: land theft, the role of *la Francophonie*, and what can be called a crisis of subjectivity

---

[6] See also Ella Tsitsi Jaji (2014).

largely experienced by – but suffered beyond – Senegal's native elite. In *Xala*, Sembène grapples with the limits of seeking out one racial identity (Senghor's 'black soul') or one national culture, preferring to depict instead what Mike Wayne dubs a Lukácsian 'extensive totality of life' (2001, 39). *Xala* urges sight of the relationship between structures and subjectivities under conditions of neocolonialism, speaking to the configurations of power that authorise elites as well as holding accountable the actions of individuals within all classes of Senegalese society (albeit some more than others). In this way, despite its criticism of Francophile West Africans – which also speaks to his emphasis on class consciousness over *Négritude*'s racial consciousness – Sembène insists on the ontological and structural decolonisation that land redistribution still promises in the context of 1970s Senegal.

While post-independence West African films never translated into a single 'type' of filmmaking, as Roy Armes (1987) observes (be that along thematic, contextual, linguistic, generic or formal lines), many – including Med Hondo's *Soleil Ô* (1970) and Sarah Maldoror's *Sambizanga* (1972) – attended to developments that were taking the continent further away from the promises of decolonisation. Situated among them and deeply attuned to the contradictions, hidden agendas, and over-simplifications behind many avowedly national aims, Malian director Souleymane Cissé's second feature *Baara* (translated as 'work' from the Bambara language) considers the role of urban space in the reproduction of capitalist norms – as well as its incubation of resistance to the very same. Cissé's Mali was suspended between French colonial economic structures, failed attempts at nationalisation, and various state and non-state actors pursuing different agendas. Cissé's compatriot Manthia Diawara recalls an anti-capitalist march on the National Assembly building in Bamako in 1969 in response to General Moussa Traoré, who was at the time promising Malians that 'once everything was privatised, the French, the Americans, the World Bank, and the IMF would help us' (Diawara 2003, 70). In another event that took place in the national football stadium that same year, Diawara recalls how Alpha O. Konaré (later president of Mali from 1992–2002) stood up in public to sing the national anthem, denounce Traoré's privatisation plans and hand in his resignation. As such, in a telling choice of setting, *Work*'s story revolves around a textile factory in 1970s Bamako. For Mali, cotton is indelibly tied to survival. As one of two key commodities for its economy then and today, Malian cotton was being exposed to the volatility of world prices and the effects of American cotton subsidies around the time Cissé was filming.[7] As in its precursor *The Girl* (1975) and its successor *The Wind* (1982), the exploitation of these productive

---

[7] See also Alexis Roy (2010).

and social reproductive labours is central to Cissé's *Work*. Through a chronologically linear and relatively simple plot, he explores how place can transform people's ways of relating to themselves and others, even as it can also reproduce classed and gendered exploitation – speaking directly to the turbulent period of economic transitions that post-independence Mali was experiencing, as well as the ongoing political potential in labour organisation and urban dissent.

One of the most socially and politically consequential of the questions raised by decolonisation, asked with different emphases throughout post-independence texts, is that of women's conditions in the new nation-state. And yet the tendency to posit, for example, African women's experiences as silences now uncovered by scholarship, to then hold them up as opposite to hegemonic (patriarchal, imperialist) historiographies, not only assumes that what was not heard by historians was silent, but also reduces a diversity of experiences into one narrative. Nigerian author Buchi Emecheta's little-studied civil war novel, *Destination Biafra* (1982), not only takes the reader beneath the surface of standard nationalist histories, but incorporates women's psychic lives into the narration of political life in the post-independent nation. *Destination* situates women's subjective experiences of the devastating Nigerian Civil War (1967–1970) as sources from which those geopolitical dimensions of the war, customarily thought of as objective facts, can be understood. Although Emecheta changed most names and included a disclaimer in *Destination* about its fictional status, her characters' educational backgrounds match their real counterparts in Nigerian history. The ruler of Nigeria during the civil war, General Yakubu Gowon, was Sandhurst trained, and the leader of Biafra, Chukwuemeka Odumegwu Ojukwu, was a graduate of Lincoln College, Oxford. Nigerian–Biafran leaderships were often participants in a British-controlled transfer of political power, and Emecheta presents these men's myopia on the way to war as another product of, among other things, the fact that their class have largely been cocooned from the social violence of resource extraction in Nigeria. *Destination*'s women, however, understand the civil war as a process of incorporating any economically vital outliers – like secessionist Biafra – into the 'single, asymmetrically loaded system' (Krishnan 2018, 12) of capitalism in its neocolonial form. In Emecheta's novel as in Ghatak's *Cloud-Capped Star*, the diverse tools available to literary and cinematic realisms are put to understanding the relationship between violence, gender and the post-independence nation-state. Affirming that subjective experience carries political weight, Emecheta attempts a new historiography of the Nigerian Civil War, starting and ending with the experiences of women of various ethnicities and classes.

Where the historical record shows that women participated directly in independence struggles, as in the so-called 'Mau Mau' uprising against British colonialism in mid-century Kenya, gender can still remain an irresolution at the heart of decolonisation and nation-building. Ngũgĩ's vision of the Kenyan anti-colonial nationalist struggle and beyond is itself a complex and at times contradictory one. On the one hand, his early novels, such as *A Grain of Wheat* (1967), belong to a period of African literature that Ngũgĩ himself calls 'really a series of imaginative footnotes to Frantz Fanon' (1993, 67). Yet others have pointed out that this period of his writing was engaged in a multi-dimensional manner with questions of political and social transformation after independence. Ngũgĩ offers why both may be true, proposing that the African writer in the post-independence period 'was still limited by his inadequate grasp of the full dimension of what was really happening in the sixties: the international and national realignment of class forces and class alliances' (1986, 11). *Wheat* reflects these mercurial dynamics backdropping the 1950s and 1960s in Kenya, which gained its independence from Britain on 12 December 1962 after militant struggle. For a start, as Bethwell A. Ogot (2003) describes, Mau Mau was not an exclusively Gĩkũyũ anti-colonial movement; several Gĩkũyũ leaders who occupied positions of power after independence did not accept the radical agenda of the Mau Mau, so a generalisation cannot be made about one 'kind' of Mau Mau strategy, recruit or experience. Neither have, as Evan Mwangi notes, 'gender and sexuality as analytic categories in Kenyan historiography of decolonisation as presented in art . . . been systematically explored' (2009, 90). Writing in the first decades of the Jomo Kenyatta era, Ngũgĩ's novel highlights these complicated afterlives of Mau Mau, and the importance of social re-integration and psychic healing for those who were directly involved in militant anti-colonial resistance. But as *Wheat* explores how Gĩkũyũ men are to transform their subjectivities and re-integrate into community after the traumas of detention, the novel struggles to identify a role for Gĩkũyũ women beyond the facilitating of men's psychic healing. A such, it importantly gestures to the gendered limits of the psycho-political powers of anti-colonial nationalism.

These four novels and four films are thus richly diverse in their historical backdrops, formal techniques and cultural contexts. However, all are also concerned, with different inflections, with the problem of how, and why, decolonisation should address the means for people to re-constitute their subjectivities. They not only prioritise aspects of psychic or social life in need of transformation, but variously affirm a mutually effectual relationship between the material conditions of mid-century decolonisation and the 'decolonising of minds'. Doing different things with this relationship, they present political contexts and aesthetic explorations that narrate, and in doing so concretise, this problem. This does not mean, however, that they contain blueprints for the complex psycho-political process this implies (Chapter 1 is dedicated to giving the book's contours clearer definition with the aid of Fanon). But taking its cue from the rich preoccupations of these literary and cinematic texts, the book's chapters do define a set of research questions in order to focus its interest in subjectivity into four cross-disciplinary discussions. As the final section of this introduction will summarise, these research questions arise both from the texts themselves, and attend to an array of historical post-independence realities, several of which have been summarised above. This book deliberately moves away from organising its comparatisms by area ('the African texts') or by form ('the films'). As Craggs and Wintle lament, 'the value of comparative work on the end of empire is increasingly being acknowledged, but the wider historiographical trend of placing the bounded nation at the heart of decolonisation studies persists and is particularly noticeable in studies of cultural forms' (2015, 7). In refraining from placing 'the bounded nation' at the heart of its readings, this book seeks to investigate the full complexities of decolonisation, with both its surprising commonalities and its fruitful divergences across geographical contexts. The approach promises a way to interrogate and re-interrogate large frameworks under which myriad questions still remain to be asked, as well as 'highlight[ing] the value of analysing diverse cultural forms alongside one another' (Craggs and Wintle 2015, 8). With this in mind, this introduction will now seek to address some of the definitions and clarifications raised by the two conceptual words in the title of this book, subjectivity and decolonisation, in order to delineate why and how both together prove a critically useful lens through which to approach post-independence texts.

An Unfinished Project

Novels and films of the post-independence or 'early' postcolonial period (1950s–1980s) emerge from decades that Fanon called 'a program of complete disorder' (1961, 36),[8] that is, 'a time when things are decomposing or dissolving, or when the inherited metaphysical distinctions between ethics and politics, say, or sovereignty and subjectivity, are being put under erasure' (Marriott 2011, 34). The term post-independence 'invokes an achieved history of resistance, shifting the analytical focus to the emergent nation-state,' as Ella

---

[8] My use of 'postcolonial', as in 'postcolonial texts' or 'postcolonial governments' is, as Ella Shohat proposes, intended to indicate 'less an "after" than a following, going beyond the moment' (1992, 108) of independence. It points instead to 'living with the legacies of', in a broad sense. This understanding of 'postcolonial' differs from the narrower use to which I put the term 'neocolonial' throughout, in that the latter refers to conditions in direct continuity with colonialism in substance, if not in appearance.

Shohat argues (1992, 107). In its focus on the nation-state, the term also makes the postcolonial nation-state accountable to whether it fulfils or pursues the economic, social and psycho-political demands to be found within those histories of resistance. This book's investigation is set within this generative contradiction. On the one hand, the term points to a period of thwarted national experiments and derailed promises of liberation, where 'the logic of coloniality was being transformed into capitalism' (Bose 2019, 681) with the participation, tacit assent or inaction of postcolonial elites. On the other, it evokes a period that saw the articulation of a common subjection to, and struggle against, imperialism. The 1950s, 1960s and 1970s constituted a period where the decolonising nation-states of Africa and Asia were pursuing autonomy under the converging pressures of nation-building and neocolonialism. 'Third World as a category of relations along horizontal axes, between colonised, postcolonial and diasporic cultures' (Chrisman 2003, 7) was being recognised and analysed within political traditions of Third Worldist internationalism, pan-Africanism and socialism.[9] This extended, at the time, to popular cultural expression across Africa and Asia in pockets of what Khadija El Alaoui (2016) has termed 'street Bandung' – a reference to the revolutionary energies of the first Afro-Asian Conference of 1955 in Bandung, Indonesia – which saw writers, artists and filmmakers engage with the possibilities and challenges of this emergent Third World internationalism through poetry, poster art, narrative film and more. Backdropped by these possibilities and tensions, post-independence texts necessarily, if often implicitly, ask: where to, decolonisation?

'Inside decolonisation itself,' Aimé Césaire wrote, 'there are degrees; all forms of decolonisation are not equal' (1959, 128). The Martinican poet and philosopher stresses a 'good decolonisation' is 'without aftermath' (126). This warning brings into view multi-dimensional questions around decolonisation. What does it encompass? Who is it for? How is it to be pursued, and where to situate national independence on its trajectory? In the two African cinematic texts considered, Ousmane Sembène's *Xala* (1975) and Souleymane Cissé's *Baara* (1978), these uncertainties find articulation in class critique. Their main concerns include post-independence labour exploitation; corruption in the public sector; and 'the national bourgeoisie discover[ing] its historical mission as intermediary' (Fanon 1961, 100) for Western business interests. Meanwhile, in several of the South Asian texts discussed, we will see that when postcolonial state-led transformations are pursued, they often generate dire circumstances for those already marginalised by the legacies of colonialism. The Bengali refugees in Ritwik Ghatak's film *The Cloud-Capped*

---

[9] See also McCann et al. (2019), and Mahler (2018).

Star and the tenant farmers in Kamala Markandaya's novel *Nectar in a Sieve*, for example, are dispossessed by the 1947 partition of Bengal and by the industrialisation of rural South India, respectively; both events overseen by a state-led decolonisation of sorts.

In agreement with a critical mass of scholarship, the 'decolonisation' in the title of this book begins from the premise that colonialism is a structure rather than an event. This shifts the notion of decolonisation away from the episodic, despite the granted particularity of the mid-century flag independences. It instead points towards something yet ongoing, where 'the supposedly unfinished (democratic) project of modernity . . . ought actually to be understood as "the unfinished project of decolonization"' (Bhambra 2016). The same grows clear in the thought of many who participated in mid-century anti-colonial struggles, including Fanon's in *Toward the African Revolution* (1964) and *A Dying Colonialism* (1959); Amílcar Cabral's in his writings and speeches about the anti-colonial praxis of PAIGC;[10] Aimé Césaire in his *Discourse on Colonialism* (1950); Ngũgĩ wa Thiong'o in his essays in *Homecoming* (1972) and *Decolonising the Mind* (1986), among others; Kwame Nkrumah's analyses in *Neocolonialism: The Last Stage of Imperialism* (1965); and Thomas Sankara in various speeches like his 'Déclaration du 4 août 1983'. Decolonisation emerges in this body of thought as a process unfinished, for 'common to every kind of imperialist domination is the negation of the historical process of the dominated people' (Cabral 2016, 169). So long as economic and political conditions of continued subjugation to imperialism exist, that negation continues. As such, decolonisation must somehow also challenge and transform epistemic and ontological conditions, as much as the colonisation of resources, labour power and territory. According to Basil Davidson (1993, 80), Cabral's comrade, the poet and politician Viriato da Cruz, even offered the slogan *vamos descobrir Angola!* as a masthead for the Angolan struggle. It is a call to psycho-political power that goes well beyond military victory: 'let us discover ourselves'.

While this gives some more definition to 'decolonisation' in the context of the novels and films here considered – and indeed why the post-independence period provoked such searching – its relation to nation as a political, economic and social reality remains ambiguous. As Imre Szeman argues, if 'failing to deal with the nation in postcolonial literature, we are in danger of misunderstanding the significance of the aesthetic and political problems confronted by the writers of the fifties and sixties' (2003, 29). As such, in reading post-independence

---

[10] African Party for the Independence of Guinea and Cape Verde, founded by Amílcar Cabral, Luís Cabral, Aristides Pereira, Elisée Turpin, Fernando Fortes, Henri Labéry and Júlio de Almeida in 1956.

texts, this book will remain attentive to the ways in which that necessitates 'dealing with the nation'. The idea of the nation, and nationalisms, exist in dynamic relationships with approaches to subjectivity and decolonisation in these texts. The national question in these novels and films often becomes a way of thinking about liberating colonial subjects by transforming people's relationships: the relationship between leaders and people, the country and the city, the peasant and worker. Begüm Adalet posits Fanon a 'scalar thinker' on decolonisation, whose dialectics can be understood as 'the relationality between the body, infrastructure and globe' (2022, 2). Bringing in this concept ('scalar thinking') from Critical Geography to bear on Fanon's dialectics, she proposes that Fanon offers a 'vision of worldmaking less as a question of political and economic institution-building spearheaded by leaders than as a multi-scalar project that permeates the production of the built environment and the creation of selves' (3).[11]

I propose that the 'national', within this multi-scalar project, is one fluid conduit for thinking about that transformation and its effects at the level of subjectivity and interiority. In Ngũgĩ's *Wheat*, for example, the work of 'imagining that is required to produce the defined space of mutual identification and group solidarity that is the nation' (Szeman 2003, 42) is attempted by Gikonyo and his fellow detainees in order to achieve a sense of ontological and interpersonal security. In detention, they recount the Gĩkũyũ creation myth in defiance, and confide in one another their psychic distress about the outcome of the trial of the Kapenguria Six.[12] In Sembène's *Xala*, a similar space emerges for this kind of imagining in his motley crew of farmers-turned-beggars. They ensure one another's survival as they perpetually move around a hostile Dakar in post-independence Senegal. Ayi Kwei Armah's *The Beautyful Ones Are Not Yet Born*, on the other hand, deploys tropes of inertia and backwards movement to speak both to the failures of national independence and to the 'things

[11] While this viewpoint helpfully relates colonialism's powers of shaping space to a problem fundamental to this book ('the creation of selves'), it is perhaps too dismissive of Fanon's specifically national considerations about what the decolonisation of space can look like in the everyday life of the postcolonial nation-state. See also Stefan Kipfer (2005) on Fanon's theorisation of the role of a broad socio-spatial alliance in decolonisation (so as to span the colonially administered divide of city and countryside) for a convincing argument that is constrained by the early context (in terms of post-independence conditions) of the 1950s in which Fanon was thinking.

[12] Although some members of the Kapenguria Six, who hoisted the Kenyan flag on independence day, have been excluded completely from politics and the public domain by successive regimes since, Mbũgua wa Mũngai stresses that 'the identities and poses assumed by the founding fathers have had a significant bearing on how successive generations of Kenyans have viewed themselves and others' (2010, 58).

that continue unsatisfied inside' for those who still hope for a nation otherwise (Armah 1969, 100).

In yet other post-independence texts, nation is triangulated with subjectivity and decolonisation via the confrontation of hegemonic historiographies. Considered in Chapter 4, Ghatak's *The Cloud-Capped Star* challenges Indian state-sanctioned historiography with its focus on East Bengal refugees, who were excluded from free citizenship in independent India 'either through active sanctions or unofficial prejudice and exploitation' (Raychaudhuri 2009, 475). However, his disillusionment exists alongside the intense presence of Bengali classical musical traditions in *Star*. Ghatak gestures towards the possibility of the nation-that-could-have-been, alongside the pain of those struggling within the nation-that-is. On the other hand, Emecheta's protagonist in *Destination Biafra* finds the 'patterns of political affiliation' (Boehmer 2005, 15) she first sought in the fantasy of a post-ethnic One Nigeria prove fruitless as the civil war rages on. The protagonist surprises herself when she instead realises her own 'political affiliation' with the inter-generational resistance practices of West African women at a lower class position than herself.

As these narrative snapshots suggest, there is no easy identification between decolonisation and nation-building. But nation is still the formation that largely determines the circumstances within which these texts negotiate the pending tasks of decolonisation, including wealth redistribution and disalienation. Decolonisation turning into a mere project of national incorporation into global markets on a higher (more exploiter than exploited) rung is always a danger within this negotiation. But so will nation be negotiated in these texts as a locus of unfulfilled potential for 'decolonising the mind', because it yet remains possible to conceive of it as a popular activity. In referring to it as an 'activity' I am thinking with Fanon when he writes that, if anywhere, nation exists where 'the massive commitment of men and women to judicious and productive tasks gives form and substance to [national] consciousness' (1961, 144). These tasks are not meant to be patriotic abstractions, but concrete work done against very clearly defined, material things: 'against hunger and darkness, poverty and stunted consciousness' (144).

A Dialectic of Self and World

Arriving at a working definition of subjectivity in relation to decolonisation is a longer task, and informs the rationale of Chapter 1. There is a wealth of scholarship that has made inroads into the relation between the psychic conditions and the material conditions of colonialism. Some of these bring conceptualisations of subjectivity with an anti-colonial lens to bear on psychoanalysis,

Existentialist philosophy and Africana philosophy. To name but two key interventions that do so: Ato Sekyi-Otu has described how and to what effect the relationship between 'bodies, space and action' was 'brutally truncated of its dialectical possibilities' under the coercions of colonialism (1997, 82), while V. Y. Mudimbe's notion (1988) of 'epistemic insurrection' explores this relationality within the context of what decolonisation may then entail, given that 'a particular type of knowledge or episteme conditioned the possibility of representing and knowing about Africa' (Orrells and Fraiture 2016, xxvi). More recently, Pascah Mungwini's survey of African philosophy's recent and emerging tendencies emphasises throughout that 'self (re-discovery) . . . Who we are and from where we speak' (2022, 111) is the ontological consideration that gives substance and direction to a landscape in which 'things are beginning to change concerning the subordinate role accorded to other knowledge systems outside the Western epistemic tradition' (110). A range of approaches have also focused on psychoanalysis, consciousness and culture in relation to colonialism, as in the work of Ranjana Khanna (2003), David Marriott (2018), Emmanuel Chukwudi Eze (2008) and Achille Mbembe (2017); these are also complemented by scholarship that draws particularly from Fanon's thought in order to discuss embodiment and political resistance, as do Lewis Gordon (2015), Neetu Khanna (2020), and Pramod K. Nayar (2019).

Approaches to the 'self' have also come from Postcolonial Discourse Theory (Bhabha 1985; 1994); from studies on realism in postcolonial literature (Sorensen 2014; Lazarus 2011) and from postcolonial feminisms (Mohanty 1988; Jayawardena 2016), demonstrating that, rather than something to be 'resolved', interrogating subjectivity has often driven important disciplinary ambitions and political convictions in Postcolonial Studies. Its discursive approaches to subjectivity have had applicability to problems such as 'the double vision that a peripheral existence in the world engenders' (Schwarz and Ray 2008, 96) – which some have proposed as a critical approach with the scope to consider both that 'doubleness' (subjectivity) and the 'world' (materiality). Well known among these is Homi Bhabha's argument that a hybrid (post-)colonial subjectivity 'intervene[s] in those ideological discourses of modernity that attempt to give a hegemonic "normality" to the uneven development and the differential, often disadvantaged, histories of nations, races, communities, peoples' (1994, 171).

Whereas Bhabha's readings of power as purely textual have been cogently challenged (Callinicos 1992; Parry 2004), points like the above do demonstrate that post-structuralist approaches have helped illustrate certain links between a colonialism 'out there' and its effects 'within'. But these have relied largely on the study of post-1980s anti-realist texts, which open up questions of subjectivity within the contexts of diasporic experience (Gilroy 1993); globalism (Appadurai 1996); and cosmopolitanism (Appiah 2007). As E. San Juan Jr. highlights, a problematic use of the relational nature of subjectivity can drive this aspect of the field: 'postcolonial theory seeks to explain the ambivalent and hybrid nature of subjects [. . .] to prove that the colonial enterprise was not just a one-way affair of oppression and exploitation, but a reciprocal or mutual co- or inter-determination' (1998, n.p). Subjectivity here becomes a non-dialectical space of inscrutable interiority on account of those colonial subjects who could 'face two ways without being two-faced' (Bhabha 1985, 77) – or contain their difference and indifference in heart and mind. The historical and geographic specificity such claims require, especially given the centrality of nineteenth-century India to textualist criticism, can sever subjectivity from its material moorings and leave little more to analyse beyond the various contents of these 'differentials' between 'disadvantaged nations, races, communities, peoples' (Bhabha 1994, 171).[13] That the approach gives particular consideration to anti-realist and post-1980s texts is perhaps therefore unsurprising, as earlier and realist postcolonial texts do not treat subjectivity as something assumed to exist primarily in the discursive realm (more later on realism).

Rather, subjectivity itself as a philosophical category is pressured and transformed when read with and through the making of racialised and colonised subjects under the material conditions of colonialism and anti-colonial struggle. Provocations like Anuja Bose's, who locates in Fanon's internationalism the possibility of 'a collective subject of the Third World' borne of 'common subjection to and struggle against imperialism' (2019, 674), and Anna Agathangelou's (2018), with her discussion of Fanon, Hegel and the political subject, are recent examples. Less often read alongside the above, but also relevant to approaching subjectivity in contexts of decolonisation, is work within Liberation Psychology like Daniel José Gaztambide's *A People's History of Psychoanalysis* (2019), as well as Marxist approaches to psychology in the traditions of historical materialist epistemology (Reed 1996) and Critical Psychology (Maiers and Tolman 1996). While this book does not attempt a philosophical treatise on a notion of subjectivity, it engages with some of the above genealogies of study to offer, in Chapter 1, a working definition of subjectivity as it will be used throughout. This definition is conceived of in materialist and anti-colonial

---

[13] British colonialism in India was unrepresentative, developing as it did a sizeable 'native' civil service and education system. As Laura Chrisman cautions, 'it is unsurprising that this geo-cultural terrain [of postcolonial India] should correspond so neatly with Foucauldian theoretical priorities of epistemology or governmentality' (1995, 206).

terms, and will be guided by Fanon's psycho-political vocabulary. Some of the below scholarship will help pursue this approach.

Those who stress the psychological components of Fanon's thought as part of his wider dialectics of liberation, including Lewis Gordon (2015, 2022) and Jock McCulloch (1983), and those who think with Fanon on the political subject, nation, decolonisation and history, such as David Marriott (2011) and Richard Curtis (2019), offer critical frameworks within which subjectivity is of material and political consequence. Complementing this is scholarship on Fanon and embodiment; it includes work on colonial violence and the body by Pramod K. Nayar (2019) and Majid Sharifi and Sean Chabot (2019); affect and emotion in relation to the body (Khanna 2020); and on Fanon's sociogeny, which Nelson Maldonado-Torres describes as 'modes of subjectivity, meaning, and power relations with attention to the interplay between subjectivity and sociality' (2017, 434). As the above suggests, even narrowing this book's approach to subjectivity by centring Fanonian thought leaves much to work with. Many, however, mobilise the idea of the 'psychic', and a 'psyche' to aid their discussions. Attending to the psychical strife of an arrested decolonisation, particularly via considering character development and narrative/cinematic form, will be one means by which this book will 'read' for subjectivity.

Important ground has also been cleared towards situating terms like the 'psychic' within contexts of anti-colonialism and decolonisation, which this book will use throughout. The categorisation of human societies under colonialism and the formation of the modern psychoanalytic subject were inseparable. This mutual implicatedness is historically undeniable, and anti-colonial thought counter-evidences claims that 'the psychoanalytic has functioned as an unexamined critical force' (Anderson et al. 2011, 3) with regards to questions pertaining to postcolonial contexts and political legacies. These ideas were very much an examined 'critical force' in the period of the independences, including through (though not uncritically *via*) some of the tools provided by European psychoanalysis (as Fanon does in *Black Skin, White Masks*). In considering subject constitution and culture, African Philosophy and Black Psychology have produced critical confrontations with colonialism's epistemic racism – or, in Emmanuel Chukwudi Eze's words, 'the color of reason' (1997).[14] Ranjana Khanna has proposed we can think with the category of the psychoanalytic as a theory of nationalism, arguing that 'psychoanalysis is a product of a time when nationalism was being theorized, when the self was understood increasingly as a national self, and when nations were being

---

[14] See also V. Y. Mudimbe (1988), Ato Sekyi-Otu (1996), Kopano Ratele (2019) and Augustine Nwoye (2022).

formed and formulated in tandem with the expansion of colonial interests' (2003, 100). Daniel Gaztambide (2019) and Ankhi Mukherjee (2022) draw attention to the ways in which 'psychoanalysis – from Freud and beyond – became involved in, and contributed to, social justice discourses and leftist politics from Europe and America to the "Global South," serving as a source of repression and liberation depending on whose hands held this tool' (Gaztambide 2019, xxi).

So, while the complicity of European psychoanalysis in the fortification of colonial hierarchies around race, class, gender and sexuality cannot be minimised, its histories, tools and methods have always been confronted, transformed and corrected by those to whom it initially denied interiority. An inability – or indeed, imperialism's politically expedient refusal – to 'imagine the psychic sovereignty of the colonised individual' (Anderson et al. 2011, 4), while a reoccurring component of dominant strands of European psychoanalysis, was challenged when it encountered those peoples whom its early assumptions denigrated. Fanon, trained in the French colonial psychiatric school but innovative and critical with this material in his own thought and practice, and Ignacio Martín-Baró (1994), who applied Paulo Freire's (1972) pedagogical practice to a clinical context, are only two examples of anti-colonial psychiatrists who sought a psychoanalysis bent towards an emancipatory project.[15] More recently, Robert Beshara (2020) has examined the theoretical links between Freud and Edward Said, while Elizabeth Danto (2007), Gaztambide (2019) and Mukherjee (2022) have all drawn attention to how socialist psychoanalysts sought to implement free clinics in the early to mid-twentieth century (in the understanding that psychic disorders cannot be thought of separately from poverty, war and colonialism).[16] The self as having a psyche that can be analysed and can be intervened with in some way is therefore not a category mutually constitutive with liberal (neocolonial) governmentality alone, but also with anti-colonialism and anti-imperialism. These demonstrate the continued relevance of some kind of category of the 'self', and the 'psychic',

---

[15] In doing so, Gaztambide summarises, 'liberation psychology asks us to consider what kinds of psychotherapeutic and pedagogical relationships will foster a more holistic consciousness, a more integrated sense of self, a greater awareness of political dynamics, and a greater sense of freedom among historically marginalised communities. It asks us to place culture in a dialectical relationship with its immediate social, economic, and political context' (2019, xxxiii).

[16] 'Freud's pronouncements on free clinics helped to create a dozen cooperative mental health clinics, from Zagreb to London,' Mukherjee writes, but the movement was 'short-lived', with Freud's books burned in Berlin and the psychoanalytic institute shut in 1933 (2022, 8).

to decolonisation. Guided by the above, Chapter 1 seeks to situate subjectivity within the stakes of decolonisation via an emphasis on historicity, corporeality and creativity in Fanon's thought.

I do not propose we read these texts as solely about the inner psychologies of characters dealing with the afterlives of colonialism. Context and form will prove as important as character-driven narrative. However, post-independence novels and films will bring us a step closer to understanding how colonialism functioned not with a structural and a psychological component, but as a total system. If decolonisation must somehow see 'the experiential energies of a fractured psychic life mobilized into the very engine of an emancipatory consciousness' (Khanna 2020, 3), such 'energies' are a result of transformations at the level of subjectivity, in tandem with one's ever-changing material reality. The creation of economic and socio-political conditions that sustain anti-colonial ways of being and relating to one another have concurrent processes within, which are illuminated by the narratives here explored.

Subjectivity in Literary and Cinematic Realisms

From the rhythms of sowing and reaping in Markandaya's *Nectar in a Sieve* to the interpersonal dynamics of a love triangle in Satyajit Ray's *Home and the World*, how the 'everyday' plays out proves crucial to how post-independence texts illustrate these processes. As something where, in Henri Lefebvre's words, 'the sum total of relations which make the human – and every human being – a whole takes it shape and its form' (2008, 97), the everyday often brings political problems, such as the troubling continuities between pre- and post-independence life, into view. Kipfer notes how Fanon's analysis of the organisation of colonial social space, for instance, 'stretches' (Fanon 1961, 40) Lefebvre's Marxism in recognition of the importance of understanding the reproduction of everyday life under colonial conditions as a pursuit intimately linked to the 'arsenal of complexes' (Fanon 1952, 19) which a 'good decolonisation' (Césaire 1959, 126) must confront. Given that 'what Lefebvre calls abstract (both homogenizing and fragmenting) space in "neocapitalist" France is even more immediately shaped by state violence and a formally racialized commodity form in the colonies' (Kipfer 2007, 715), the potential of daily spatial practices and embodied experiences to incubate psycho-political change proves a major preoccupation in post-independence texts.

When, for instance, the everyday rhythms of rural life in her South Indian village are disrupted by the arrival of an industrial tannery, the narrator of Markandaya's *Nectar in a Sieve* comes to the realisation that she is being alienated from the land that helps constitute her sense of self. Her spatial experiences help reveal a wider post-independence context of nation-building-through-dispossession. Armah in *The Beautyful Ones Are Not Yet Born* likewise pays special attention to narrating the everyday experience of his unnamed protagonist, his highly visceral language shuttling back and forth between describing 'the man's' everyday life and accounting for its effects upon this character's interiority. This relation constitutes both the central tension of Armah's novel and illustrates for the reader how and at what cost Armah's protagonist has to constantly refuse acquiescing to a Ghanaian state bureaucracy with neocolonial characteristics. As Charles Mills argues, colonialism is a process through which space was 'normed and raced' at the level of countries, continents, neighbourhoods, and 'even the microlevel of the body itself' (1997, 43–4). The continuities between its spatial practices and those that occur ostensibly 'after' colonialism (in the independent nation-state) are examined in all eight texts through attention to everyday life. The tools employed by film versus literature mark different approaches to this exposé, but a unifying rationale behind all here studied is that they turn to realism as the form to carry this representational task.

There has been an ongoing scholarly reconsideration of realism in the field of Postcolonial Studies for some time, but the issue of representation in particular is 'perhaps the single most fraught and contentious term within postcolonial studies' (Lazarus 2011, 114).[17] It is also especially relevant to the literary representation of subjectivity. Eli Park Sorensen points out how 'postcolonial theory eventually developed a sustained infatuation with a "struggle against representation itself"' (2014, 240), and goes on to delineate the kinds of text that 'accord well' with this theoretical perspective. Agreeing with Neil Lazarus's argument in *The Postcolonial Unconscious* (2011) that 'the vast majority of "postcolonial" literary writing' reaches towards a 'deep-seated affinity and community, across and athwart the "international division of labour"' (2011, 19), I want to pause on the question, then, of what we allow the realism of post-independence texts to be, and to do. 'Post-independence' kinds of text, Sorensen proposes, have been perceived as a problem by a theoretical perspective that seeks 'so-called self-reflexive texts', and have often been 'transformed into historical or ethnographic documents (typically, "mimetically naïve" texts)' (2014, 241). On the other hand, compartmentalising post-independence texts as attempts to 're-orient literature towards its political-utopian project' (Brown 2009) does not intuitively suggest that these texts' attention to ques-

---

[17] See also Ato Quayson (1997); and the Warwick Research Collective (2015) for summaries.

tions of subjectivity and psyche may be related to such 'political-utopian' goals.

Yet realism has long been understood as having capacities of representing the subjective effects of those systematising forces within the reality that it depicts. György Lukács attributes an expansiveness to the mode that takes the subjective experience of objective conditions into its representational remit. He highlights a 'new immediacy' that is created by the 'twofold labour' of the writer who 'uncovers the deeper, hidden, mediated, not immediately perceptible network of relationships that go to make up society' then 'artistically conceals these relationships' (1938, 1042). What he calls the 'appearance' of reality (the lived psychic and embodied effects that it creates differently within each) is a vital component of understanding the 'laws governing objective reality'. These latter, such as the conditions of colonialism and neocolonialism, do not of course change solely by virtue of shifts in how individuals perceive them. But the (artistic) labour of mediation between that reality, and reality as it is perceived, is what makes realism possible. To highlight this relationality, Lukács evokes both Naturalism and Expressionism as 'one-dimensional' (1938, 1045) – that is, undialectical – in their respective ways, where for him the former is devoid of reality as subjectively perceived, and the latter can be emotive self-expression without necessarily referring to any social reality.

The post-independence literary texts here considered reach for the representational potential of this Lukácsian dialectic of 'appearance and essence'. Their narratives reveal the contradictions between the 'what is' of the post-independence everyday, and what decolonisation had promised. The effects of this contradiction are fundamentally linked to things that help make sense of oneself. For Markandaya's protagonist in *Nectar*, for example, these effects include the erosion of community as one way of making sense of oneself: 'others were reconciled and threw the past away with both hands that they might be the readier to grasp the present, while I stood by in pain' (1954, 33).[18] For others, this dissonance can shatter illusions. Buchi Emecheta's upper-class protagonist in *Destination Biafra*, arrives at political commitment through a war experience that challenges the differences she assumed between herself and Igbo peasant women. Though differing across context, inflection and emphasis between this book's novels, the affirmation of neocolonial conditions as shared, and the subjective effects they engender as a material oppression, gives

---

[18] While the term 'intersubjectivity' has various theorisations across Psychoanalysis, Philosophy and Anthropology, my usage in this context is best summarised by Susan Reynolds Whyte in *Postcolonial Subjectivities in Africa* as 'the way people are interdependent in trying to pursue goals' (2002, 182).

form to these narratives. Their committed but critical literary realism treats subjectivity and its constitutive forces as a political problem, and therefore a terrain full of potential towards decolonisation.

Co-representing the subjective and the material was also of interest to other applications of realism during the post-independence decades. Cinema was quickly recognised as politically consequential in the formerly colonised world.[19] Ideas about how post-independence circumstances should be illustrated and critiqued informed cinematic realism in South Asia and Africa. Articulated in Latin America and taken up by radical filmmakers whose national contexts ranged from Türkiye to Vietnam, Mozambique to Cuba, Third Cinema set out a vision of a guerrilla cinema that foregrounded collaborative production, democratic screenings and the concerns of societies struggling with the effects of Western hegemony.[20] These are all utilised to different degrees by Ousmane Sembène, Satyajit Ray, Ritwik Ghatak and Souleymane Cissé, the directors behind this book's film selection. Ewa Mazierska and Lars Kristensen point out that a characteristic of Third Cinema is that its 'active character', or its goal of developing people's understanding of their own conditions, means they 'do not address the "human subject" and "human condition" as such, but a [person] entangled in specific historical circumstances and affected by many factors, of which class is the most important' (2020, 3). Sembène and Cissé, for example, all draw on the dialectical montage of Soviet classics like *Battleship Potemkin* (1925) and *October* (1927) to critique exploiters and express solidarity with the exploited.[21] But theirs, as well as Ray's and Ghatak's works, are all a partial subscription to different facets of Third Cinema, rather than straightforwardly Third Cinematic works. While grouping directors of such different geographies and styles may raise the question of whether it is useful at all to loosely unite them under Third Cinema's ideas, both the characteristics of this movement and the shared tenets within these directors' visions render this association possible, even as many of them push its boundaries.

A cinema with Africans at its helm emerged on the continent against the backdrop of anti-colonial nationalist sentiment in the 1960s, where 'within international film culture [there was] a mutual awareness among African and non-African "third-world" filmmakers concerned with decolonisation, national

---

[19] See especially Odile Goerg (2020) on film culture and anti-colonial struggle in the 1950s.
[20] See also Solanas and Getino (1969), Martin Stollery (2001), Frank Ukadike (2014), Mariano Mestman (2011) and Matthew Croombs (2019) for some of the histories, contexts and debates on Third Cinema.
[21] That said, as Lindiwe Dovey explores, 'Sembène reveals his uneasiness with adopting any party line through using the power of sound, something that was not available to Eisenstein during the silent cinema period' (2020, 381).

liberation and critiques of neocolonialism' (Rosen 2010, 255). An avant-garde seeking to *décolonisez les écrans* began to form in West Africa with the establishment of FESPACO and FEPACI,[22] and Sembène's *Black Girl* (1966) is widely credited as the first feature-length film by a sub-Saharan African (though shorter films by both Sembène and others pre-date this). His and Souleymane Cissé's formative career years saw them receive training in Moscow, growing conscious of the internationalist dimensions of anti-colonialism. Cissé was trained as a film projectionist on a three-month scholarship in 1961, returning in 1963 to study filmmaking at the State Institute of Cinema until 1969. Sembène was nearly forty years old by the time he studied cinematography at the Gorki Studios in 1962, but his prior working life – as a docker and labour union organiser in post-war Marseilles – charged his artistic convictions with an internationalist politics.[23] The urgent need for economic and political decolonisation therefore takes precedence over gestures of cultural return in his *Xala*, discussed in Chapter 3.

Cissé's social realism, meanwhile, foregrounds the cultural heritage of the Bambara, while sustaining Pan-Africanist gestures. 'The first task of African filmmakers,' he has said, 'is to affirm that people from here are human beings, and to communicate those values that could serve others. The generation that will follow us will open itself up to other aspects of cinema' (Cissé and Senga 1987, 135). A looking outwards is there, as befitting the internationalist aspirations of Third Cinema, but Cissé here anticipates the work will take a long time. The no less important foundation he and his generation could provide their successors is a cinema that represents African contemporary realities in their full complexity and humanity. Here, the everyday is no static depository of culture for cinema to draw on, but ever the dynamic source of the filmmaker's imagination. This speaks to several anti-colonial thinkers' insistence that the changing social, cultural and political currents among a society are what both 'modifies, and gives precision' (Fanon 1961, 239) to the aesthetic production of an intellectual from and of that society. In maintaining that a sense of social justice emerges from daily experiences – wherein gender, religion, culture and value intersect and are negotiated – *Xala*'s and *Work*'s hybrid cinematic practices locate subjectivity as both constituted by, and one location of, social transformation.

What is sometimes called Indian Parallel Cinema, on the other hand, is more often grouped under the category of World Cinema than Third Cinema.

---

[22] Festival Panafricain du Cinéma et de la Télévision de Ouagadougou, and La Fédération Panafricain du Cinéastes, respectively. See also Colin Dupré (2012) on FESPACO's history.
[23] See also Samba Gadjigo (2008) for biographical material on Sembène.

The cinematic realism of one of its significant contributors, Satyajit Ray, is frequently traced back to Western variations of the form. Rather than taking this at face value, however, it is important to recall that there is a political context to declaring certain films World Cinema. As Mazierska and Kristensen recount:

> At the same time as Third Cinema, rightly or (more often) wrongly came under attack, new terms and concepts entered into circulation in film studies, such as transnational cinema and even more so world cinema, on occasion written in capital letters, to underscore its distinctiveness. (2020, 9)

They point out that the seemingly post-political positioning of World Cinema as simply 'the cinemas of the [non-Western] world' (Nagib 2006, 31) does not sufficiently address hierarchies within global film production and discourses.[24] Although Ray's work does not overtly align with the political and social manifesto of Third Cinema, this does not set him up in opposition to the intentions or aesthetics of someone like Sembène.[25] Ray's is another partial subscription to Third Cinema: he takes on some of its tenets, such as non-actors and social realism, and makes other choices more commonly understood within the vein of avant-garde aesthetics. Among those who stress Ray's homegrown influences, Moinak Biswas (2005) also offers a more convincing argument about the impact of the naturalism of the Bengali novel on Ray's use of temporality and landscape. However, it is an analytically meaningless task to seek to trace Ray's aesthetics back to one tradition in film theory or one cinematic geography. They can easily be found, for instance, in both the Soviet and Weimar schools respectively of Sergei Eisenstein and Siegfried Kracauer – an

---

[24] World Cinema conceived as a value-free category celebratory of plurality and inclusion can be, at worst, a method in which 'trans- and pan-nationalism is often used as a cover to introduce neoliberal order', while at best it 'does little to help the masses excluded from participation in politics and culture due to their poverty and colonial legacy . . . to [analyse] their condition' (Mazierska and Kristensen 2020, 11–12).

[25] While Roy Armes promisingly discusses Ray alongside Third Cinema veterans like Sembène, Glauber Rocha and Yılmaz Güney, he concludes that, though far from a neutral artistic quality, '[Ray's humanism] can be seen as the product of a tradition created by a middle class that has come to terms with colonization' (1987, 242), suggesting that Ray sits within this value-free 'World Cinema' and therefore refrains from the kinds of psycho-political questions asked in this book's introduction. Some critics seem to concur: Amit Chaudhuri traces the influences of John Ford and Jean Renoir on Ray (2008, 54); Ben Cardullo explores Ray's so-called Chekhovian style (2008, 33); and Lalitha Gopalan (2015, 266) cites Italian neo-realism and the French New Wave at Ray's formative influences.

amalgam that Keya Ganguly identifies as singularly suited for representing the 'crises of experience' (2010, 19) that Ray's characters negotiate. The results are often astute explorations of the subjective experience of social and historical contradictions in an everyday where Bengali cultural norms and the afterlives of the British Raj intersect. My discussion of Ray's 1984 adaptation of Rabindranath Tagore's 1919 novella *Home and the World* will refer to these historically inflected aesthetics, but ultimately focuses on how Ray genders the two kinds of anti-colonial nationalism that emerge in the story.

While extremes of interpretation have come Ray's way, Ritwik Ghatak has provoked perhaps too little contention. Unlike Ray, his lived experience of refugeedom 'launched him directly into the here and now of unemployment, destitution and the disintegration of the family' (Dasgupta 1985, 263), but Tagorean influences animate his realism as they do Ray's. His realism has a complexity that stems from a striking attention to how the material conditions of Partition double in their detrimental effects through their psychic ripples. In Chapter 4's discussion of *The Cloud-Capped Star* (1960), which depicts the plight of a refugee family from East Bengal, the systemic oppressions of poverty and patriarchy manifest in crippling psycho-social effects such as nostalgia and depression. Ghatak is committed in that film to representing these phenomena as material, in direct engagement with social themes related to Indian decolonisation. This helps explain what some have deemed his excesses of form, such as the non-diegetic and 'melodramatic' (Herbert 2010) use of sound, as an experimental realism that seeks the expressive register of the psychic effects of Partition dispossession and poverty.

The Structure of this Book

The differences between the national contexts of the works in this study, which comprise a selection that spans West Africa, East Africa and South Asia, are undeniable. This is not only in the sense of differences in pre-colonial and colonial histories, languages, cultures and religions, but also in terms of trajectories towards independence and the decades after (certainly between the French and British ex-colonies, and also between those ruled by the same power). Comparatisms concerned with these differences and divergences continue to be examined in historical and anthropological scholarship.[26] Yet aesthetic and political connections are also constantly unearthed. Recent research collaborations have traced how South Asian networks – a 'Greater India' within the

---

[26] Such as the work of the Afro-Asian Networks Research Collective (2018); Anne Garland Mahler (2018); and Richard Werbner (2002).

imperial Indian Ocean – served as the first conduits of Afro-Asian political connection in the early twentieth century.[27] The Bandung Conference and its afterlives have also generated a significant body of work on the polytonal but adjacent politics of the 1950s and 1960s across the so-called Third World.[28] Nationalisms – more specifically those 'derived from an alternative nationalist standpoint' of the kind Neil Lazarus (1993, 72) attributes to Fanon, as opposed to 'imperialist nationalisms . . . projects of unity on the basis of conquest and economic expediency' (Brennan 1990, 58) – are also a shared political impulse in the geographies covered by this book's texts. While discussing one novel and one film per chapter may seem a heterogenous assemblage, it is not an arbitrary one. The political commonalities to an arrested decolonisation in Africa and South Asia as discussed above is its historicising rationale; a Fanonian approach to subjectivity is its conceptual guide. As a comparative approach, however, it is also purposefully experimental. Putting into conversation texts otherwise usually grouped by region or medium reveals four shared, though multi-valanced, queries that facilitate these texts' engagement with post-independence circumstances. The below chapter structure seeks to parallel them with an eye on subjectivity, rather than reconcile contrasts in content and form.

Chapter 1, which sketches a theorisation of subjectivity drawn from close critical consideration of Fanon's dialectics, has already been outlined above. Granting anti-colonial nationalism's ideological effectiveness in building the momentum of liberation struggle, Ngũgĩ's *A Grain of Wheat* (1967) and Ray's *Home and the World* (1984) are discussed in Chapter 2 in terms of how they engage with the charged relationship between these nationalisms and patriarchy. Do anti-colonial nationalisms facilitate – or even allow – the transformation of *all* subjectivities? Exploring how *Wheat* brings the relationship between nativist politics and hegemonic masculinities into view, the chapter traces where and how a Fanonian treatment of subjectivity also emerges. However, the novel then grapples with how to incorporate women's subjectivities into this treatment – and in doing so places its dialectical vision for Kenyan liberation on shaky ground. In Ray's *Home and the World*, meanwhile, gender again circumscribes the effects, reach and consequences of anti-colonial nationalism. In this film's case, the latter takes the form of the early twentieth-century

---

[27] They paint an Afro-Asian 1950s 'shaped by shared arenas of anti-imperial possibility and experimentation . . . multivalent linkages that include but go beyond sites of South Asian diaspora in Africa' (McCann 2019, 5). See also the work of *Another World? East Africa and the Global 1960s*, available at <https://www.globaleastafrica.org/welcome> (accessed 15 August 2021).

[28] On Bandung's resonances and beyond, see Christopher J. Lee (2010); Robbie Shilliam and Quynh N. Pham (2016); and Adom Getachew (2019).

Swadeshi movement in India. Examining how the story's female protagonist finds herself negotiating the contradictions between the ideological, the domestic and the subjective in these texts, Ray's adaptation of Tagore's 1919 novella captures the (gendered) limits of nationalism in transforming the home, let alone the world.

Where Ray's and Ngũgĩ's texts ask questions about the course and afterlives of Swadeshi and Mau Mau anti-colonialisms respectively, Chapter 3's novel and film bear witness to the transformation of West African liberation into mere rhetoric after independence. Armah's *The Beautyful Ones Are Not Yet Born* (1969) and Sembène's *Xala* (1975) examine subjectivity under the socio-economic and political pressures of neocolonial conditions facilitated by the Ghanaian and Senegalese elite, respectively. These conditions inform the sometimes bitter and often satirical bent to these narratives. In Armah, disillusionment gestures to what a resistant subject may be under circumstances that demand participation upon the pain of complete social exclusion. *Xala*, on the other hand, expands explicitly on what a counter-institutional and counter-cultural response to these socio-political circumstances could look like, but uncertainly. Both texts eventually affirm that intersubjectivity nurtures the grounds upon which decolonisation may yet be pursued.

As Chapter 4's works illustrate, however, the post-independence decades were too often a period of conflict, during which violence did damage to one's ontological and social moorings. Territorial partition and displacement marred the post-independence decades of India and Nigeria. Ghatak's *The Cloud-Capped Star* (1960) and Emecheta's *Destination Biafra* (1982) narrativise these traumas, addressing the Partition of Bengal (1947) and the Nigerian Civil War (1967–1970) respectively. In them, the structural conditions of an imperialism that did not die with the independences include extraction, forced migration and violent communalism. *Star*'s Hindu refugees, who have fled to the environs of Calcutta from the newly created East Pakistan, relive the trauma of their geographical displacement and class descent through relationships that are premised upon guilt, emotional labour, fear and escapism. Emecheta's *Destination Biafra* sets up a similar relationality from the perspective of its diverse female characters, but demonstrates how women's subjective experiences can challenge and correct state-sanctioned historiography. In both works, subjectivity emerges as subject to historical causation and social experience. While the psychic effects of violence are minimised when collectivised in Emecheta's novel, in Ghatak's film, their effects re-entrench 'a choice between dependence and inferiority' (Muhkerjee 2022, 36) for the dispossessed.

Finally, works that are a decade on from their respective independences – as is the case for Markandaya's *Nectar in a Sieve* (1954) and Souleymane Cissé's

Work (1978) – inform Chapter 5's analysis of displacement without migration. The need to fundamentally redefine people's relationship to themselves under any project of decolonisation extends, socially and psychically, to the spatial. As Ato Quayson writes, 'everywhere, colonial space-making also involved the intellectual appropriation and symbolic reconfiguration of the relationship between the colonised and their natural environment' (2010, 970).[29] Markandaya's novel *Nectar* shows the applicability of this idea of spatial continuity by addressing the effects of a Nehruvian model of development on rural India's dispossessed.[30] Meanwhile, in *Work*'s urban spaces, the spatial and economic promises of African socialism are fast being negated by the realities of the global production line. Cissé's film pursues a visual and narrative connection between spaces of labour and the (re-)constitution of subjectivities, in order to ask whether cross-class solidarities can still be forged within the hyper-exploitative urban nodes of a capitalist globalisation that disrupts West African local production.

Guided by a problem theorised through a key thinker who shares the milieu of my cinematic and literary case studies, it is my hope that this book demonstrates the interdisciplinary and comparative possibilities of placing more texts from this politically and aesthetically important period into conversation. As Elleke Boehmer argues in *Postcolonial Poetics* (2018), juxtaposition is an inferential poetic that operates through performing 'a movement across gaps' (41). It can create disruptive effects that invite readers to seek new possibilities – particularly when their attention is directed to 'finding relationships in the discontinuities' between the juxtaposed elements. This juxtaposition can work internally within a text itself, but also across texts; effective examples include Brigitta Isabella's (2022) readings of 'Bandung chronopolitics' – historical memories of a 1960s Tricontinentalism – in contemporary protest poetry. This book's pairings of texts spanning Africa and South Asia, literature and film, are pursued in this spirit of 'finding relationships in the discontinuities' (Boehmer 2018, 41).

The taking stock characteristic of diverse post-independence texts has them asking questions such as 'how did we get from colonialism to here?' and 'where even is here?' As a result, such texts have with some accuracy been

---

[29] Space, as Etienne Balibar and Immanuel Wallerstein propose, underwent 'realisation for' colonial accumulation (1991, 89), and in turn for neocolonial accumulation. These later included ostensibly developmentalist moves, whose 'significant threads of continuity' with colonialism 'are masked by a complex shift in vocabulary and the persistent narration of historical rupture' (Biccum 2005, 156).

[30] See Brij Kishore Sharma (2012) on Jawaharlal Nehru's conceptual framework for India's development in the post-independence period.

called 'literatures of disillusionment' (Lazarus 1990, 18). But they also mark a practice of representation that is driven by the hope that constructing societies permanently transformed out of the structures and legacies of colonialism is still possible – once the new guises of these structures are exposed, and their psycho-political effects upon people are challenged. On that basis, these texts ask some of the most politically consequential questions of their moment: can people who are each day negotiating the conditions of an arrested decolonisation act upon such conditions? What has to happen at a social and a psychic level for someone to act in resistance? And where can people find the ontological resilience for confronting these conditions? In asking such questions, these stories look beyond independence to recognise a world that is yet to be decolonised, and they position the transformation of our very selves squarely within this unfinished undertaking.

1
Reconciling Us To Ourselves: Decolonisation and the Question of Subjectivity

In *A Dying Colonialism*, originally published as *L'An V de la Révolution Algérienne*, Frantz Fanon thinks on the dynamics of colonial oppression from the vantage point of the fifth year of the Algerian War of Independence against French occupation. 'The Algerian people have decided that, until independence, French colonialism will be innocent of none of the wounds inflicted upon its body and its consciousness', he declares (1959, 118). Although he is speaking in relation to a politically specific moment and movement, he is also naming two sites of the effects of colonialism that go beyond the Algerian context: 'body' and 'consciousness'. The link between them signals what much of Fanon's work examines: how colonialism undertakes material and psychic assaults that are inseparable from one another. The social, political and economic structures that European colonialisms implemented around the world for the extraction of natural resources, the occupation of land, the creation of captive markets, and the exploitation of human labour were in a mutually effectual relation with the exercise of power over people's ways of understanding themselves and others. Turning these two loaded words ('body' and 'consciousness'), and the phenomena they describe, into colonialism's judge, jury and executioner, Fanon implies that justice here includes the means for people to re-constitute their subjectivities. This claim rests on a conceptualisation of subjectivity that enables Fanon in his context to understand the self and its material conditions as ever only transformed together. This chapter seeks to set out the problem of subjectivity – its constitution, and the conditions of its transformation – with Fanon as its primary guide. The inroads that emerge will, I hope, give greater definition and direction to how Chapters 2 to 5 use this idea in their discussions of eight post-independence texts.

As the routes of critique summarised in the Introduction suggest, the relationship between the psychic conditions and the material conditions of decolonisation has animated scholarship in fields ranging from Liberation Psychology to Fanon Studies, decoloniality/colonial modernity theory to Africana philosophy. Major anti-colonial thinkers, including but not limited to Fanon, Aimé Césaire, Amílcar Cabral, B. R. Ambedkar, Ngũgĩ wa Thiong'o, Chinua Achebe and Thomas Sankara, were undeniably the products of different contexts and geographies – not least in the obvious sense of differences in the historical contexts of their geographic origins, languages, cultures and belief systems, but also in terms of the different trajectories of colonisation, anti-colonial struggle and independence between them. But the forms of resistance they witnessed and participated in, and the political, social and economic structures they were working within after flag independences, often crystallise upon this aforementioned relationship between the transformation of material structures and the transformation of subjectivities. Whether it is to the contexts of Fanon's writings we look – a 1940s Martinican middle class for whom proximity to whiteness equals self-worth, then a 1950s Algeria in the thick of anti-colonial struggle – or to those of Ngũgĩ, where we often find a postcolonial Kenyan state repressing its own, we find these writers and political actors looking through and beyond independence.[1] The effects of colonialism as well as those of a neocolonialism that soon followed the flag independences on people's social, economic, political and psychic ways of being in the world are variously noted by Sankara, Achebe, Fanon and others as 'mental colonisation' (Murrey 2018), 'inferiority complexes' (Fanon 1952), and a lack of 'reconciliation with oneself' (Achebe 1975). Among their many other concerns, they are preoccupied with the psychic effects and possibilities of the ever-shifting and constantly besieged project of decolonisation in the mid- to late twentieth century.

Biodun Jeyifo rightly emphasises that a 'theme of epistemic, cognitive crisis' is discernible in many texts that 'preceded the attainment of formal independence, indeed coincided with the inception of the movement toward decolonization' (2007, 126). But it would be remiss to collapse the particularly complex and heightened forms that this 'crisis' took after the flag independences into a kind of *longue durée* beginning with pre-independence decolonisation movements and ending with the global order of late capitalism in the postcolonial world. The causes and courses of any 'epistemic crisis' represented in pre- and post-independence texts (of much temporal, geographic and formal diversity among themselves) included but extended beyond the fact that 'lifeworlds in

---

[1] Detained without trial in 1978 for writing and staging *Ngaahika Ndeenda* ('I Will Marry When I Want') in rural Kenya, Ngũgĩ's *Detained* (1981) recounts this experience as a tactic of many a postcolonial state at the time: that of 'breaking progressive nationalists', to ensure no popular activity could raise mass consciousness (Ngũgĩ 1981).

which "old," hitherto stable meanings, codes, inscriptions and significations no longer [sufficed] to make experience easily or reassuringly cognizable' (Jeyifo 126). Indeed, some thinkers on decolonisation such as B. R. Ambedkar actively repudiated any notion that 'old . . . meanings' (in his case, those of a traditional Hindu knowledge system dominated by Brahmins) had ever made 'experience easily or reassuringly cognizable' for an oppressed majority.[2] More broadly, there is a particularity to the independence decades that animate, worry and propel the writings of those like Fanon and Ngũgĩ with the notion that people's very subjectivities remain to be transformed out of colonialism's debilitating psychic states. One aspect of this can be described as the work of understanding the ways in which imperialism and colonialism have produced subjectivities; the other is the question of what conditions beget what kinds of transformations therein.

That a qualitative transformation of consciousness is a component of any qualitative transformation in the economic foundations of societies is well-trodden territory in various schools of Marxist thought. The production of subjectivity – the manner in which relations of production produce ways of thinking and living – is at the centre of what Louis Althusser dubbed Marx's transformation of philosophy towards a new way of doing philosophy. Conceptualisations of 'the production of subjectivity' – understood both in the sense of being produced by the relations of production and by ideology, but also in the sense of 'producing effects that exceed the production and reproduction of capital' (Read 2022, 2) – are often indebted to a variety of philosophical approaches not necessarily in agreement with one another, from post-structuralist thinkers like Gilles Deleuze and Michel Foucault to the Frankfurt School. However, seeing first-hand how subjectivities were produced by the conditions of colonialism, and living with the urgency of changing these processes, revolutionaries in the midst of anti-colonial and/or anti-imperialist guerrilla wars in Latin America, Africa and Asia also brought this problem to bear on the practical conditions of struggle and nation consolidation. From Che Guevara's pedagogical work in Bolivia and the Democratic Republic of the Congo, to those engaged in rural community *conscientização* like Paulo Freire, efforts put towards decolonisation had to consider ways through and out of how imperialism and colonialism produced, and everyday continued to produce, subjectivities that have internalised their imperatives.[3] As much an obstacle to decolonisation as the lack of public infrastructure in

---

[2] See also Shivam Agrawal (2021) on Ambedkar's views on education and more in colonial India.
[3] See also John D. Holst (2009) on the pedagogy of Che Guevara.

a new postcolony were what Fanon called colonial 'inferiority complexes' at once 'epidermal' and 'economic' (1952, 4), and what Aimé Césaire called a 'skilfully injected' mix of 'fear, inferiority complexes, trepidation, servility, despair, abasement' (2001).

While debating Eurocentrisms in Marx and the postcolonial critique of Marxism are beyond the scope of this book, several of the above names – not least Fanon and Césaire – self-identified as committed, with various inflections, to historical materialist approaches to understanding the trajectories of colonialism.[4] They also unequivocally understood decolonisation as a revolutionary process, with dynamics that produced and resolved a variety of contradictions as local and international conditions evolved. Fanon's 'stretching' (1961, 5) of some of Marx's analyses, to find its avenues of theoretical and practical application in contexts of anti-colonial struggle and nation-building,[5] is also applicable to his treatment of subjectivity constitution and transformation. He offers a dialectics that this chapter will attempt to trace. But he also applies it in altogether original ways to a problem he sees in psycho-political terms, which is why he will remain the key thinker for the problem at the heart of this book.

How then, and along what lines, is the transformation of subjectivities – whatever particular conditions for this each context may produce – related to the material processes of decolonisation: the dismantling of the economic, political and social structures inherited from colonialism? Is the former a precursor or successor to the latter? Are they to occur simultaneously? Does pursuing one result in the other? Before I turn to Fanon to examine this nebulous but crucial inter-dependency, it is important to recall – especially given the philosophical inflections of some of the below – that the contextual backdrop, or political stakes, to these considerations are specifically related to that aforementioned question of 'whither decolonisation' after the independences. These decades saw the consolidation of new actors and bureaucratic structures that cultivated 'new' dependencies, even as 'old' colonial structures, sustained by Europe and the United States, lived on in various guises.[6] As such, what 'nation' could do, did, and was failing to do – as it existed alongside a new, emergent reality of a neocolonialism with myriad faces – is a preoccupation that cannot be disentangled from the relationship between decolonisation and the transformation of subjectivities. Many of the above mid-century figures

---

[4] For a summary of some of these critiques of Marxism, see Kolja Lindner (2022).
[5] See also Sara Salem (2019) on Fanon's Marxism discussed in the context of Egyptian decolonisation.
[6] Susan Williams (2021) extensively relates the involvement of, among other actors, the CIA in Africa during and beyond the independences.

were thinking within a context of what Anna Bernard calls the 'political desire for autonomy and self-determination in a world where the nation remains unforgoable as a site of liberation struggle' (2011, 79).

For now, this chapter turns to three organising (but intersecting) ideas that help delineate how Fanon emplaces the self, in material terms, into a dialectical relation between itself and the world. My aim is not to claim heretofore unstudied insight into this densely studied figure, but to orient select critical work towards answering why 'living through' (Macey 2000, 162) and out of colonialism can also be understood as an ongoing process of subjectivity constitution. Rather than provide a definitive answer to this question, Fanon's thinking on subjectivity brings into view three broad aspects to it: historicity, embodiment, and creativity. These characteristics or conditions make possible the transformation of people's ways of relating to themselves and to one another – the re-constituting of their subjectivities – in contextually determined ways. The decolonisation Fanon speaks of is one where independence is merely one stage of an ongoing and manifold process, which is a key political context uniting the eight texts under consideration here. Alongside lasting material change like wealth redistribution and reparative justice, it touches and transforms people's ways of relating to themselves and to one another. Better understanding what the 'subjectivity' undergirding this link is illuminates what decolonisation promises, but has not yet delivered, in the post-independence novel and film.

The Historicity of Subjectivities

Prathama Banerjee writes that 'the colonized were recast as lacking valid modes of practice and thus lacking politics . . . Colonial historians and ethnographers criticised the colonized for lacking in historical acumen and living in an uneventful, changeless social continuity' (2020, 69). This reinforced the so-called 'impossibility' of the colonised having subjectivities that were historical – ever-changing through their lived experiences across time – and agential – able to act upon the structures of material reality. As *Black Skin, White Masks*, in Lewis Gordon's words, follows 'a quasi-anonymous black hero' who tries in good faith, chapter by chapter, to live 'simply as a human being' through the 'options offered the black by modern Western thought', he soon discovers its 'impossibility'. All available options call 'for living simply as a white', for they re-inscribe 'whiteness as the "normal" mode of "humanness"' (Gordon 2015, 22–4). The protagonist then decides, with the tone of one assuring the reader that this is the erroneous conclusion that such a world at first gives rise to, that he 'will quite simply try to make [himself] white: that is, [he] will compel the white man to acknowledge that [he is] human' (73). As *Masks* proceeds, however, the pain and rage of this attempt lends itself to Fanon's actual task: that of analysing colonialism's systemic and subjective machinations for the goal of, in his words, freedom from the 'arsenal of complexes that has been developed by the colonial environment' (Fanon 1952, 19).

As creations of concrete environments, to transform these 'complexes' that circumscribe subjectivities will entail what Fanon calls the 'restructuring of reality' (34). A need to 'restructure reality' can only be identified from the understanding that, foremost, there are historical actors within that reality. A relationship between one's material conditions, and one's lived experience of those conditions over time, must be asserted and examined. To that end, Fanon sets out to reclaim the subjectivities of the colonised as an accumulation of history, with agency. Among and through its critiques of French thinkers who have written on colonialism, including Jean-Paul Sartre and Octave Mannoni; its consideration of inter-racial relationships within the context of a stratified anti-black society like 1930s Martinique; and the painful 'journey' of its narrator through and out of the internalisation of his racialisation, *Masks* will politicise every stage, whether a dead-end or success, of a transformation in his protagonist's subjectivity – in his way of relating to time, his body and to others.

Fanon first seeks to understand how the colonial world at every turn renders disalienation for the colonised – their being in 'human reality in-itself-for-itself [*la réalité humaine en-soi-pour-soi*]' (218) – out of reach. This provokes questions of how and to what end colonialism has constructed, and maintains, the appearance that its own inventions – such as race – set the terms for subjecthood. When in *Masks* he provides corrective to Octave Mannoni's ethnopsychiatry by analysing Mannoni's 'pernicious misunderstanding, [which] gives the native no choice between dependence and inferiority' (Mukherjee 2022, 36), Fanon is also pinpointing the ahistoricity of this view. The apparent timelessness of its structures is an insidious but potent claim of colonialism. Demonstrating how colonial ethnopsychiatry's ethnicity-based differentiations between human psyches always rests on what Ankhi Mukherjee calls 'concept metaphors' that exist only in relation to the European, Fanon illustrates its fundamental irrationality, then counters these so-called differences by thinking on the historicity of the subjectivities of the colonised.

To help concretise this, we can look to a frequent refrain in Fanon Studies: Hegel's 'Lordship and Bondage' in *Phenomenology of the Spirit* (1807), and Fanon's engagement with its ideas within the contexts of slavery and colonialism. My aim in underlining this here is not to open up a comprehensive discussion on Fanon and Hegel, of which there are several,[7] but to raise Fanon's historicising approach to subjectivity at 'the point of realisation' where Hegel 'falls silent', in the words of Susan Buck-Morss (2000, 843). What the dissatisfied protagonist of *Masks* is incensed by is the dead-end that mutual recognition amounts to in a colonial world. Seeking to transform one's subjectivity within an unchanging environment is not only a paradox, but it only leads one to conclude that, 'for the black man there is only one destiny. And it is white'. As David Marriott offers, 'to see whiteness as the destiny of blackness means to question everything', and this begins to render historicisable what colonialism presents as static and timeless: the colonised subject (2011, 33). 'There is in fact a "being for other," as described by Hegel, but any ontology is made impossible in a colonized and acculturated society', Fanon argues (89). His confrontation of the paradox that is 'the Slave [reaffirming] the Master's exclusive right to give rights' (Harfouch 2019, 143) by awaiting his recognition makes possible abandoning the notion of achieving subject-status under the same social order that makes people objects.

Fanon instead pushes his reader to think dialectically about the relationship between questions of ontology and the historical processes that have led to a set of concrete and intersecting conditions. Looking back, he writes in *The Wretched of the Earth* that since 1954 (shortly after becoming *chef de service* at the Blida-Joinville Psychiatric Hospital in Algeria), he has 'drawn the attention of French and international psychiatrists in scientific works to the difficulty of "curing" a colonized subject correctly, in other words making him thoroughly fit into a social environment of the colonial type' (1961, 181). He points out what he feels should be self-evident to his fellow practitioners: that the opposite of subjectivity constitution (reconciliation to objecthood) is what indicates 'health' in such an environment. 'What the Colonial Master wants from the Slave is not recognition but rather labor,' Harfouch points out (144), and this has implications for the trajectory of decolonisation, given that, for example, 'anti-colonial national movements who seek recognition from colonial hegemons' may not necessarily be a threat to the 'ontological horizon' of empire (Harfouch 143) – a critique that will reoccur in post-independence texts. Giving rights to formerly colonised subjects on empire's own terms may be one way to secure continued access to their labour. While this may seem a pessimistic diagnosis, it gestures towards a dialectic involving the self and the world. In the case of the above example, Fanon illustrates this dialectical relation at work for colonialism, producing and reproducing oppression.

---

[7] See, for example, Zahid Chaudhary (2012), Andreas Krebs (2007) and Charles Villet (2011).

However, thus associating 'self' and 'world' has now opened up not only new psychiatric questions – questions to which a colonial medical establishment has given him no answers – but also political ones.

This relation proves vital in post-independence texts like Armah's *Beautyful Ones*. State power, more diffuse forms of social power, and their effects entwine subjectivity and subjugation in the post-independence Ghana of Armah's novel. The taken-for-granted autonomy in personal self-formation is called into question as his protagonist experiences multiple temporalities, seeing his disappointing present through the lens of the pre-independence promise of African socialism. When nausea sets in for the protagonist who cannot entertain progress and regress as distinct, Armah leaves his reader with a sense of the fallibility of individuals in the face of the structural entrenchment of colonialism – as well as how they can either perpetuate or change structures. Far from 'living in an uneventful, changeless social continuity' (Banerjee 2020, 69), Armah's protagonist becomes a resistant subject through the very fact that his personal experience of post-independence time reveals the social effects of a colonial-capitalist extraction that seeks its own continuation; or, how '[w]hat had been going on there and going on now and would go on and on through all the years ahead was a species of war carried on in the silence of the long ages' (Armah 1969, 15).

Recalling Armah's protagonist, in seeking psychoanalytic answers for the colonised subject's state of alienation and distress, the fact that Fanon begins from the colonised having subjectivities that they can intervene in and transform in some way is a crucially historicising move. 'As soon as I desire I am asking to be considered. I am not merely here-and-now, sealed into thingness. I am for somewhere else and for something else,' he says (170), pointing away from mutual recognition and towards a 'somewhere and something else' – towards the material world, in other words, both as it is and as it could be. This is the generative place from which *Masks* can pursue the 'question of direction' (Ahmed 2006, 42), as its protagonist can now seek out what – if not recognition ('becoming white') – one becomes *for*. As imperialism's refusal to imagine the psychic sovereignty of the colonised individual is revealed to be politically and economically expedient for sustaining its own structures, Fanon lands upon the future as the direction ('I am for somewhere else and something else'), that is, both a future world rid of colonialism, and his future self in that world. Such temporal reorientation also speaks to Emecheta's plot line in *Destination Biafra*, where the refugeedom and violence experienced by her upper-class, Itsekiri protagonist serves to shatter the class barriers between her and the peasant Igbo women alongside whom she survives the Nigerian Civil War. Emecheta's protagonist Debbie's decision to turn women's already extant (albeit in oral and mnemonic form) history of the war into a written one is not only her 'refusal of a passive role as victim for the testimony-giver' (Harlow 1996, 73), but also a means of disrupting the nation-time of official Nigerian state-sanctioned history. The war has rendered Debbie unable to bear children, and the future 'she is for' instead becomes that of the future of Biafran women, via the part her pen can play in keeping historical amnesia at bay. In many ways, the once-elite Debbie encapsulates Fanon's implication that subjectivities which emerge changed in unpredictable ways upon encountering the conditions of colonialism are subjectivities contiguous with liberation, because to be able to change is to be historical.

Fanon holds colonialism's effects upon the self's capacity to create itself (as Emecheta's protagonist eventually does), and to act from its experiences of material reality over time (as Armah's protagonist insists on doing at the expense of his own material comfort), to be psychically and politically consequential at an altogether different level to isolated acts or utterances of domination. To counter the former looks different in different contexts, as *Beautyful Ones* and *Destination*, among other texts here, will show. But all require the discovery and assertion of the historicity of the subjectivities of the colonised. The protagonist of *Masks*, who 'cannot hope to win' on terms that make 'any ontology impossible', must instead reorient his actions towards a future beyond colonialism as the place and time that 'he is for' (170). Becoming, thus historicised, can be in dialectical relation with the material world, instead of with the oppressor's misrecognition or lack of recognition. Although the latter, too, shapes the world, the colonised must not mistake it for the world.

Embodied Experience

Fanon's emphasis on the body, and on embodied experience, offers a further pillar to his conceptualisation of subjectivity. Studies that take up questions of embodiment in Fanon include Majid Sharifi and Sean Chabot on biopolitics, violence, and dignity (of the body); Carolyn Ureña's work from a Disability Studies perspective; and Lewis Gordon on masculinity, manhood, and the 'zone of nonbeing' in *Masks*.[8] Others like Neetu Khanna incorporate affect and emotion in relation to the body in order to explore a set of relations between embodied experience and political feeling, within the context of decolonisation. While agreeing that such sets of relations are fundamentally related to how 'a collective revolutionary consciousness must both arise from

---

[8] Sharifi and Chabot (2019), 251–71; Carolyn Ureña (2019), 233–51; Lewis Gordon (2015), 19–47.

and transform the psychic trauma of racialisation',[9] Fanon's attention to corporeality suggests that this notion of the 'visceral' (embodied experience and political feeling) is always already implied by his understanding of subjectivity as only ever an embodied subjectivity.

A phenomenological view of the self, as understood through one of Fanon's influences, Maurice Merleau-Ponty, posits that it is formed through our daily, and mostly mundane, physical encounters with the world around us.[10] But, Fanon argues, embodied experience in a colonial world that creates the social category of race, then locates it upon the body so as to secure an economic system as normative, is oppressive of the very possibility of consciousness of oneself as an embodied, yet still unified and coherent, whole: the latter becomes 'solely a negating activity' (Fanon 1952, 85) for a non-white body. In seeking to apply phenomenology's mutually constitutive interaction between subjective consciousness and the materiality of the world to his own body, Fanon is left asking why the embodied subject yielded by these interactions is assumed to have what Gayle Salamon terms 'an "underneath" that is untroubled by dramas and dilemmas of racial or sexual difference' (2006, 97), given that the (colonial) space that body inhabits is oriented, or rather disoriented, by the latter differences.

Sara Ahmed argues that there is a glimpse of such an 'underneath' in *Masks*, found in Fanon's description of his body 'at home' in the process of directing his arm to reach for his cigarettes when he wishes to smoke. It shows, Ahmed posits, 'the body before it is racialised', before 'the disorientation affected by racism diminishes capacities for action' (2006, 111). This disorientation occurs in the next, much discussed scene: '*Maman*, look – a Negro! I'm scared!' (91). However, Fanon tells us prior to this scene that 'the black man on his home territory is oblivious of the moment when his inferiority is determined by the Other' (90). Even when 'at home' in his body, Fanon insists that 'the world', and especially location, effects self-perception. For example, although there do exist 'minor tensions between the cliques of white Creoles, Mulattoes, and Blacks' in the Antilles, he reflects, 'when we were given the occasion to confront the white gaze . . . an unusual weight descended on us. The real world robbed us of our share' (90). This is not, then, a straightforward description of moving from an experience of 'a body before it is racialised' to a body 'made black' then 'weighed down' accordingly. Where one stops and the other starts is more ambiguous here; Fanon is suggesting that there is more than one racial-historical schema that bodies inhabit simultaneously, effecting

---

[9] Neetu Khanna (2020), 3.
[10] See also Maurice Merleau-Ponty, *Phenomenology of Perception* (1962).

one's self-perception. Rather than whether or not there is a 'body before racialisation' – before it exists emplaced in a particular historical and social location – what Fanon finds a more urgent consideration is that European colonialism has done something altogether different ('an unusual weight') thanks to the social, political and economic power of imperialism. It turns one of many fluid racial-historical schemas into a rigid racial-epidermal schema, and thus stops some bodies from becoming.

As Ato Quayson describes, the '*Maman*, look!' incident generates an 'affect of terror', which is crucially also an immobilising affect (2021, 17). The powerful image of dismemberment Fanon paints by describing his now-unrecognisable body being 'given back to [him]' is a moment of total mundanity on the one hand – a child doing what a child does, unself-consciously speaking – and a towering power imbalance on the other, where we witness the implosion of a man's phenomenological experience of his own body. In that moment, he is no longer able to 'intellectualise differences' between his own and others' bodies so that there is 'nothing dramatic about them' (90) – which is not quite the same as no longer being in 'a body before it is racialised' (Ahmed 111). Rather, as Lewis Gordon describes, 'the n——r who awaits his or her appearance' in the mind of 'the white' is interpellated into existence, unconsciously, by the child, and Fanon unconsciously turns in response (2021, 22). Rather than the unsurprising fact of this white child's early socialisation into anti-blackness, or that colonialism instructs us in the meanings to be ascribed to some bodies ('I'm scared!'), what Fanon's analysis prioritises here is why his body responds in seeming confirmation of this racial-epidermal schema. Part of the shock of the event for him is his bodily reaction. 'I thought that what I had in hand was to construct a physiological self, to balance space, to localise sensations' (178), he says. These are elements of proprioception: a process through which we apprehend and make sense of our own bodies. Upon being interpellated, Fanon queries why his proprioceptive process is overridden by an 'internalised inflection of a social reflex', which causes him to turn in response to the child's description (Quayson 16).

This moment yields more than what is already known to Fanon from both his lived experience and his professional practice: that a social invention (race) inscribes various meanings upon his and others' bodies, which helps its founding structure – colonialism – propagate itself. Any psychic effect of such a world, like 'inferiority complexes', Fanon ascribes to the same process in the same order: 'First, economic. Then, internalisation' (xiv–xv). When the resources to be drawn for one's subjectivity constitution (resources consisting of experiences in the material world) indicate at every turn that you are an object, or a subject-yet-to-be, there seems to be no escaping what Pramod K.

Nayar calls colonial biopolitical regimes. There, 'the body is the centre from which the dehumanization and loss of dignity proceeds' (2019, 224). This is especially evoked in Ritwik Ghatak's visceral aesthetics in *The Cloud-Capped Star* (1960) in order to narrate the experience of Partition dispossession. *Star* is singular in many ways, but Ghatak's extra-diegetic conventions lend themselves to particularly visceral representations of the gendered dimensions of oppression. His experimental realism, among other things, brings to life the corporeal experience of his protagonist Neeta's dire circumstances. Particular sequences stand out in communicating her psycho-economic suffocation; in one scene, for example, Neeta's caregiving and wage-earning burden is multiplied to devastating extent after her father's accident, and Ghatak's shot shows Neeta turning away from her family and wearily looking up a dark staircase. Low light and dramatic depth-of-field renders the staircase an endless upward spiral, and the slow pan to the vortex-like sight above evokes the sensation of vertigo. In these and many more moments, Ghatak's film treats the body as the main location of this historical experience that displaced millions on the Subcontinent and confined many more, like Neeta, to the corporeal wear and tear of poverty. What emerges in that location (trauma, longing, nostalgia, despair and guilt) are fundamentally embodied knowledges that counter the triumphalism of state-sanctioned independence narratives, turning the psycho-somatic legacies of Partition into its historical truth.

However, Fanon's treatment of the body, even where he describes such abjection as comparable to Neeta's, is also affectively charged by the dialectical relationship between self and world that it sustains. This charge has liberatory potential, though it is not to be confused with a teleological narrative of liberation in itself. Fanon's example of the Algerian *fellah*'s so-called 'indolence' in the face of being put to labour illustrates this distinction. In this example, Fanon suggests that embodied experience can give rise to resistance, but not necessarily sustained resistance informed by knowledge of the powers structuring that experience: 'The duty of the colonized subject, who has not yet arrived at political consciousness or a decision to reject the oppressor, is to have the slightest effort literally dragged out of him' (Fanon 1961, 220). Embodied experience as conceptualised by Fanon is not foundational because of some self-evident authenticity, but because it yields knowledge of 'the raw material with which we construct identities' (Mohanty 1997, 205). And in this way, it may be contiguous to say, it sustains the possibility of psycho-political shifts. While Ghatak's protagonist arrives at resistance too late – as her brother Shankar visits a dying Neeta in a sanatorium for the terminally ill, Neeta can only utter 'but I really wanted to live!' – other post-independence texts use it as a source of political energy and social transformation. Souleymane

Cissé's extreme close-ups (forehead to chin) in *Work* (1978) evoke a tactile connection between the spectator and the subjects on film, channelling what Laura Marks has termed 'haptic visuality' (2000). Having the eye function as a faculty of touch in moments that are particularly sensorial, Cissé's shots of Bamako's workers impart a heightened sense of what enduring the manual work of the textile factory, and going through its motions, does to the mind and body. But his combination of haptic shots with medium shots that take in broader settings, like the street, the mosque courtyard, the factory floor, and the middle-class home, foremost situates Cissé's characters within their environments via their bodies. The cuts from an activity (self-grooming, welding, reading a magazine, etc) to close-ups of the people and objects involved generates a sense of how socio-spatial practices, and the embodied subjectivities of its participants, are mutually constituted. In this way, Cissé maps place via the people that make it what it is, gesturing to fault lines in the totalising effects of a global capitalism that, by the late 1970s in West Africa, had begun to transform colonial extraction into the neocolonial production line. This latent, embodied political energy explodes at the end of the film, where the textile factory workers form a human barrier to stop their criminal boss from escaping the police.

This difference between the fates of *Star*'s and *Work*'s characters return us to Fanon, who insists that only via a double confrontation with the world's racialisation of his body, and with his body's learned response to that world, can embodied subjectivity become a location for the critical evaluation of this colonial mechanism. 'The *eye* is not only a mirror, but a correcting mirror. The *eye* must enable us to correct cultural mistakes,' Fanon insists (1952, 178) (original emphasis). A mirror may prove corrective by way of the comparison it makes possible between what appears, and what is actually out there: a world of experiences, such as political action, available via your body. As Stephanie Clare describes, 'life in Fanon's writing is the quality of being directed toward the future through action' (2013, 62). And when life is tied to embodied movement and action, the possibility of decolonisation persists through it. This is no blueprint for what a possibility may become, but it is a state of relationality between the material world, embodied experience and subjectivity constitution that renders visible what Fanon calls 'the world I am heading for' (Fanon 1952, 204). Corporeality can therefore be understood not just as an arena of colonialism's oppression, but also as a starting point of anti-colonial knowledge. It is still that life itself in which the stirrings of decolonisation can be sought, through an embodied subjectivity that engages with the world in order to change it – and is changed in the attempt.

Creative Agency

What is emerging so far is a repeating upon the idea of subjectivity as formed and re-formed through actions that confront the colonial world. But if the negation of one's subjectivity is to be countered through embodied knowledge of colonialism's workings, which then informs action done upon the world, what to make of Fanon's elevation of 'freedom', as in: 'I have one duty: the duty never to let my decisions renounce my freedom'? (1952, 204) This freedom – which I propose to interpret as creative agency – is that which must exist for the radically new to be a constant possibility. However, it is not unmoored: we shall see that it is given direction, constraints and purpose by the fact that many are still unfree. Wherever oppressive social, political and economic conditions can be challenged, there also will be a series of choices that may (re-)constitute your self. Here, Fanon's approach to subjectivity intersects with his theorisation of the process of decolonisation itself as the creation of 'new' men,[11] informing the third component of his material conceptualisation of the self.

As '[decolonisation] infuses a new rhythm, specific to a new generation of men, with a new language and a new humanity' (Fanon 1961, 2), this social, psychic and political becoming crucially involves exercising agency ('my freedom') in dialectical relation to the historicity and corporeality of subjectivity, which delimit it. As such, far from a declaration of individualism, this is said within the context of how colonialism structurally redirects embodied action towards cyclical reaction to oppression. That 'quality of being directed toward the future', of being both agential and creative, is systematically blocked. Violent anti-colonial struggle, while generative in many ways for Fanon and which saw many colonised peoples through to the seizing of political and economic power, is one such form of agency that does not alone transform subjectivities in ways that translate into a changed relationship with the material world. This emphasis on the psycho-political outcomes of a necessarily violent struggle is shared by several post-independence texts. In *A Grain of Wheat* by Ngũgĩ wa Thiong'o, it informs a major, if often latent, preoccupation in the novel: can those who participated in armed anti-colonial struggle necessarily assume to have 'decolonised their minds' (Ngũgĩ 1986)? As many readers of *The Wretched of the Earth* have elaborated, the 'new concepts' that such political, interpersonal and pedagogical work gives rise to are enriched and enabled by collective struggle.[12] But consciousness of both one's material world

---

[11] Fanon, *The Wretched of the Earth*, p. 239.
[12] For an early critical consideration of this that still holds, see Neil Lazarus (1993).

as not yet transformed, and in what ways transform it must, are foundational to these pursuits. This sustains 'freedom as a difficult question that cannot be resolved' (Marriott 2011, 64) in Fanon, but it does not foreclose the specificity and enduring relevance of armed anti-colonial struggle to independence and beyond. As such, while Ngũgĩ's *Wheat* condemns collaborators like its antagonist Karanja for having betrayed the cause of Kenyan independence, it also gestures to a problem that includes peasant freedom fighters like the characters of Gikonyo and Mugo. Looking to undo the emasculating experience of detention by enacting gendered violence brings Gikonyo no peace. Individuals who are 'involved in the active work of destroying an inhibitive social structure and building a new one begin to see themselves', Ngũgĩ writes in *Homecoming* (1972, 10), and Gikonyo's mother Wangari, who sides with her daughter-in-law, draws attention to this pending task when she calls for her son to 'know [himself]' (172). Wangari here sees through her son's rage and knows it to be a misplaced attempt at dealing with his 'thingification' under detention: a word with psycho-political inflections coined by Aimé Césaire (1950, 43) and echoed later by Fanon as 'the "thing" which has been colonised' (1961, 37). Wangari's warning is a discomfiting but important one to make for a novel that maintains that to live in, and for, community is the condition of collective transformation. Her reprimand underlines how, while a moral victor of the Kenyan independence struggle, Gikonyo is not yet thinking in terms of Fanon's 'real leap' of 'introducing invention' (1952, 204) for a future world decolonised. An ontological re-alignment with others and commitment to (self-)transformation is necessary, too, of those who participated in violent anti-colonial struggle – indeed, perhaps especially from those who participated, because the social transformation promised by decolonisation cannot be realised by men who 'thingify' women because they themselves were once 'thingified' by colonial violence.

The emphasis on creativity persists throughout *Wretched*, where Fanon describes anti-colonial struggle as 'opening up spheres [people] never even dreamed of' and 'awakening people's intelligence' (130). While Ariella Aïsha Azoulay puts forward a persuasive caution about how calls for new beginnings can often serve to enhance and reproduce hegemonic violence (2019, 334), it may be disingenuous to interpret Fanon's emphasis on novelty here as wholly dismissive of pre-existing socio-cultural resources for resistance (such as those found in 'old', or customary, practices). In keeping with his prioritisation of the psycho-political, I suggest the emphasis serves to sustain that the only conditions under which subjectivities can 'become' through and out of colonialism is collective and agential creative action within the colonial world, so as to effect the structures of that world. Fanon argues that, even after the ostensible end of colonialism, people must 'exercise their authority and express their will' as they go about co-creating the new conditions of life (149). If this creative will is blocked after independence, then 'the moment for a fresh national crisis is not far off,' he diagnoses (150). The social and psycho-political resources those creative actions may draw on, and the methods collectivities may employ, are open, drawing as they do from 'all the material means which make possible the radical transformation of society' (250). They crystallise at certain times in dynamic relation to the changing contexts of the struggles at hand.

As with the political limitations to reactive versus creative action, so too with the former's ontological limitations. This is articulated as early as the charged conclusion to *Masks*, where Fanon propounds that the uncovering of cultural, social and intellectual histories destroyed, erased or suppressed by colonialism is to be celebrated only insofar as the liberation of the 'eight-year-old children working in the cane fields of Martinique or Guadeloupe' is also being fought for (205). One's humanity in a colonial world is expressed when – in the face of their own subjection – one 're-claims the subjects and peoples that one encounters in the world and who live in precarious conditions'. Majid Sharifi and Sean Chabot discuss how Fanon's clinical writings, too, maintain the idea that 'selfhood cannot be complete without the arduous process of humanizing the Other' (2019, 254). This creative leap in intention and focus is the difference between power substitution and liberation, and between the internalisation of colonial conditions and the search for 'a new language and a new humanity' (Fanon 1961, 36). In the former, the 'new man' of decolonisation is a master, because there has been 'no breach of the colonial master's ontological horizon or the material expressions of that horizon' (Harfouch 2019, 145). Fanon does not give the new human content, but as the outcome of a dialectical process, that 'ontological horizon' or that gaze on the world cannot be just another variation on the relations of the hegemonic colonial order. While it cannot be pre-determined, it cannot come into being without engaging in a confrontation with the world for the purpose of freeing others. This is about inventing what becoming 'free' is, when it will no longer equate to becoming (like) a master.

Practical Actions

As this vision of collectivity and embeddedness in material conditions suggests, while Fanon does mobilise creative agency, he maintains that the (re-)constitution of subjectivities must also emerge through a rejection of colonialism's logic that agency equals the drive for individualism: 'the only way to break this vicious circle that refers me back to myself is to restore to the other his human reality' (1952, 192), because 'only conflict and the risk it implies can make human reality, in-itself-for-itself, come true' (193). I raised the point above that the transformation of subjectivities involves the creative work of conceptualising through and out of the limited possibilities offered by 'becoming (like) a master', but this does not mean a de-linking from, or a non-confrontation with, the 'master's ontological horizon and its material processes'.[13] Fanon affirms that one cannot pick and choose those elements in one's own conditions that are somehow 'non-colonial' or 'non-Western' – themselves unstable notions – ensuring that only those phenomena shape one's psyche, one's intersubjective relations or one's embodied experience of the world. Marco Vieira rightly cautions against all-too-easy espousals of 'reconnecting with non-Western ways of "being in the world"' (2019, 150) – not for their valuable attempts to challenge Eurocentric ontology and epistemology, but for the assumption of the existence of fully isolated, 'non-Western' (ante-capitalist or non-neocolonial) ways of 'being in the world'. The 'asymmetrical encounter between the colonised and the coloniser has fundamentally and extensively redefined human subjectivity', given the 'all-encompassing penetration of Western coloniality (in its political, economic and cultural representations)' (Vieira 150). Some completely pre-colonial or non-colonial form of subjectivity cannot be uncritically assumed, because most of the world has been in asymmetrical contact (if not outright destructive and violent contact) with a capitalist globalisation that has risen out of colonial domination.

In fact, Markandaya's 1954 novel *Nectar in a Sieve* tackles exactly this encounter. Even where it first seems to present a semi-romanticised view of rural southern India after independence, the novel concludes as Fanon does – that the psycho-political means available for people's 'dis-subjection [*désassujettissement*]' (Cherki 2016, 262) are replenished through confrontation with the world's colonial structures. Throughout cycles of difficulty and respite, Markandaya's protagonist Rukmani sees her environment and herself bound in an exchange of labour, nourishment, destruction and renewal, which helps constitute her sense of place and self. This has sometimes aided interpretations of *Nectar* as a story of archetypal peasants in the Subalternists' sense: entirely community-oriented, unconscious of exploitation, and indeed unconscious altogether of a self, as they apparently live for community. But when Rukmani's environment is transformed, *Nectar* opens out onto questions of its effects upon subjectivity, and whether these can be resisted or, at the

---

[13] On constructively critical notions of pluriversality in decolonial approaches, see also Gianmaria Colpani (2022), 54–72; Katrine Smiet (2022), 73–88.

very least, whether some agency can be exercised over them. 'Change I had known before, and it had been gradual. But the change that now came into my life, into all our lives, blasting its way into our village, seemed wrought in the twinkling of an eye,' Rukmani narrates (24), describing the coming of an industrial tannery to the nearby village, growing it into a town. The family still pays rent to some absentee *zamindar* as part of a socio-economic bind they know and fulfil. But they are now also squeezed by the higher prices and environmental degradation that follow the waged new workforce in their midst. It is her environment's industrialisation that yields Rukmani the knowledge that no rural idyll ever existed, given its feudal oppressions, and that resistance under these circumstances is to survive and wrest some agency over her conditions. In the end, Rukmani refuses to turn away her daughter, who has borne a child from sex work, and adopts the orphan Puli who helped her survive the city. Her resistance is not manifest in the form of a wishful 'return' to a life before post-independence industrialisation, but rather in confronting the faceless and dispersed workings of capitalist extraction upon her social and ecological bonds.

Putting into conversation various pieces of Fanon scholarship and attempting to synthesise some of their inquiries can never make claims to comprehensiveness or closure. Fanon's works and life – their interpretation, and their instrumentalisation – are live debates. Taking up three intersecting investigations, this chapter has sought to arrive at a working, though by no means final, conceptualisation of Fanon's relationship between the (re-)constitution of subjectivities and the material conditions of colonialism. As emphasised throughout, in its contextually determined dynamic, this conceptualisation is if anything precursor and condition, rather than determinant, outcome or revolutionary praxis itself. Colonialism, blackness, racialisation, and their intersecting structures did not, do not, look the same everywhere. What subjectivities and societies emerge from anti-colonial struggle depend on the specific historical, social, economic, cultural and political contexts of colonialism within which Fanon's so-called *damnés* find themselves, and the methods they employ. As Alice Cherki, who worked alongside him from 1955 to 1961, writes: 'the idea that a master discourse, colonial in this instance, could shape the constitution of the individual subjective unconscious is of paramount importance to the entire body of work that has been attributed to Fanon' (2016, 22). While Fanon's dialectics cannot circumscribe all outcomes, it illustrates why the material for becoming cannot be anything but that which is found in the reality of engaging with that world, in all of its constituent parts, as one seeks those means best suited to the context within which one is looking to liberate others.

Understood in this sense, 'the link of liberation to realised identity' in Fanon does not always 'equate the experience of post-independence with a new sovereign identity' (Marriott 2018, 53), but rather enables a critical understanding of liberation as ongoing and non-linear experiences of confrontation with oppression. It is a movement more akin to what Laurie L. Lambert describes as 'the queer temporality of revolution' (2020, 127), where 'ideas of revolution as a chronological project of achievement' must be disrupted in order to expand what constitutes everyday resistance, political struggle, and decolonisation. This is the grounds from which the psycho-political problems articulated by post-independence texts are asked. What are concerns around 'mental reconditioning' (Sankara 1988) and 'decolonising the mind' (Ngũgĩ 1986) if not questions about where the possibilities for lasting change through and out of colonialism lie (beyond national independence), guaranteed as these changes are only through the ongoing 'practical actions [*action concrète*]' (Fanon 1961, 190) of people who are themselves changed in this process? To approach the historically and geographically specific inquiries this large question poses, recourse to a philosophical and political conceptualisation of the relationship between the colonial world we live in, and the people it produces, is necessary. Fanon's materialist approach to subjectivity as historicisable, embodied and creative is therefore this book's fruitful point of departure when speaking of the self in its narrative and cinematic texts.

Engaging with the trials, contradictions, failures and hopes of the independence periods in their respective countries, the four novels and four films examined in the following chapters seek to understand how decolonisation is both being arrested and pursued in their own contexts. To this end, these narratives ask questions that necessarily rely on, and draw from, the above conceptualisation of subjectivity as historical, embodied and agential. Where do the possibilities of real change lie, they ask, now that the coming of the independent nation-state has irrevocably shown that the material and psychic work of decolonisation still lies ahead? In exploring the avenues of further inquiry this raises through a range of themes – from gender to conflict, memory to place – post-independence novels and films understand subjectivity in Fanonian terms. As a material phenomenon that is effected by and effects change on the world, the self is ever in their line of vision as a terrain of transformation fundamental to Césaire's 'good decolonisation, without aftermath' (1959, 126).

2
Women and Anti-Colonial Nationalisms: Gendering Subjectivity in Satyajit Ray's *Home and the World* and Ngũgĩ wa Thiong'o's *A Grain of Wheat*

In a 1975 essay, Chinua Achebe writes: 'the nationalist movement in British West Africa after the Second World War brought about a mental revolution which began to reconcile us to ourselves' (145). Achebe here singles out the revolutionary impact that nationalist movements could have at the 'mental' level, possibly going a great way in bringing about what he calls 'a reconciliation with oneself'. Mid-century decolonisation gathered much of its momentum from such anti-colonial nationalist mobilisations across Africa and Asia. As Achebe records, the power of nationalist movements at a psycho-political level were undeniable, and they induced many colonised subjects to be actional. 'Creat[ing] a real dialectic between [the] body and the world' (Fanon 1952, 83), such mobilisations were conducive to remaking people's ways of relating to themselves and their world. Yet the contextually diverse attributes and processes of anti-colonial nationalisms also had uneven effects. Their Janus-faced aspects have been a key preoccupation of Postcolonial Theory. Sometimes, as Neil Lazarus (2009), Crystal Bartolovich (2002) and Benita Parry (2004) have discussed, this has been to the detriment of understanding its role in sustaining anti-colonial momentum up to and beyond independence, but also to the benefit of examining the darker outcomes of some nationalisms in post-independence contexts (such as territorial secessions or ethnic conflict).[1] The latter have been immortalised in cultural production ranging from novels to plays, films to poetry. Unresolved and riven with contradictions, the lived experience and subjective effects of anti-colonial nationalisms are grappled with time and time again in post-independence texts.

A Grain of Wheat by Ngũgĩ wa Thiong'o and the 1984 film *Ghare Baire (Home and the World)* by Satyajit Ray, within their Kenyan and Indian contexts respectively, acknowledge complex and politically urgent questions around

[1] On this, see also Said (1993); Chrisman (2003); Barrington (2006); and Spivak (2009).

the possibilities and limits of anti-colonial nationalisms for 'decolonising the mind'. This chapter will explore how they set up, to different degrees, a Fanonian framework within their narratives via characters that, through a 'dialectic between [the] body and the world' (Fanon 1952, 83), change their relationships to themselves, each other, and to the nationalist energies that mark their historical contexts. Following the social and psychic struggles of its two male protagonists Gikonyo and Mugo, *A Grain of Wheat* unveils how people carry an accumulation of multiple histories, with these – among other things – providing resources to draw on during, and after, protracted nationalist struggle. But as Gikonyo and Mugo resolve the psychic effects of this struggle through re-integration into community, the chapter will bring into view how women's subjectivities remain something outside, or other than, what the novel's dialectical vision affirms. This makes visible important fault lines in the relationship between the experience of anti-colonial nationalist struggle – even with its powers of 'mental revolution' – and its actual outcomes at a psycho-political level. Reading for the transformation of *Wheat*'s characters' subjectivities over time reveals the gendered circumscribing of this transformation. The novel leads to different outcomes in political consciousness for men and women, despite their ostensibly shared material conditions.

The critical significance of this, and its relevance to an unfinished decolonisation, will grow clearer as this chapter proceeds to its cinematic text. In *Home and the World* (1984), Ray adapts Rabindranath Tagore's 1919 novella with a focus on the gendered dichotomy of home/world against the backdrop of the nationalist Swadeshi movement of 1905–1917 in colonial Bengal. From the antagonist Sandip's Pompadour cigarettes to its female protagonist Bimala's Anglicised saris, the materials of the 'home' – which the story's two central male characters assume to be a sphere of Hindu custom, cocooned from the nationalist movement – actually begin to provide Bimala with direct access to nation-history in the making 'outside'. *Home and the World* therefore reveals a dynamic that first comes into view in *Wheat*: that of the dialectical relationship between the constitution of subjectivities and their material conditions. But in the Kenyan novel, the subjectivities of characters like Njeri and Wangari – Gĩkũyũ women who are vital for the recuperation of the kind of anti-colonial history *Wheat* celebrates – are not entirely realised. Nor are their actions integrated into the novel's dialectical vision of national liberation.[2] Similarly, in

---

[2] This is not to say Ngũgĩ espouses the nationalism of the native male elite: he suggests disapprovingly throughout *Wheat* that 'in Kenya, during the Mau Mau insurrection no known nationalist claimed he was a member of the movement or attempted to defend it' (Fanon 1961, 71).

Home and the World, the effectiveness of nationalism as a source of 'mental revolution' (Achebe 1975, 145) remains contingent upon caste, class and gender. While allowing for their differences, considering the Ngũgĩ and Ray texts together brings into view a certain failure to imagine the historicity of women's subjectivities – and this, in both texts, weakens anti-colonial nationalism as a force capable of expediting 'reconcil[iation] [with] ourselves' (Achebe 145).

'Unwilling husbands to Queen Elizabeth'

In Ngũgĩ's *A Grain of Wheat*, published barely one decade after the Kenyan Emergency, the charged relationship between anti-colonial nationalism and gender is latent. It requires, as Brendon Nicholls proposes, reading against the grain of Ngũgĩ's main narrative preoccupations in the novel, working both 'strategically within, and against, the dominant symbolisms of *A Grain of Wheat* and the marginalia of Mau Mau histories in order to discover the spaces that these texts make available to a female sexual and revolutionary subject' (Nicholls 2010, 115). Featuring flashbacks and diversions into 150 years of Kenyan history, *Wheat* focuses on the protracted liberation struggle of the Kenya Land and Freedom Army ('Mau Mau') against British colonial rule from 1952–60. The main narrative takes place four days before Independence in 1963, leading up to the Uhuru celebrations that will honour the fallen fighters of the anti-colonial struggle.

Several of *Wheat*'s characters, however, are still grappling with the psychic afterlives of this period referred to as the Kenya Emergency in colonial records. They try to reconcile personal traumas with a collective narrative of victory. Various histories (including Gĩkũyũ and Christian myths) are woven throughout the novel into the ongoing rhythms of daily life, informing these characters' relationships with their past, themselves, and one other. The novel articulates the principle of community unity, but also foregrounds the lasting effects of the violence of anti-colonial struggle on individual psyches. It argues that decolonisation is only possible if cycles of betrayal are disrupted, yet gives us characters who struggle to move past having betrayed or been betrayed. And it 'critically investigate[s] the links between nativist politics and hegemonic masculinities' (Hammond 2011, 115), but cannot entirely sever its dialectical vision from certain patriarchal supports. While all of these are related, the latter is this chapter's particular focus; it is within that tension that we best see Ngũgĩ approach subjectivity in a Fanonian manner, and explore the ambiguous status of decolonisation after flag independence.

Many have already read gender as a blind spot in Ngũgĩ's revolutionary vision, but for reasons as different from one another as Elleke Boehmer's

(2005), who examines Ngũgĩ's accentuation of class at the expense of gender, and Peter Mwikisa's (2006), who proposes that 'Ngũgĩ [is] ultimately grappling with issues of his Christian faith' rather than advancing revolutionary gender ideals. I propose that, in using a critical lens that incorporates the novel's approach to subjectivity, the implications of this gender blind spot grow particularly consequential to its politics of decolonisation. The novel's attempt to position Gĩkũyũ women as both the moral facilitators of post-independence reconciliation and the symbols via which Gĩkũyũ male subjectivities may be re-configured, results in the dissonance of *Wheat*'s vision of the process from individual to community. This is a process that turns out to be crucially related to the transformation of subjectivities. The novel does reimagine Gĩkũyũ malehood in new ways that serve social healing and nation-building, as Kenneth Harrow (1985) and Andrew Hammond (2011) have explored. However, its project of a new masculinity eventually reverts to a defence of the 'old' Gĩkũyũ masculinity – one that was undone when Gĩkũyũ males became 'unwilling husbands to Queen Elizabeth' (Ngũgĩ 1967, 137). Of greater analytical import than raising this in order to determine the author's personal inclinations with regards to women is exploring why and how the novel's partial granting of women's subjectivities as historical, embodied and agential – characteristics discussed in Chapter 1 – excludes women from the Fanonian dialectic between self and world that facilitates *Wheat*'s politics. Presented as driven either by exclusively political-heroic motivations (Wambui, Mary Nyanjiru) or exclusively sexual-romantic ones (Njeri, Mumbi), women's actions in *Wheat* seem to exist outside the dialectical 'becoming' (from states of solitary distress to collective healing) that its male characters experience. That the former are also shaped by political experiences, which in turn can and do prove consequential for the trajectory of decolonisation, remains under-examined.

Collective Histories

Both recent (Emergency-era) history and distant history (Gĩkũyũ and biblical mythologies) are consistently woven into the ongoing rhythms of daily life in *Wheat*'s setting, a village called Thabai. Indeed, reiterating these collective pasts, as the recruits do throughout the Mau Mau uprising, often becomes a means of resilience: 'Karanja and others collected [in Gikonyo's workshop] in the evenings, hurled curses and defiance in the air, and reviewed with pride the personal histories of the latest men to join Kihika' (Ngũgĩ 1967, 101). Recalling recent history allows *Wheat*'s male characters to reassure one another of their loyalty to the anti-colonial struggle, and to imagine otherwise. The latter, to recall, characterises the temporality of decolonisation for Fanon:

For the colonised, he writes, 'disalienation will come from refusing to consider their reality as definitive' (1952, 201). That 'being for somewhere else and something else' (Fanon 170) functions in this moment of *Wheat* almost exactly as Fanon proposes. Here, men living daily with the fear of being captured by the British substantiate their subjectivities under colonial conditions of terror. They remember the past and present of Gĩkũyũ resistance, implying its sure futurity. Fanon's theorisation in *Masks* as to where the 'raw material' (1952, 113) for processes of disalienation may be found here takes the form of the relational and psychic power of shared histories.

The men's collective emotional investment in the trial of the Kapenguria Six, for example, functions in this way. Facing the sham trial's predictable outcome galvanises the detainees at Yala, where our protagonist Gikonyo is being held, into action. First hiding their shame about their feelings of distress, they then begin to redefine what it means to share this wrenching experience:

> They refused to look into one another's eyes in order not to read what the other was thinking . . . Then one night, suddenly, they believed the news, all of the detainees to a man. They did not say their belief to one another, it was only that they gathered together in their compounds and sang. (104)

Although some members of the Kapenguria Six, who hoisted the Kenyan flag on independence day, have been excluded completely from the public domain by successive regimes since, Mbũgua wa Mũngai stresses that 'the identities and poses assumed by the founding fathers have had a significant bearing on how successive generations of Kenyans have viewed themselves and others' (2010, 58). The inmates sing the Gĩkũyũ creation myth; the connection between mythological past and political present, performed through song and the collective memory it sustains, helps these men 'look into one another's eyes' (104). There, they encounter the same secret desire for life over martyrdom in the name of national liberation. Only in doing so can they resist the deliberate function of their detention, which is to break their unity and resolve.

Christian mythology also grounds the novel's notion of subjectivity as, among other things, a location of shared histories. In a scene describing the Uhuru celebrations, biblical parallels are written into the community's recitation of recent history: 'They sang of Jomo (he came, like a fiery spear among us), his stay in England (Moses sojourned in the land of Pharaoh) and his return (he came riding on a cloud of fire and smoke) to save his children' (214). Despite occasionally bordering on messianic declarations, resistance leader Kihika also frequently adopts biblical myth into a materialist understanding of colonial Kenya. Kihika's strong personal faith is the prism through which he chooses to understand how he, as one man, is connected to the decolonisation that must be delivered to all. He exclaims:

> Can't you see that Cain was wrong? I am my brother's keeper. Take your whiteman, anywhere, in the settled area. He owns hundreds and hundreds of acres of land. What about the black men who sweat dry on the farms to grow coffee, tea, sisal, wheat and yet only get ten shillings a month? (96)

With such strong links gestured towards between subjectivity and history, *Wheat*, however, then withholds the same accumulative and relational subjectivity from its women. Where the former should result in the narrative presenting us with women's subjectivities of a similar historicity, we will see that they are instead static. This re-routes what could have been a radical politics of decolonisation in the novel: one that may have brought full circle the novel's psycho-political investment in anti-colonial nationalism.

The Symbol of Woman

Wheat configures women's bodies as sites of male reconciliation and national salvation. It does so with what can even be read as an investment in women as society's depositories of a latent reconciliatory potential. As Boehmer points out,

> It is by singling out female voices, by fixing women beneath the evaluative epithets 'vibrant' and 'beautiful', that Ngũgĩ gives way to that tendency to objectify women which qualifies his attempt to grant them a leading role in the revolutionary struggle for Kenyan liberation. (2005, 42)

One way this occurs is through the novel's reliance on positioning 'Woman' as symbol, with the function of making or breaking male bonds. That Mumbi, for example, 'arous[es] other characters to a better knowledge of themselves' (Sharma 1984, 207) and 'is the catalyst that prompts [Mugo] to public confession' (Nnolim 1984, 219) renders her a disembodied symbol that can take on various meanings. These include becoming a stand-in for psycho-political hope in conversations that facilitate the relationship between Gatu and Gikonyo, and between Mugo and Gikonyo.

During their detention, Gikonyo experiences a 'terrible bond being established between [Gatu and himself]. He struggled against this but in the end gave up, so that it was he who first opened his heart to Gatu' (107). This confession centres around Mumbi, or rather, around all the imaginative weight

Gikonyo has assigned her. Through recounting their marital bliss, Gikonyo is able to confess (via the sign that is Mumbi/Woman) his feelings of guilt about the fact that returning to domestic life, rather than Kenya's political freedom, is what sustains him throughout imprisonment. This facilitates a bond between the two men, who share many characteristics that Ngũgĩ seems to envision for a new, revolutionary Gĩkũyũ masculinity. These include (for him) the most important aspects of traditional Gĩkũyũ masculinities, such as sexual potency and community loyalty – while also allowing for vulnerability and emotional expressiveness. When Gatu answers Gikonyo's confession with a disclosure of his own about a missed opportunity at marriage – where, again, Woman functions as symbol of 'all our losses for the cause' – Gikonyo thinks: 'weak, weak like any of us' (108). Gatu, who seemed to have purely ideological motivations, turns out to be too much like Gikonyo for Gikonyo to idolise. The having of 'Woman' and the loss of her becomes a stand-in for what they have sacrificed by joining the resistance: patrilineal futurity, sexual comfort and psychic unburdening.

Gikonyo's 'reformed' masculinity recalls that of Nikhil's in Ray's *Home and the World*, where Sandip's and Nikhil's differing attitudes to Swadeshi nationalism seem to map onto a difference in the kinds of masculinity these two men suggest. Nikhil frames his desire that his wife Bimala emerge out of *purdah* (seclusion) as a suggestion of enlightened reason: 'Here you are wrapped up in me. You know neither what you have, nor what you want [. . .] I would have you come into the outer world and meet reality'.[3] Much as Gikonyo is able to re-constitute his subjectivity throughout *Wheat*, growing vulnerable without emasculation thanks to the usefulness of Mumbi/Woman as a symbol, Bimala functions similarly for Nikhil. She serves, in Ashis Nandy's words, as a kind of 'embodied amalgam or link between (male) patriotisms' (1994, 14). Ray's adaptation, however, will expose this gendered function through Bimala's own arc towards political consciousness – on which more later.

Sam Radithalo (2001) proposes that, in *Wheat*, Ngũgĩ invites us to see women's facilitatorship of male bonding as a vital role that benefits all of society. In his anthropological studies, Richard Werbner similarly argues that it is often the very undergoing of subjection which constitutes a 'persuasively influential and dignified female subject in postcolonial intersubjective relations' (2002, 8). The asymmetries of this, however, are stark. Throughout the novel, it is Mugo who is assumed by others to be a facilitator of reconciliation, on the basis of an incorrect rumour. This is later resolved in Mugo's narrative;

---

[3] All subsequent references are from *Ghare Baire*, dir. by Satyajit Ray (Criterion Eclipse Series 40: Late Ray, 2014), DVD.

he confesses his betrayal of Kihika and subsequently feels 'a load of many years lifted' (232). Via re-integration into community, he grows free to become: to now re-constitute his subjectivity. Mumbi, on the other hand, finds means of psychic resilience during the Emergency – emerging from hunger, extra-marital pregnancy and rejection – without forsaking community. Yet Mumbi is not recognised as warranting a similarly dialectical transformation throughout the narrative as Mugo. Instead, we witness a symbolic elevation of the character more akin to Werbner's observation of women as 'dignified and influential' guides, confidants and healers of men.

In addition to the promise of communal re-integration for men, it is not insignificant that Mumbi-as-symbol also becomes the site of a struggle between Gikonyo and the novel's antagonist, Karanja. The representation of land in *Wheat* speaks to a historical crux of the Kenyan anti-colonial struggle: the demand for the redistribution of the fertile central uplands in Kenya (still sometimes called 'The White Highlands'). The British colonial government's Swynnerton Plan, a colonial agricultural policy aimed at expanding cash-crop productions, was implemented in Kenya in 1954. It concentrated land ownership with the strategy of establishing a new middle class of loyalists in response to the 'Mau Mau' uprising. The result was that 'a new Gĩkũyũ society was born – propertied and propertyless – and left to face an uncertain future in face of the politics of independence' (Ogot and Ochieng 1995, 25). Mumbi's body is laden with land symbolisms that speak to these tensions. Unless her body is utilised by the man with the 'right' to do so (her husband, the peasant revolutionary Gikonyo), the implication is that it could, vassal like, be claimed by the 'wrong' kind of man (the middle-class loyalist, Karanja). Eventually, Gikonyo's successful claim upon Mumbi's body symbolically maps onto (for Ngũgĩ) the righteous claim of the Gĩkũyũ peasant to the land. To that end, the novel's final moments feature Gikonyo's political-sexual fantasy: 'He had never seen himself as father to Mumbi's children. Now it crossed his mind: what would his child by Mumbi look like?' (241). The questionable legitimacy of this land claim – especially given the majority advantages of the Gĩkũyũ after independence – diverts the reader from the class irresolutions of Kenyan independence.[4]

Some scholars argue that we misinterpret Ngũgĩ's 'marked sensitivity to women as nationalists' (Radithalo 2001, 9) if we miss the autonomy in the female characters' sexual choices, like Mumbi's choosing of Gikonyo over Karanja. But it may be inconsistent to reach for this limited lens to read *Wheat* – a novel that, as discussed above, otherwise sustains a dialectical relationship

---

[4] See also Boone et al. (2021) on land politics in Kenya since 1962.

between history and subjectivity. In fact, considering reproductive sexuality in the novel reveals a flip side to the seemingly empowering final reconciliation between Mumbi and Gikonyo. While '[Mumbi] was now really aware of her independence' and 'Gikonyo was surprised by the new firmness in her voice' (242), this hint at her transformation in consciousness is overshadowed by the image that closes the novel: 'I will carve a woman big – big with child', Gikonyo thinks to himself (243). This prophetic pronouncement on the nation-about-to-be-born counterpoises the woman with the 'new firmness in her voice', and what the latter could mean for the future of decolonisation.

Sexual Politics and/in Resistance

While 'Woman' functions as a sign useful for homosocial relations, or a vassal for the reproduction of a certain kind of masculinity, Mumbi complicates this. As do *Wheat*'s secondary cast of female characters. Applying Nicholls's (2010) idea of an 'interested reading' that must to an extent 'work strategically against' the novel's dominant symbolisms, we can explore this paradox as an irresolution: one potentially fruitful for understanding the complex triangulation between gender, subjectivity and history in this post-independence novel. Wangari, Gikonyo's mother, becomes an important character in this regard. Whereas Wanjiku, Mumbi's mother, admonishes her daughter for excessive pride when Mumbi goes back to her childhood home after Gikonyo slaps her, Wangari challenges her son. 'Wangari stood up and shook her front right finger at him. "You. You. If today you were a baby crawling on your knees I would pinch your thighs so hard you would learn,"' (172) she says to a raging Gikonyo, who has returned home after their quarrel to find Mumbi gone. Wangari reminds Gikonyo that he must re-constitute his subjectivity: 'Let us see what profit it will bring you, to go on poisoning your mind [. . .] Read your own heart, and know yourself' (172). In not 'knowing himself', his mother seems to imply, Gikonyo is losing sight of the pending task of his own 'dis-subjection' [*désassujettissement*] (Cherki 2016, 262) – of refusing to 'thingify' others through domestic violence because he himself was 'thingified' by colonial violence. Wangari thus raises a question the novel does not pursue: did what the male Mau Mau recruits go through during the Emergency indeed beget a psycho-political transformation within? In light of ambiguities around what Mau Mau was and how it continues to be narrated,[5] Wangari's warning to Gikonyo implies that those who fought in anti-colonial nationalist struggle cannot straightforwardly assume to have 'decolonised their minds' (Ngũgĩ 1986).

---

[5] See also Bethwell A. Ogot (2003) and Evan Mwangi (2009).

Bethwell A. Ogot (2003) describes how Mau Mau was not an exclusively Gĩkũyũ anti-colonial movement, pointing out that several Gĩkũyũ leaders who occupied positions of power after independence did not accept its radical redistributive demands. As such, a generalisation cannot be made about one 'kind' of Mau Mau strategy, recruit, or experience. In light of these ambiguities around what Mau Mau was and how it continues to be narrated, Wangari's question is a discomfiting but important one to ask – especially for a novel that maintains that to live in, and for, community is the condition of collective transformation out of the legacies of colonialism. An ontological re-alignment with others and commitment to (self-)transformation is necessary, too, of the moral victors of the struggle.

The novel's treatment of the character of Njeri, meanwhile, genders the politics of nationalist motivation. She is one of few in a story deeply occupied with the notion of loyalty – to oneself, to one's community, and to anti-colonial struggle – who emerges perhaps faultless. Njeri, we are told, is cat-like (Ngũgĩ 1967, 100), recalling both colonialist degradations of African womanhood as animalistic, and a woman guerrilla whose stealth proves an asset in warfare. She taunts Kihika's lover Wambuku for expecting Kihika to remain out of the action. Instead, 'letting loose her long-suppressed anger . . . [Njeri pledges,] "I will come to you, my handsome warrior," trembling with the knowledge that she had made an irrevocable promise to Kihika' (101). Honouring her sexual and political promise, she joins Kihika in the forest and dies as Mau Mau. Where does this leave the subjectivity of a militant character like Njeri, whose actions we are told stem from 'long-suppressed anger' towards the trappings of her gender on the one hand, and from her sexual desire for Kihika, on the other?

Njeri's loyalty and passion (which other characters like Gikonyo wrestle with trying to sustain, then grapple with the shame of failing to do so) seem the 'wrong' kind for national becoming. Indeed, Njeri's actions are written through the assumption of their stemming from a rage that emasculates. Despite her reputation as a fighter preceding her knowledge of Wambuku and Kihika's relationship, the novel suggests that her political militancy arose out of jealousy: '[Njeri] felt superior and stronger and she could not help her contempt for Wambuku' (100). Whereas the narrative affirms that Mau Mau men's lived experiences – of land dispossession and torture at the hands of the British – motivates their resistance, it cannot approve of the same consciousness in women. The combination of rage (at her social powerlessness) and desire (for both Kihika the man and the political ideal) that motivates Njeri's actions is deemed inappropriate at a time when Gĩkũyũ masculinity is fragile.

Recent scholarship has established that Mau Mau women's detention and punishment were similar to that of their male counterparts. The British detained approximately 8,000 women under the Emergency (Bruce-Lockhart 2014). Why, then, would Njeri's anger and loyalty mark her an outlier? Sociologist Srila Roy's discussion of gender as central to the moral economy of radical political violence helps illuminate this: 'Given that women have been historically and conceptually excluded from the public realm, and marked as "other" even upon inclusion, political participation entails varying degrees of "ontological complicity", including acquiescing in the power hierarchies within which they are located' (2014, 183–4). This raises the question of what is at stake in 'attaining "composure" through normative (political) identities' (Roy 2014, 183), which is precisely what Njeri defies when she arrives at political commitment through sexual rebellion.

In *Wheat*, 'female identities and anatomies became symbolically bound to motherhood and to the nation – at the expense of female political agency and female sexual agency' (Nicholls 101), and this makes Njeri's choice significant. Like Wangari, she presents an unfulfilled opportunity for the novel to pursue the full complexity of gender vis-à-vis radical nationalist politics. In what ways – other than requiring the 'ontological complicity' of women – could the relationship between gender and nationalism inform the transformation of subjectivities? How would such transformations effect the trajectory of decolonisation? Similar questions exist in *Home and the World*, where Bimala's initial interest in Swadeshi is entangled with her romantic feelings for Sandip. However, unlike the treatment of Njeri in *Wheat*, we will see that Ray's narrative and formal choices draw deliberate attention to how Bimala's political consciousness exists in a complex amalgam with her tenderness for Nikhil and her excitement at extra-marital flirtation. For now, *Wheat* hurries over its markedly 'other' woman, whose actions bring to mind how, for Fanon, 'the beginnings of decolonisation' are to be sought 'within life itself' (Clare 2013, 63), where we desire and act upon desires.

Wheat's problematisation of a single idea of what a man is or can be is undoubtedly a significant critical pursuit for its post-independence context. But in centring the re-socialisation of Gĩkũyũ men to the work of decolonisation, women's subjectivities are imagined only insofar as they make this masculinity/nationhood possible (as with Mumbi). When their actions are in 'excess' to this task (as are Njeri's and Wangari's), the narrative intriguingly acknowledges, but does not pursue, their challenge. Although Ngũgĩ builds a dialectic that conceives of subjectivity and its transformation as historical and embodied, the reduction to symbols of a complex set of female characters' subjectivities weakens the dialectical becoming that is at the heart of this novel.

In some of the above ways, *A Grain of Wheat* centres the re-socialisation of Gĩkũyũ men to the project of decolonisation. Despite its political vision, the novel struggles to imagine women's subjectivities in a dialectical relationship with their material conditions. The latter transform over the course of the narrative only insofar as doing so makes a revolutionary masculinity possible after the trials of anti-colonial struggle. While there is no doubt that *Wheat* remains a milestone in Anglophone African writing, its grappling with gender invites deeper reading into the possibilities and limits of understanding anti-colonial nationalism as a source of 'mental revolution' (Achebe 1975, 145) during the independence period. Ngũgĩ's text crucially brings into view how any vision of liberation must overcome a tendency to treat the re-constitution of subjectivities – of 'decolonising the mind', in Ngũgĩ's own words (1986) – as a process that men undergo, and women merely facilitate.

Turning now more closely to Ray's *Home and the World*, we can find a similarly ambivalent approach to anti-colonial nationalisms. There, the whole cultural edifice of the nation comes to rest in the home (symbolised in the physical person of the sequestered and observant Hindu woman). As we shall see, however, Bimala's overall characterisation and the film's formal choices challenge this in a way *Wheat*'s context did not quite allow.

The World in the Home

Originally published in 1916 and translated into English in 1919 with the close input of its author, Rabindranath Tagore's *Home and the World* is a story where 'home' and 'world' intersect during a period of Indian anti-colonial nationalism. The novel focuses on the 1905–1917 anti-colonial Swadeshi movement, galvanised in part by the 1905 colonial partition of Bengal by order of Lord Curzon, the then Viceroy of India.[6] While a fierce opponent of British rule in India, Tagore was both a dissenter and reformer where nationalisms were concerned. In a mode that 'seemed almost reactionary' (Dasgupta et al. 2013, 152) in its time and milieu, Tagore was opposed to rushing toward nation-formation along the Western model at the expense of histories, cultures, and systems of social and economic organisation that already existed in India. Amiya Kumar Bagchi emphasises in Tagore's writings that which is directed

---

[6] Intended to divide the Bengal Presidency on religious grounds, with a Muslim majority in the east and a Hindu majority in the west, the day of partition (16 October 1905) coincided with Raksha Bandhan day, which celebrates sibling relationships. Tagore implored Hindus to tie *rakhi* on this day, especially to Muslims, to emphasise inter-religious harmony among Bengalis (Ghosh 2017, n.p). See also Sudeshna Chakravarti (2013).

against the de-socialisation of human beings by both colonialism and blind acquiescence to Hindu tradition, seeking instead 'a sustainable, fully human condition' (2014, 42). Warning against equating decolonisation with inclusion into one unequal 'machine' (capitalist industrialisation), operating advantageously for European empires while the rest play catch-up, Tagore asks: 'When, instead of being numerous separate machines they [become] riveted into one organised gregariousness of gluttony, commercial and political, what remotest chance of hope will remain for those others'?[7]

This preference for cultural polytonality and a geopolitically multipolar world undergirds *Home and the World*. Both 'home' and 'world' in this story oscillate between being physically and culturally fixed spheres (at a given time), and porous, unstable notions on the whole. The novella follows Bimala, a young woman who emerges from seclusion at the urging of her British-educated husband Nikhil, a *zamindar* (feudal landlord) in Bengal. Bimala at first seems a repository of all that affectively charges the notion of 'home' in a Swadeshi nationalist imaginary. Her total pre-occupation with domesticity renders her at one and the same time a shorthand for the Bengali upper-class woman; Hindu spirituality; and customary sexual and gender norms. Nikhil's boyhood friend Sandip, one of the leaders of the Swadeshi movement, certainly embraces this idea. For him, the 'world' is the realm of capital, intellect and political struggle. Currently dominated by British colonialism, it must be recaptured by the upper-caste Indian man. This man, in turn, can draw strength from the spiritual power and emotional succour of the Hindu home – the one sphere, Sandip implies, that colonial power cannot touch. Sandip and Bimala's meeting sets in motion the dissolution of this apparent distinction between the two spaces; as Bimala grows attracted to both Sandip and to Swadeshi ideology, she is faced with a choice between enabling Sandip's methods and following the dictates of her own growing political consciousness.

Satyajit Ray's 1984 film adaptation sustains the contours of Tagore's plot and thematic interests, but emphasises the story's connections between Indian (bourgeois) nationalism, gender and colonial capital. Completed by Sandip Ray due to his father's ill-health, *Home and the World* triangulates these three structural forces to reveal how both nationalist politics and colonial capitalism shapes the 'home' at this historical conjecture.

---

[7] Anita Desai calls this 'a particular native meaning given to the political struggle against imperialism' in her introduction to the Penguin Classics edition of *Home and the World* (2005, xxii), but Tagore's observation that 'for the production of wealth on a gigantic scale', a nation has both 'qualities of abstraction' and the 'callous perfection of an automaton' (Tagore 1917, 15) also gestures towards characteristics that Lenin (1917) theorises as that of finance capital.

While set in the colonial period, the film's own context of the early 1980s could be described as late post-independence India. Going into the 1980s, India's political landscape was on constantly shifting ground, with the hardships and horrors of the Emergency (1975–1977) still fresh.[8] Proponents of globalisation in both India and the West, meanwhile, are unable to decide whether it was a lost decade or one that laid the groundwork for capitalist transformation.[9] Why, then, would this period drama that returns to '[Bengali] cultural nationalism's gendered project' at the turn of the twentieth century (Quigley 2018, 55) relate to post-independence Indian conditions? By representing the invisible long-term structures of gendering that Swadeshi nationalism fails to transform, the film reveals nationalism's investment in patriarchy (as *Wheat* does). But with its antagonist Sandip, who remains invested in colonial class hierarchies while resenting Britain's control over it, and its protagonist Bimala, whose subjectivity is transformed upon gradually realising this contradiction, Ray's film speaks to India's post-independence questions around leadership, the role of the nation-state, and power. Whereas *Wheat*'s characters are all largely the Kenyan revolutionary peasantry, with gender being a key blind spot for Gĩkũyũ nationalism in this particular context, *Home and the World*'s leading nationalist Sandip assigns Bimala an altogether special realm of experience due to her gender. Not only does this surface the culturalisms in Indian nationalism, it also – much like *Wheat* – denies that women's subjectivities are also produced through their conditions, their embodied experiences, and agency (ideas so keenly emergent in Fanon's thought on decolonisation).

The Materials of a Colonial Economy

An early scene introduces Bimala as intelligent and headstrong, with a degree of political awareness that exceeds her husband Nikhil's expectations. When Bimala correctly answers him about what Swadeshi is, Nikhil exclaims, 'you know so much!' in surprise. Bimala responds with, 'I read the newspaper'. Her confinement exists to a degree in Nikhil's mind, where he fails to assume that the newspaper that informs him of the world – a particularly 'national' form of media, in Benedict Anderson's theorisation (1983) – has also informed Bimala's understanding of her present. The objects in this scene function with as much meaning. Setting in *Home and the World* is rarely if ever merely indicative of where or who characters are, but also of 'structures of feeling' in

---

[8] This period has since been a major consideration in the Indian contemporary novel; see also Merivirta (2019).
[9] See also David Lockwood (2015) on the Indian Emergency in economic context.

Figure 2.1 Our Struggle. *Ghare Baire [Home and the World]*. Dir. Satyajit Ray, 1984.

Raymond Williams's sense (1977) – of what Ray's characters are preoccupied with, what social forces are present, and what 'affective elements of consciousness and relationships' (Sharma and Tygstrup 2015, 5) are being suggested. One scene, for example, has the camera slowly zooming into an assortment of Bimala's sewing materials, under which a pamphlet titled 'Our Struggle' is momentarily visible (Figure 2.1). In a similar vein, in the above-mentioned bedroom conversation, an abundance of textiles – cotton Edwardian blouses and silk saris – lie draped on the furniture, 'worlding' the intimate sphere. Ray's camera shoots in close-up the myriad objects in the room as Nikhil points out, one by one, that Bimala's comb, mirror, perfumes, dressing table and four-poster bed are all imported.

Although the Swadeshi movement aimed to put pressure on the British primarily via the boycott of Manchester cotton, historians have pointed out that there was little alternative. Indian textile markets only expanded sufficiently to meet domestic demands after the 1930s.[10] This scene hints with historical accuracy at a certain misalignment between the economic reality of India of the

---

[10] See also Abigail McGowan (2016).

time and the strategy encouraged by Swadeshi's elite proponents. Seeing her material surroundings anew in light of this information, Bimala immediately understands that she is implicated, and demonstrates her political will in asking: 'then what should we do?'. Bimala then agrees to venture into the semi-public space of the sitting room to meet Nikhil's childhood friend Sandip, a Swadeshi leader, who is on a nationalist campaign trail around the countryside. The significance of props and set design return to the fore in this crucial meeting of the two. A crowded *mise-en-scène* highlights the characters' class separation from the politics that is the subject of their conversation. Material indicators of English tastes, and therefore colonial capital, are everywhere; these objects, Ray's direction suggests, have reached a degree of familiarity from use, and now exist in a 'homegrown' register. Bimala adorns the English silver vases with local flora, and Nikhil serves his guests Darjeeling tea in Derby porcelain. The heavy Edwardian drapes, the patterned silk of the couches, the men's *dhotis* and *kurtas*, and Bimala's fiery red sari all saturate this scene with textiles, crowding the eye (Figure 2.2). It is clear just how, for this class of Bengalis in this particular period, 'non-clothing textiles helped to negotiate the novel conditions of urban life, where homes were increasingly open to non-kin visitors, and men and women shared space in new ways' (McGowan 2016, 518). Dedicated close-ups of particular objects (vases featuring miniatures of Victorian women, ornate mantelpiece clocks, a deck of playing cards, a pianoforte) situate the characters, Bimala included, within the multi-directional flows of colonial capital within their lives, as oppressed colonial subjects from an oppressive class and caste (Figure 2.3). With the home being populated by these objects, Ray renders it as an always already historicised, 'worlded' space, in the sense of colonial capital's penetration.

These material surroundings – with their particular emphasis on textiles – are also utilised actively for constituting the self. A scene in which Nikhil surveys his lands on a white horse, dressed like a British colonial officer, is perhaps the most unmistakeable example of how his subjectivity exists in tension with the political commitments expressed in the previous sitting-room scene. Nikhil's choice of linen suit and colonial pith helmet to observe his Muslim tenants speaks to how his own subjectivity is produced through a certain class position, over and above any feudal or religious affiliation (Figure 2.4).[11] He pauses to listen in on a sermon at the local mosque; the imam is warning his tenants that Swadeshi is a predominantly Hindu movement, and that they should instead remember that, 'by the grace of Allah, Muslims are the majority in Bengal. You are the farmers. The wealth of this country comes from this

---

[11] On the imperial connotations of the pith helmet, see also Victoria L. Rovine (2022).

WOMEN AND ANTI-COLONIAL NATIONALISMS 67

Figure 2.2 Textiles of the home. *Ghare Baire [Home and the World]*. Dir. Satyajit Ray, 1984.

Figure 2.3 Colonial capital. *Ghare Baire [Home and the World]*. Dir. Satyajit Ray, 1984.

Figure 2.4 The humanist sahib. *Ghare Baire [Home and the World]*. Dir. Satyajit Ray, 1984.

land'. Nikhil can only watch in incomprehension and concern, far removed from the context of his impoverished tenants. To them, their *zamindar* here would look much like an English *sahib*; and sure enough, the two forms of authority, colonial and feudal, overlapped in pre- and post-independence India. Changing but not entirely destroying the feudal relations it found in India, British colonialism re-moulded native economies. As Sumit Sarkar notes, 'the link with a semi-feudal land system did not prevent bourgeois aspirations, but it did inhibit radical thought and action on agrarian issues – a limitation of ultimately momentous consequence for Bengal, with its large Muslim peasant population' (2000, 254). As empathetically as the story portrays Nikhil, the materials of a life built upon this feudal-colonial-capitalist exploitation of the Indian peasantry produce his subjectivity.

Deifying the Nationalist Woman

While Tagore's story is primarily interested in exposing Sandip's 'bad' nationalism and comparing it to Nikhil's 'good' nationalism, Ray's adaptation devotes more scenes to unpicking the thwarted expectations of both men in terms of moulding Bimala's subjectivity upon her emerging from *purdah*.[12] Ray chooses to make visible – although passes no final judgement on, as is his style – both the dichotomy Sandip is trying to construct between Man/thought and Woman/feeling, and Nikhil's patronising enthusiasm for 'cultivating' Bimala's mind. In both symbolisations, the future of the nation requires that the subjectivities of its women are available for moulding through instruction. For Sandip, elite Bengali women are promising embodiments of *Bhārat Mātā* (Mother India): their sexual and spiritual labours will ideally socialise Indian men into becoming anti-colonial nationalists. Sandip's deification of Bimala as the goddess Kali to that end can seem empowering, but as Indrani Mitra argues, 'even as the principle of feminine strength (Kali) was often evoked in nationalist writing in resistance to the aggressive masculinity of imperial culture, the potent sexuality embodied in this figure was to remain a lingering cause of discomfort for the middle-class ideologues of anti-colonial nationalism' (1995, 256). Sandip's mode of nationalism relies on the idealist notion that women 'intuit' nation-love, anchored as they apparently are to their bodies through reproductive capacities. There is no subversiveness in Sandip's woman-worship, but rather the belief that women's subjectivities are formed through phenomena anterior to the Fanonian dialectic between self and world; it must be 'nature' at work. For Sandip, men, in contrast, are burdened with questions, doubts, politics and principles, formed dialectically as they are by the interplay between their concrete realities and their agency.

Significantly, Sandip's ahistorical assumption that women live purely sensory lives actually throws his own ideology into question. What are his motives, if his nationalist feeling does not arise from a place of embodied experience, as he so performatively celebrates in Bimala? Sandip's *bhadralok* social and economic privileges, and even his 'modernising' zeal, align with an Indian middle-class historical self-consciousness. Anirudh Deshpande writes that the 'national project of this middle-class was made problematic by the colonial conditions confronting it' (2009, xi), but also by the colonial value systems through which they viewed this project. This is particularly discernible via the terms in which Sandip defends Swadeshi songs: 'Don't you remember the significance of *La Marseillaise* in the French Revolution?' he asks a cynical Nikhil reproachfully. Liberal-capitalist interpretations of the Enlightenment as

---

[12] This is not as apparent in Tagore's original, which is in keeping with what Kumari Jayawardena (2016) writes of Tagore's attitude to women's liberation. Aligning with most male Bengali reformers of his time, he 'came out strongly against some customs and practices' but believed there to be 'some special female qualities imperative for social harmony' (Jayawardena 85).

a vehicle for progress are integral to Sandip's understanding of nationalism, the former with which he is more familiar than the conditions of production in his own home of Bengal.

Much scholarship on both Ray's and Tagore's versions of *Home and the World* agrees on Nikhil's 'good' nationalism as opposed to Sandip's 'bad' nationalism, stressing its humanist inflections.[13] But Nikhil, too, hopes for the selective liberation of Indian women, who (if bourgeois) should be allowed to become educated companions to their 'absolutely modern' husbands (Tagore 1919, 3). In one scene located in the symbolic space of a balcony, where the film's colour scheme is striking in its meaningful duality of warm and cool in tones (Bimala stepping away from the home fires and out to the world), Nikhil asks, 'those things you said tonight: were those your own thoughts?' If the now 'free' Bimala is not arriving at his own European Enlightenment humanism, Nikhil imagines this must be due to his rival Sandip's skills of persuasion. His question suggests how upper-class patriarchal control of Indian female sexuality 'changed from what was seen as the coercive system of the *zenana* to the more contractual form of companionate marriage' in this period (Sarkar 2000, 55). In the modern/colonial gender system, Maria Lugones argues, 'women racialised as inferior were turned from animals into various modified versions of "women" as it fit the processes of Eurocentered global capitalism' (2008, 13). This may not recall *Home and the World*'s central couple at a surface level, given the gentle demeanour of Nikhil. But while Sandip's imaginary realm of pure 'feminine intuition' may be entirely unable to conceive that women's subjectivities are historical, Nikhil's stems from a similar failure, conceiving of them as a blank slate awaiting the liberal man's pedagogy.

As Priyamvada Gopal remarks, the temptation to gender space as home/feminine and world/masculine vis-à-vis nationalisms, as does Partha Chatterjee (1993), works in favour of 'the assumption that "the nationalist mind" was always already male and that the issue of national "self-identity" was fundamentally a crisis of masculinity' (Gopal 2012, 61). Ashis Nandy rejects this separation, offering that 'Bimala's personality incorporates the contesting selves of the two [male] protagonists' (1994, 14). However, configuring her as an embodied link between male patriotisms does not entirely break with the gendered 'nationalist mind', even if it positions women's subjectivities as shaped by their 'world'. This point of contention is about why a woman's experiences must be managed and contained by separating the two environments (private and public) of one colonial-capitalist reality. As such, the nationalist visions

---

[13] See, for example, Sunita Peacock (2011) and Jayita Sengupta (2012).

of both Sandip and Nikhil jeopardise decolonisation as a multi-valanced and dialectical project of the kind conceptualised by Fanon. It will in fact be the growing instability of these demarcations between 'home' and 'world', and the overlapping spheres of experience within these spaces, that begin to expose how the two men's professed forms of nationalism have done little to 'decolonise their minds' (Ngũgĩ 1986).

Consciousness and Action

Towards the climax of the film, Bimala begins to see Swadeshi's contradictions through the framework of her own emerging political consciousness. Amulya is an important character in accelerating this. A promising youth derailed from his education, he is one of the generation who, in Sandip's vision, will put 'the Swadeshi flame' to building the nation that has been won. Honest, if naïve, Amulya is finally deterred from his role of *provocateur* by Bimala, who dissuades him from armed robbery. Sudeshna Chakravarti notes that 'it is this horror story in the mouth of an innocent boy which finally convince[s] Bimala of the evil of Sandip' (2013, 162). As Chakravarti's emphasis suggests (though 'evil' perhaps overstates Sandip's petulant narcissism), Bimala actually sets aside the revelation about Sandip's hypocrisy here (it turns out he spent Bimala's Swadeshi donation on personal luxuries). This scene is about the Amulyas grappling with a moral universalism that cannot be entirely silenced in service of a hypothetical future good, especially when the nature of that good is decided by men from a class with little skin in the game. It is also about our protagonist, whose political consciousness, at this point, is able to hold contradictions while still recognising a certain universal (here, the moral wrong of the violence to be disproportionately suffered by the poor, like Amulya, through this particular nationalist strategy). Bimala's subjectivity had already been of the 'world' even while it was located in the 'home'. The 'world' has now again 'induced [her] to be actional' (Maldonado-Torres 2017, 435). She does not retreat into her husband's Enlightenment humanism, but rather intervenes to change Swadeshi nationalism's local strategy.

That some anti-colonial nationalisms invest in future neocolonialisms when they work to minimise the risk to patriarchy is a necessary and uncomfortable thread running through *A Grain of Wheat* and *Home and the World*. While their differences are clear in context and form, both Gĩkũyũ anti-colonial nationalism and Swadeshi nationalism respectively fail in these post-independence texts to conceive of women's subjectivities as formed by historical-material experiences. Read together as this chapter has attempted – without collapsing their differences but with an eye to their common preoccupations – Ngũgĩ's and

Ray's works underline the problem anti-colonial nationalisms have in situating women's subjectivities as equally shaped by, and as agents of, history. This produces several anxieties in the two texts, not least about the kind of nationalisms that should and should not be fostered in post-independence contexts still reaching for decolonisation. However, in grappling with why and how anti-colonial nationalisms can expedite 'mental revolutions' (Achebe 1974, 145), Ngũgĩ and Ray place a very Fanonian emphasis on creative agency. The forms of creative agency exercised by women like Wangari, Njeri and Bimala challenge and even redirect those nationalist energies that diverge from the radical goals of decolonisation.

In the following chapter, the stakes of such divergences will become particularly clear. It considers the novel *The Beautyful Ones Are Not Yet Born* (1969) by Ayi Kwei Armah and the film *Xala* (1975) by Ousmane Sembène; both paint a politically bleak post-independence picture that delves into the neocolonial set-ups in Ghana and Senegal, respectively. Their narratives explore the crises of subjectivity that their postcolonial bourgeoisies experience as a result of their own colonial education and their comprador activities. Armah and Sembène emphasise the all-too-material effects that such crises among elites can have upon the wider populace in newly independent nations. But both *Beautyful Ones* and *Xala*, in their different ways, also turn to various elements of Fanon's understanding of subjectivity in order to illustrate the potential avenues for grappling each day with the causes and consequences of neocolonialism. Over the course of both stories, the daily psychic and social confrontations these grapplings entail come to define what a resistant subject may be, even under such disappointing post-independence circumstances.

3

Neocolonialism's Subjects: Complicity and Resistance in Ousmane Sembène's *Xala* and Ayi Kwei Armah's *The Beautyful Ones Are Not Yet Born*

This chapter examines two narratives of hope, betrayal, resistance and renewal set in post-independence West Africa: Ousmane Sembène's 1975 film *Xala* and Ayi Kwei Armah's 1969 novel *The Beautyful Ones Are Not Yet Born*. Both ask what happens to people's subjectivities under these circumstances – seeking to understand, in particular, the relationship between a state that has not delivered the social, political and economic goals of national independence, and the effects that this arrested decolonisation have on people's psychic and social lives. The central allegories of this film and novel hold to account the national Senegalese and Ghanaian bourgeoisies respectively. They also yield a profound interest in the relationship between subjectivity and decolonisation along lines that complement Fanon's approach to the self. In both *Xala* and *Beautyful Ones*, the loss of the hope that independence would facilitate a process of decolonisation provokes a search for the causes and extent of the present decay.

Enriched and strengthened by its ability to hold contradiction, Ousmane Sembène's cinematic practice sustains what Sam Okoth Opondo identifies as 'the ambiguity and multiplicity of African times and lived experiences' (2015, 41), while centring Africans as agents of their own representation. Sembène's fourth feature-length film, *Xala* (1974) addresses the betrayal of the promises of Senegalese independence within the space of a decade, attempting to diagnose why, and how, these hopes have not borne fruit. For Sembène, as for Fanon, the nation is if anything a collective state of motion: it is society tackling shared challenges in ways that, little by little but inevitably, (re)make that society itself. To recall from *Wretched*, Fanon consistently implies that nation-building is a popular activity before it is a space or a political body: 'The nation deserts the false glitter of the capital' where 'flags and government buildings' sit as static and symbolic objects (1961, 144). If anywhere, it exists where 'the massive commitment of men and women to judicious and productive tasks [gives] form and substance to consciousness' (1961, 144). The ways in which various material conditions give 'form and substance' to the subjectivities of *Xala*'s characters informs the crux of the film's critical thrust.

Although Ghanaian writer Ayi Kwei Armah's novel *The Beautyful Ones Are Not Yet Born* (1969) is dark where Sembène's *Xala* is often comical, it too considers how the crises of subjectivity of the powerful (particularly in Ghana's post-independence context) can have serious material ramifications on wider society. Armah was among the very first African writers to question the meaning of independence from colonial rule, and to address the continent's continuing dependence on former colonial powers. Laden with the disappointment of what began as a potentially socialist Ghana turning into a cumbersome and corrupt bureaucracy, *Beautyful Ones* follows an unnamed, working-class man who is a clerk in the Railway Traffic Control Office.[1] Armah's protagonist seems to neither count himself entirely as one of the 'suffering sleepers' around him, nor among those who have 'found in themselves the hardness for the upward climb' (Armah 1969, 23). Within his socio-psychic limbo, he muses that 'it was not so difficult to forget the self and the world against which it had to live' (182). But forgetting and remembering the self, or experiencing cycles of refusal and temptation, is to become the man's trajectory of movement in the novel. Paired with *Xala*'s analysis of the comprador bourgeoisie's internalisation of colonial structures, Armah's exploration of the effects of such structures on the subjectivity of his protagonist will reveal the political stakes of this relation.

Cinéma Engagé

The filming of *Xala* took place within the context of the neocolonial state of affairs it satirises: a context at once a powerful motivator for Sembène, and a constant practical challenge. France's anxieties around the power of film in shaping public opinion in West Africa was evident in colonial decrees such as Le Décret Laval, which sought to 'control the content of films that were shot in Africa and to minimise the creative roles played by Africans in the making of films' (Diawara 1992, 23). Despite this and colonial distribution hurdles, cinema's pedagogical and ideological value, along with its close affinity to African oral traditions, could not be forgone. As Sembène wrote:

---

[1] I use 'working class' within its African contexts and positions, which include, in the example of Armah's protagonist, a wage labourer involved in metals transportation within a post-independence, single-commodity export economy. See also Leo Zeilig's edited volume, *Class Struggle and Resistance in Africa* (2008), for essays covering various markers of 'working class' as understood in its contemporary African contexts.

Since ours is an oral culture, I wanted to show reality through masks, dance, and representations. The publication of a book written in French reaches only a minority, whereas via film one can do as Dziga Vertov did with his 'Kino Pravda'. (Levieux 2004)

Some have therefore suggested that Sembène's cinematic language even 'fulfils the same function as the Gĩkũyũ language does for Ngũgĩ' (Messier 2011, 4). His work's commitment to African futurity certainly bears parallels to Ngũgĩ wa Thiong'o's political rationale for setting aside English, but Sembène's films may not quite share the same emphasis on ethnocultural return. The film disapproves of the substitution of diverse, dynamic, quotidian kinds of African cultures for the fictitious monolith that the Senegalese elite in *Xala* applaud as 'Africanity'. Sembène more closely aligns here with Fanon's critique of the post-independence state's tokenistic attitude towards African cultures: '[the native elites] will surround the artisan class with a chauvinistic tenderness in keeping with the new awareness of national dignity' (Fanon 1961, 119).

Lifelong Marxists like Sembène and Sarah Maldoror also disapproved of adopting wholesale the Soviet approach for filmmaking in Africa.[2] Whereas both felt indebted to the dialectical montage of Sergei Eisenstein, they believed that socialist realism constricted the forms they could explore. For Sembène, this especially meant the freedom to explore a dialectical cinema that could nonetheless include some African oral storytelling techniques. *Xala* pursues these in its tale of an unlikeable businessman, El-Hadji Abdoukader Beye. As he grows obsessed with his sudden onset of erectile dysfunction, paying several *marabouts* extortionate amounts for a cure, he is stripped of the financial and social markers of his status in post-independence Dakar. Drawing from the earlier interpretations of Fredric Jameson (1986) and Roy Armes (1987), scholarship on *Xala* has traced how El-Hadji's behaviour is dictated by a class 'whose meaning and purpose are determined by forces apparently coming from the outside' (Sorensen 2010, 223), proposing that the film draws 'a relation between the private and public: stories of individualised characters or configurations figure a broader public, collective context whose signified is national' (Rosen 1996, 35).[3]

Broadly agreeing with these analyses of *Xala* as an example of *cinéma engagé*,[4] this chapter pivots to Sembène's relatively under-explored but related interest in the relationship between these aforementioned neocolonial conditions, and

---

[2] See also Lindiwe Dovey (2020).
[3] As also discussed by Guneratne and Dissanayake (2003); Mushengyezi (2004); Kilian (2010); and Lindo (2010).
[4] More on this from Landy (1984); Gadjigo (2008); and Opondo (2015).

the formation of subjectivities. One of Sembène's core investigations throughout his early cinematic *oeuvre* – from *Black Girl* (1966) to *Mandabi* (1968) – is that of West Africa's thwarted decolonisation. But the inseparable, albeit varied, relationship between this structural problem and the problem of the different effects these structural injustices have upon the interiorities of West Africans of all classes is also key here. Continuing apace from the 1980s onwards, but already in motion in the early 1970s of the film's making, the separation of Africans from the products of their labours was underway. Accompanying this was neocolonialism's manufactured separation between the individual-subjective and the collective-social. Through its protagonist, *Xala* exposes how this separation depends on conflating purchasing power with ontological security. The antidote, for Sembène, lies in redirecting the psycho-political work of decolonisation away from the task of reforming a Francophile African elite, and towards the land- and kinship-based networks that help sustain everyday life for the wider populace.

As El-Hadji's class enacts mere spectacles of nationalist resistance to legitimise their lifestyles of mimicry, they are also transforming the former's demand for economic self-determination into the freedom of consumer choice. They, in Fanon's words, are not only 'set in the mould of the former mother country' themselves, but also 'hasten to send the people back to their caves' after independence because their class has not taken the 'primordial task' of raising popular political consciousness 'to heart' (1961, 145). As Fanon's psycho-social terminology implies, the threat to decolonisation is not necessarily that this class has hinged the constitution of their subjectivities upon consumer capitalism. They are 'set in their moulds' already, given their colonial education, and after independence, they simply go about undertaking 'their historic mission – that of intermediary', in Fanon's biting diagnosis (152). The critical concern of *Xala* is that a majority are internalising what they see. Under the guise of nationalisation, which in this case is 'simply the transfer into native hands those unfair advantages that are a legacy of the colonial period' (Fanon 152), the populace in *Xala* is distracted from the actual crime at hand: the theft of collective wealth. Building on work like that of Matthew H. Brown (2015), which argues that *Xala*'s allegory constructs characters' subjectivites in relation to collective concerns, I add that it is by seeing this relationality as *Xala*'s starting point, rather than its representational goal, that we can understand how and why the film utilises the problem of subjectivity constitution to deepen its political critique.

Africanity's New Clothes

Self-fashioning, in the very literal sense of clothing intended to indicate certain characteristics about oneself that are socially understood, is of political consequence in *Xala*. The persisting effects of colonial ideologies on Senegal's post-independence ruling classes are unmistakeable in the sartorial choices of the president of the Chamber of Commerce, El-Hadji, and in those of their fellow 'socialist' businessmen. Although their European suits, and the French dresses sported by El-Hadji's second wife Oumi N'Doye, have been discussed as indicative of the native ruling class's alignment with Western interests,[5] less has been said on how this also reveals a self-fashioning based on the idea of imitation, rather than full assimilation into neocolonial power structures. Costume changes here work largely to signify El-Hadji's mark of belonging to the Chamber of Commerce as a space cut off both from the life of the nation, *and* from where the flows of Western capital are decided. The businessmen's self-delusion – infantile in its satisfaction with the mere cosmetics of power – is affirmed when Sembène shows that these men essentially play dress up on independence day when they don their *boubous*. The next day, they suit up to receive a designated amount of francs in briefcases from white French deputies.[6] This class mimicry without economic autonomy signifies a loss (or indeed, sale) of self, cemented via a banal exchange where El-Hadji proclaims to his fellow businessmen that 'modernity mustn't make us lose our Africanity'.[7] This prompts the president of the Chamber, dressed in an extravagant white tuxedo, to applaud and respond enthusiastically: 'Too right! Long live Africanity!'

The moment is reminiscent of the critique Fanon makes in an essay published in *Toward the African Revolution*, wherein he warns of an 'absence of ideology' as 'the greater danger which threatens Africa' in the independence and post-independence period (1964, 196). Amílcar Cabral echoed this concern at the time, with his observation that 'Africa's postcolonial history is one of unfulfilled missions because the national leadership has been lacking in revolutionary theory and ideology' (1966, n.p.). El-Hadji and his class borrow seemingly ideological terms like 'modernity' and 'Africanity', but not out of some attempt to find syntheses between the two (if that is what their proclamations are meant to suggest, and if we were to grant any stability to these two concepts).[8] They do so instead to capitalise on 'ideology as smorgasbord', in Barbara Foley's words, wherein 'ruling-class hegemony, as well as enhanced possibilities for capital accumulation, can be secured by any number of routes

---

[5] See Messier (2011, 14) and Gugler and Diop (1998, 149).

[6] A scene that was censored by the Senegalese Board of Censorship (Chamley 1991).

[7] This and all subsequent references from *Xala*, directed by Ousmane Sembene (1974, New Yorker Video, 2005), DVD.

[8] See also Paul A. Beckett (1980) on Fanon's critique of the 'absence of ideology' among post-independence African governments and leaders.

of ideological transmission' (2019, 70). The men in this scene, chameleon-like in their quick succession of changes in self-stylisation, dip into being harbingers of 'modernity' (possibly some vague celebration of capitalist growth), and then being defenders of 'Africanity' (possibly some vague celebration of nativism). The latter they understand through a dubious interpretation of what the Qur'an contains on the subject of polygamy.[9] What brings Sembène's critique full circle here is the question of who these men even are – what are the cultural, social and economic affiliations constituting their subjectivities? Their use of 'ideology as smorgasbord' not only secures them mere petty accumulation (without political or economic autonomy), but also makes answering this question impossible. El-Hadji and his class have no ideology, whether 'modernity' or 'Africanity'. Nor have they received any real power in exchange for their cipher-like subjectivities, as the viewer is reminded by the white French deputy who looms silently behind the president of the Chamber. Instead, they resort to rhetorical flourish as a global order takes shape to which 1970s Senegal is bound via the terms of neocolonialism.

Self-fashioning in *Xala* connects the constitution of subjectivities to the material circumstances of neocolonialism not only on these negative terms of mimicry, but also on promising terms, through examples of effortless cultural fusion. The film introduces an array of characters who prefer the fez or the head wrap, including a farmer whose storyline merges with the beggars; Adja Awa Astou, El-Hadji's devout first wife; and characters who, according to the spaces they move in, switch between *boubous* and the fashions of a global 1970s youth counter-culture, such as El-Hadji's daughter Rama.[10] However, as *Xala*'s sartorial choices set up what may be examples of subject-positions that arise from lived experience, so do they complicate any simple pairings such as elites/falsehood and masses/authenticity. For example, one somewhat tragicomic scene undercuts such binaries, drawing the viewer's attention to the mutually effectual relationship between subjectivity constitution and the material conditions of post-independence Senegal. A young man who looks neither poor nor desperate steals a farmer's money in the midst of a street commotion, then goes to a tailor to spend his stolen funds on a strange new outfit: a dark suit reminiscent of the French businessmen's, paired with an American cowboy hat (Figure 3.1). The viewer soon finds out that what he stole were the precious savings of a farmer's entire village. The sequence cements how *Xala*'s sartorial allegory is also about the relationship between people's

---

[9] See Vartan Messier on this misinterpretation (2011, 13).
[10] See also Ophélie Rillon (2018) on youth fashion and politics in 1960s and 1970s West Africa.

Figure 3.1 Beggars of Dakar. *Xala*. Dir. Ousmane Sembène, 1975.

everyday self-perceptions and social behaviours, and an economic system of neocolonialism taking shape in the post-independence period. The suggestion that American capital has an entire market to gain upon any weakening of French cultural hegemony in West Africa is clear: the kitsch symbol of the US, the cowboy hat, is literally being bought into in this scene by an ordinary Senegalese citizen. With money stolen from the overwhelmingly agrarian country's most productive class, no less. Sembène suggests that those symbols and objects that the African working classes reach for in order to style themselves in the public sphere are beginning to mirror the commodity worship of El-Hadji and his elite class. It unmoors the production of subjectivity from the Fanonian dialectic traced in Chapter 1 – of the interplay of history, embodied experience and creative agency that sustains the possibility of 'decolonising the mind'. Instead, shown here is the erroneous assumption that subjectivity is something free of any social embeddedness or social obligation.

'Even the insults, in the purest Francophone tradition!'

In a 1976 interview with Noureddine Ghali, Sembène argues that '[The El-Hadji] types are alienated to such an extent . . . [that] they are always the first to say people's mentalities have to be decolonised, but it is actually [theirs] which has to be' (Sembène in Busch and Annas 2008, 73). Elsewhere, he has related this idea about decolonisation on a subjective level ('mentalities') to the functions of the French language in West Africa. In saying that he 'has no complex about using French [. . .] it is no more or less than a working tool' (Sembène in Fofana 2012, 105), he chooses a telling psychiatric term. Not making the former colonial power's language the source of 'a complex' is something Fanon, too, identifies as one of the psycho-political tasks of decolonisation. In his observation, the French language (and we could extend it to other European languages spread through colonialism) has a hand in creating the 'internalisation – or, better, epidermalisation, of an inferiority complex' (1952, 4). Due to the impossibility of dissociating a language from the cultural values it perpetuates, for Fanon, 'to speak . . . means above all to assume a culture, to support the weight of a civilisation' (1952, 89). Language in (post) colonial contexts, he reminds us, has the power to perpetuate or challenge, at one and the same time, cultural alienation (the internalisation of colonial values) and inequitable material conditions (the crushing 'weight' of European 'civilisation' upon the colonised, who built it through sweat and blood).

Particular to Sembène's observation, however, is the complexity of language politics in Senegal. While the cultural and political meaning of French in *Xala* is a point of discussion in most Sembène scholarship,[11] El-Hadji and his daughter Rama have received particular attention. The former's preference for French and the latter's for Wolof has been interpreted as a representation of, respectively, the neocolonial present and the revolutionary pan-African future. As one who has wholeheartedly embraced the economic practices of the neocolonial nation-state, French is undoubtedly 'a complex' for El-Hadji in the sense Sembène uses it above. We witness on several occasions how he insists on replying in French when spoken to in Wolof; shouts in frustration at Rama when not spoken to in French; and in his only moment of rebellion in the film, where he lists the hypocrisies of his fellow businessmen, he is cowed into continuing in French even though he began in Wolof. This is not to discount that, in having spread 'far beyond the boundaries of its core ethnicity' (O'Brien 1998, 25), a different problem of linguistic hegemony arises in twenty-first century Senegal as 'Wolof becomes coextensive with the Senegalese nation itself' (Smith 2010, 69). But the allegory's function in this 1975 film, and how it applies to Sembène's related concern – that of the 'mentalities' of the El Hadjis – is highly relevant to a materialist consideration of subjectivity in this post-independence text.

In *Xala*, the 'complexes' of the native elite, which play out in private (between father and daughter, wife and husband), influence the daily lives of the wider populace. 'We have a bourgeoisie who only feel significant when

---

[11] See Harrow (1980); Mushengyezi (2004); and Vetinde (2012).

they express themselves in French,' Sembène observes in the same Ghali interview (2008, 73). He goes on to suggest that this behaviour, borne of subjectivities that draw on closeness to the Western bourgeoisie for their ontological security, results in insidious long-term effects beyond this class. The majority of the population have urgent material needs that need the postcolonial state's attention, and they may or may not be experiencing any such cultural alienation like that of their elites. A satirical scene captures this well: 'El-Hadji may speak, but only if in French,' pronounces the president of the Chamber of Commerce after El-Hadji is voted out of his position for neglecting his debts. 'Even the insults, in the purest Francophone tradition!' he adds, in utter seriousness. This may seem comical, but as Sembène points out, it is no more so than a bourgeoisie '[who] speaks to the peasants in French. In a country with 80 per cent illiteracy, speeches, which are supposed to talk about their problems, go right over their heads' (2008, 74). This is the far more urgent critique that *Xala* seeks to make: that 'when the bourgeoisie committed this flagrant error [of aspiring to France], they drew an entire people after them' (Sembène 2008, 74). The urgency of these elites' 'linguistic drama' (Albert Memmi 2013, 108) and 'psychological drama' (Fofana 2012, 103) lie in their wider structural consequences.

A more critical approach to the character of Rama proves insightful here. If sustaining the canonical reading of her as the symbol of a politically conscious, youth vanguard of pan-African socialism, we could arrive at the interpretation that the atonement, re-education or re-socialisation of the governing class will come with the post-independence generation. There is, however, cause – in both widely available biographical knowledge of the director and in *Xala* itself – to argue that such an interpretation de-radicalises Sembène's vision.[12] In fact, *Xala*'s attention to the many dimensions of language choice in the ostensible private and public spaces of the film suggest otherwise. The 'complexes' of this class are manifest in widespread and *material* ways; they have given shape to the practices of self-stylisation and social signalling that bespeak power in post-independence society. As such, liberation (which may or may not include the disalienation of this class) cannot only lie in the transformation of material life itself. To recall from Chapter 1, the psycho-political means available for people's 'dis-subjection' (Cherki 2016, 262) cannot be sought, ready-made, from (even 'good') political leadership. It can only come about in action: in living through and out of the limited possibilities offered by the 'master's ontological horizon and its material processes' (Harfouch 2019, 145). Understood within the context of Sembène's politics, which align with the

---

[12] See also Berthomé (2007) and Gadjigo (2008) for biographical material on Sembène.

above Fanonian ideas, the character of Rama suggests that the overlapping of language and subjectivity in postcolonial Senegal leaves few out of its remit.

El-Hadji's eldest daughter prefers the common linguistic practices of Senegal (which is to use French primarily for official business) and makes a point of otherwise speaking in Wolof. Reduced to supplementariness, this recall's Sembène's own position on French as 'a working tool' (Sembène in Fofana 2012, 105). But much has also been written, not least by Fanon, on how political consciousness does not mark an end to the identity struggles of postcolonial intelligentsias, who often situate themselves in relation to two systems of cultural reference. Is Rama's reduction of French to supplementarity *Xala*'s suggested antidote to neocolonial 'mentalities' (Sembène in Busch and Annas 2008, 73)? Rama's refusal to address her father in French is certainly a declaration of political separation from the older generation. However, we can assume that the neocolonial socio-economic conditions depicted in *Xala* determine the contours of Rama's political potential. For instance, Rama's fluent French response to a police officer who stops her functions as a class-based warning to the authorities that she is not to be harassed. In yet another scene, Rama rides her motorcycle to her father's office and is welcomed deferentially by his security guard, who is also tasked with intimidating beggars away from the building (Figure 3.2). This is, on the one hand, a subject-positioning necessitated by Senegal's post-independence reality, where French and Wolof have their domains. But as Rama warns authority of her ability to

Figure 3.2 The Franco-American. *Xala*. Dir. Ousmane Sembène, 1975.

wield French in tactics of everyday domination, she becomes a more ambivalent character. If El-Hadji and his class perpetuate French as a 'locus of unconscious servility' (Trinh T. Minh-Ha 1989, 52), what are we to make of Rama, a politically conscious elite woman, exercising this power?

Although Rama's politics means that she is attuned to the substance of this everyday to a greater extent than her father, *Xala* hints at the asymmetrical oppressions of the bourgeoisie's embrace of La Francophonie (a crisis of subjectivity for them, material deprivation for the masses). It implies that the cultural imperialism of La Francophonie may not necessarily be confronted by the children of the West African bourgeoisie. This is not to say that the rejuvenation of African languages does not have an important place among the tasks of decolonisation, but rather to open up a space for recognising that *Xala* also has some misgivings about its usage as evidence of having 'decolonised the mind'. Language is a 'specific relationship to the world' and to the self (Ngũgĩ 1981, 16). Its ability to shape that relationship, the film demonstrates, still lies in its economic power, however cultural its manifestations also are. We will later witness how class markers (like language) that enable mobility in the post-independence city can in fact directly uphold a neocolonial order in Armah's *The Beautyful Ones Are Not Yet Born*. But for now, *Xala*'s decisive linkage between the constitution of subjectivities and the material conditions of neocolonialism turns on land theft: the crime at the heart of its climactic reveal.

The State of the Land

In the rising action of the film, the beggars' blind leader Gorgui reveals that he has been rendered landless by the expropriation of Lebu lands – people to whom he (and distantly, El-Hadji) belongs. The late 1970s in Senegal saw the beginnings of the commodification of land organised around family networks. The Lebu progressively lost much of their remaining land, and with it, their customary labours in agriculture and fishing.[13] 'What I am now is your fault. Do you remember selling a large piece of land at Jeko belonging to our clan? After falsifying the clan names, you took our land from us', Gorgui accuses El-Hadji. Land loss also signifies here the loss of things that reassure one's subjectivity, including lineage, family ties, place-memory, labour practices, communal knowledges and the interpersonal relations that shape a life lived from the land. The historical background to which this plot twist gestures is one that allows Sembène to make a direct link between colonial and

---

[13] See also Hannah Cross (2013) on the dispossession of the Lebu and their now forming one of the largest groups of clandestine migrants to the EU.

post-independence conditions in Senegal. The collective ownership of land in kinship networks functions in 'the space of a past and future utopia – a social world of collective cooperation' (Jameson 1986, 84). El-Hadji, and the new post-independence national bourgeoisie more broadly, have exchanged this in return for playing Western capital's intermediary. The 'clientelist strategies of political and economic control' of this rentier class in Senegal facilitated neither socialist transformation nor local capital accumulation, leaving the majority of the nation dependent upon connections to, or aspirations towards being, a member of the political class.[14]

While scholarship on this scene has foregrounded the ritualistic punishment and/or purification of the bourgeoisie by the people, it illustrates more.[15] The postcolonial elite's crises of subjectivity are not just a product of the historic colonialism that dispossessed them too (to a degree), but also of independence. Independence of the kind that sustained conditions amenable to clientelism has resulted in the El-Hadjis of the nation taking advantage of ties to their poorer kin (who may assume that their better-off brethren still sustain the socio-cultural codes they do). As such, although 'Sembène's portrayal of the beggars echoes Fanon's faith in the revolutionary potential of the lumpenproletariat rather than Marx's dismissive view of it' (Gugler and Diop 1998, 149), when we situate this lumpenproletariat as the recently dispossessed peasantry that they are, we can discern the contours of a triangulation between collective land ownership, subject-formation, and social embeddedness or intersubjectivity emerging in Sembène's climax.

This triangulation is suggested through techniques that enact a reveal and a contrast, which rely on the climax to work. The reveal is that the series of events that make up the film were triggered not by the *xala* but by an earlier act: El-Hadji's sale of his kin's land, and his subsequent running away from what Jameson coins the 'primordial crime of capitalism' (1986, 84), the theft of collective wealth. His crime is directly linked to his desubjectification. The beggars invite him to partake of the ritual so as to reclaim 'the only thing he has left' to regain: his virility. If his virility is 'the only thing left', the implication that he can have his manhood back (but that is all he will get back) gestures to the realisation that without embeddedness in the social relations and responsibilities that he has sold, El-Hadji has no real potency. In evading social obligation, El-Hadji has given away the very grounds of ontologically secure subjectivity formation.

---

[14] See also Catherine Boone (1990) on the roots of state power in post-independence Senegal.
[15] As put forward in Brown (2015); Mushengyezi (2004); and Lynn (2004).

A contrast, established throughout the film via both narrative and formal methods, also helps this crystallise. The beggars/dispossessed farmers have animated the naturalistic scenes of Dakar street life throughout *Xala*, offering blessings or playing tunes on the *khalam* as they sit on street corners in twos or threes (Figure 3.3). Their collective way of life ensures their survival. We witness, for example, the group preparing tea for everyone using a tin of condensed milk one of their number have procured. They invite the distraught farmer (who, to recall, was mugged earlier) to join them and unburden himself. Gorgui, their leader, silently hands the farmer a portion of what must have been everyone's hard-earned cash from that morning, to nobody's protest. This scene is one of several that establish that the beggars/dispossessed farmers operate via an entirely different set of values. They embody what Sam Okoth Opondo identifies as an 'engagement with the micro-political and transgressive practices of everyday life' in Sembène's entire *oeuvre* (2015, 41) – an engagement that highlights the capacities of the most powerless to create social change. Easily missed, this change includes the transformative experience their companionship has on the farmer. Having first resigned himself to the theft of the village funds as *qadr* (Allah's divine preordainment), the farmer grows to recognise that he is due reparations in this life, and joins the group in occupying El-Hadji's house.

The beggars' powerfully collectivised subjectivities under conditions of marginalisation thus allow Sembène to demonstrate an altogether different

Figure 3.3 Rama's mobility. *Xala*. Dir. Ousmane Sembène, 1975.

relation between the processes of subjectivity formation and the material conditions of neocolonialism. With the social and political meaning of their act established, the beggars transform their suffering into an act of collective refusal: they refuse to demand El-Hadji's stolen wealth as compensation for their land loss, and they refuse to await from his class a justice they cannot deliver. Sembène's film begins from an understanding that the necessary confrontation with neocolonialism may be beyond the consciousness of the West African political elite to see, and beyond its capacity (or desire) to undo. It proceeds to critique the subjectivities that neocolonial conditions – encapsulated in the primary crime of land theft – have constituted, and the social embeddedness and responsibility that promise other grounds for subjectivity formation.

With the reveal of the 'primordial crime' of collective wealth theft, subjectivity emerges in *Xala* as a conducive site of agency for the beggars/dispossessed farmers. Having demystified the mechanisms by which they have been marginalised, they refuse to be paid off in exchange for being severed from their lands and their labours. In Ayi Kwei Armah's *The Beautyful Ones Are Not Yet Born*, however, the reader is plunged into a more pervasive and psychically debilitating situation. The agency of the oppressed that crowns the ending of *Xala* will prove difficult to sustain in Armah's setting, which takes its reader via a thinly veiled allegory through life during the final year of Kwame Nkrumah's presidency.

'The self and the world against which it had to live'

In a scene just prior to the climax of Armah's first novel, *The Beautyful Ones Are Not Yet Born* (1969), the nameless protagonist and his wife are taken home in the chauffeur-driven car of their acquaintances: Joseph Koomson, a corrupt minister in an ostensibly socialist government, and his wife Estella, who rarely 'reconcile[s] herself to being an African' (Armah 1969, 155). The protagonist's mental state exhibits a particular kind of exhaustion.

> How was the man ever going to be able to fight against all the things and all the loved ones who never ceased urging that nothing else mattered, that the way was not important, that the end of life was the getting of these comfortable things? For the self, or if not for the self, then for the loved ones, for the children. (177)

What would it mean to get these 'comfortable things [. . .] for the self'? By this point in Armah's novel, we know what it would entail in post-independence Ghana: risk-taking, a lack of scruples, and artifice. But what, as the reflective voice prompts us to consider, is the relationship between the self and the material conditions of a daily life spent either in the getting of, or fighting the desire to get, these 'comfortable things'? The pursuit of wealth has become the means by which people constitute themselves as subjects, and the way intersubjective relations are conducted – how care and love are expressed, identity and recognition reinforced. In a novel that examines both the legacies of colonialism and daily life in Nkrumah's Ghana, this quiet moment of reflection demonstrates how the psycho-social and economic stakes of neocolonial circumstances are interwoven.

While Sembène's characters are in a sense settled into their own positions with regards to the neocolonial system at hand – with those like El-Hadji and his second wife Oumi N'Doye fully buying into its promises – the beggars, as discussed above, straightforwardly represent those who reject its imperatives. But Armah's ambivalent protagonist allows the reader a rich glimpse into what is the far more commonplace situation for the majority of a population under neocolonial circumstances. Every day he contemplates the ease of participating in such 'normal' social conditions for the promise of integration or financial reward that it offers; he mostly refuses, and gains nothing. Through this tension, *Beautyful Ones* harnesses the devices of multiple temporality and character interiority. Together, these chart how neocolonial socio-economic conditions and the very subjectivities of the novel's characters are mutually constitutive, explanatory and effectual. Identifying the extent to which these connections have been addressed in existing Armah scholarship, I will propose a syncretic approach to the key concerns of these critiques, which tend to consider subjectivity and economic conditions in isolation from each other. Particularly relevant here is recalling from Chapter 1 Lewis Gordon's (2015) and Nelson Maldonado-Torres's (2017) proposition that, if there is a universality to the unconscious in Fanon's thought, it is the desire for (and a dialectical movement towards) freedom. *Beautyful Ones*, which offers no narrative or political resolution, gestures at the condition grounding this movement: one's embodied experience within one's material conditions. In charting its protagonist within this relation, Armah situates subjectivity as an essential terrain in the struggle to transform society.

Armah's novel has been discussed both in terms of the individual's struggle within and against society, and its more contextually specific socio-political overtones, which emphasise the novel's allegorical depiction of the decay of revolutionary hope.[16] Armah's narrative techniques for linking the lust for

---

[16] For Derek Wright, for example, Armah's portrayal of the pervasive materialism of all classes in Ghana 'produces a socio-cultural monolith, in which the bourgeoisie [. . .] absorbs into itself a wholly emulative, sycophantic and bureaucratised working class' (1989, 36).

wealth and economic dependence on the West are interpreted by G. Ojong Ayuk (1984) as Armah's 'fictional axe [aimed] at those leaders whose thinking has unfortunately been distorted by current materialism' (33). Others, like Derek Wright, read Armah's content and delivery as being at odds with one another, arguing that the novel 'is rescued from the cartoon-like banality of its political themes, the bareness of its plot, and the suspicious simplicity of its cyclical view of history by the performance of its language' (1989, 30). Indeed, few things happen to the protagonist, whose life remains the same at the end as it was at the beginning. But the plot is hardly bare, for the man experiences changes in his relationships to himself, his wife and his own conditions. And it is, of course, the very 'banality' of the neocolonial politics depicted in *Beautyful Ones*, and the 'cyclical' history it laments, that imbue Armah's remarkable language with the depth of effect that Wright implicitly celebrates.

Neil Lazarus's (1987) interpretation anticipated two important critical threads that scholars of Armah have explored in the past two decades: analyses of the potent bleakness of the material reality depicted and its underlying causes, such as John Lutz's (2003) comments on commodity fetishism and conspicuous consumption, and those readings, such as Minna Niemi's (2017) Arendtian interpretation, that focus on the protagonist's moral resilience as an indication of Armah's grimly optimistic vision. Through an approach that incorporates both, Lazarus understands *Beautyful Ones* to be formulated on the premise that it is 'only by knowing one's world, by seeing it for what it is, that one can ever genuinely aspire to bring about its revolutionary transformation' (1987, 139). This speaks closely not only to how *Black Skin, White Masks* envisages a socially relational subjectivity that is constituted by the material, but also to Fredric Jameson's theory of cognitive mapping (1995), which centres experience. A term originally taken from the geographer Kevin Lynch's *The Image of the City* (1960), cognitive mapping effectively describes an intersection of the personal and the social, which enables people to function in the urban spaces through which they move. For Jameson, representation is made and remade in and through practice – through experiencing social reality, and allowing social reality to shape one's subjectivity. This 'necessarily includes the psychic and the subjective within itself' as part of the 'social raw material' it draws upon (Jameson 1995, 4). Since he prioritises the question of representation, however, Jameson does not pause long on his foundational assumption that material reality constitutes subjectivity. But it is precisely this mutual interaction of 'the psychic and the subjective' with 'the social raw material' in Armah's novel that yields a Fanonian conception of the self. First exploring the theme of multi-temporality, and secondly, Armah's detailed and lyrical narration of the effects on the man's psyche of his everyday life, helps reveal this interrelation and its political import.

Neocolonial Time

Armah's protagonist weaves his existence within and among a temporal incoherence that is not merely indicative of the political incoherence around him. It also reflects his subjective experience of the contradictions that characterise the transition from the short-lived promises of anti-colonial energies to neocolonial nationhood. There is a national time that is hurtling forwards: non-synchronous with the time of the majority of the governed, who are quite literally disoriented by their own dis-identification with the present. They are the 'living dead [who] could take some solace in the half-thought that there were so many others dead in life with them' (Armah 1969, 25). If, in the novel, the liberational promises of independence can be construed as a movement forwards, this is always accompanied by a reverse movement, a national time hurtling backwards to exploitation under another guise.

A valuable triangulation between nation, time and subjectivity has been proposed by Vilashini Cooppan (2009), who offers that the postcolonial nation can be thought of as an entity constructed through movement – one of spatial and temporal unevenness, interiorisation and exteriorisation, constituted as much by what it borders as by what it contains. Describing the nation's psychic locale and its 'propensity to mix up the realms of inside and outside, past and present as it constructs the narrative of [national] identity' (2), Cooppan characterises it as one of incessant movement between distinct spaces, times and attachments through which national identification (and dis-identification) comes into being. *Beautyful Ones* presents this as a state of nausea. And while nausea in this novel has been commented on frequently, interpretations like those of Alexander Dakubo Kakraba (2011) and Derek Wright (1990) focus on disgust as its sole source – a disgust the protagonist certainly feels towards the corruption and obscene wealth disparities he witnesses in postcolonial Ghana. However, Cooppan's observation reminds us of the social effects that are produced by postcolonial nation-building. In this case, affecting its subjects is a nation-time whose crony capitalist present looks much like its colonial past, causing the psychological equivalent of motion sickness. 'Here we have had a kind of movement that should make even good stomachs go sick. What is painful to the thinking mind is not movement itself, but the dizzying speed of it. It is that which has been horrible' (Armah 1969, 62).

The two temporalities at work in Armah's novel do not easily map onto distinct parallel lines (modern-versus-organic or Ghanaian-versus-African, for instance) so much as onto a circle. Circularity in the postcolonial nation-state, as Achille Mbembe points out, sustains a certain ceremonial rituality that is necessary to maintain the appearance of autonomous power, concealing its actual neocoloniality: 'consider, for example, ceremonies for the "transfer of office" that punctuate postcolonial bureaucratic time and profoundly affect the imagination of individuals – elites and masses alike' (Mbembe 2001, 65). Metaphors of circularity abound in *Beautyful Ones*: the night-man's circuit, the chichi dodo bird, the two bus journeys that bookend the plot. These are allegories of recurring political corruption, the long chain of bribes, and the replacing of one 'fat yessir-man' (Armah 1969, 96) with another. However, Armah is not interested in dissecting how and why the promises of independence were diverted into cycles that maintain the appearance of progress. Like everyone else, Kwame Nkrumah – the main political figure whose presence hangs over the novel – is framed as both a passive figure and an active agent. The protagonist thinks of the 'promise he had held out but which he himself consumed, utterly destroyed. Perhaps it is too cruel of us to ask that those approaching the end of the cycle should accept without fear the going and coming of life and death' (Armah 1969, 103). There is an unflinching clarity here as to the entrenched structures individual leaders may face.

But neither are post-independence leaders absolved; individuals have a part to play in perpetuating or changing these structures. 'How were these leaders to know that while they were climbing up to shit in their people's faces, their people had seen their arseholes and drawn away in disgusted laughter?' (96). Obscene language, Kakraba suggests, serves as Armah's 'therapeutic shock, [meant to] awaken a very decadent and dying society' (2011, 312). Such visceral imagery also relays the psychic effects of historical betrayal. Recalling Fanon's biopolitics, the graphic imagery emphasises how 'the body is the centre from which the dehumanization and loss of dignity proceeds' (Nayar 2019, 224). There is an ontological and political dynamism in the ridicule of the masses who have now 'drawn away', learning better than to expect their political class to pursue the redistributive promises of decolonisation at risk to their own comfort.

The question of agency, so crucial to Fanon's conceptualisation of subjectivity, is the real crux for any possibility of decolonisation in *Beautyful Ones*. The novel suggests that the truly disabling effect of neocolonial time can be found in its infiltration of people's subjectivities via social rituals (such as ceremonies of nationalism), and the upkeep of a new order through participation in crony capitalism. Docile acceptance of the corrupt nature of the present poses, for Armah, an even greater risk than the corruption itself. A seemingly passing moment in *Beautyful Ones* reminds of this:

> Only a few goods trains would be coming down, and there was nothing going up with which they could possibly collide [. . .] Until the old 1:50 train started up to bring Tarkwa gold and Aboso manganese to the waiting Greek ships in the harbour, this would be a time of peace. (24)

Under our protagonist's watch, a steady stream of raw material departs, with which products will be manufactured elsewhere; as Fanon describes, 'we go on sending out raw materials; we go on being Europe's small farmers, who specialise in unfinished products' (1961, 152). Armah's protagonist observes the continuation of dependency after independence with a sense of detachment and exhaustion. As serious as corruption may be, more so is how these conditions fail to 'induce [people] to be actional' (Maldonado-Torres 2017, 435). As such, the conditions that make struggle possible, which in turn gives substance to the physical world that may lie beyond it, require confrontation with conditions in the present that foreclose people's actionable capacities. That these neocolonial conditions in *Beautyful Ones* can still surface powerful emotive states in some like our protagonist – they feel 'painful to the thinking mind' (62) – speaks to the potential of an altogether different future than that implied by 'suffering sleepers' (23).

'Things that continue unsatisfied inside'

Whereas El-Hadji's cipher-like subjectivity in *Xala* evidences his full internalisation of neocolonial conditions, Armah's protagonist's interiority is a fraught terrain. He can simultaneously hold dissatisfaction towards his material reality; see why others embrace it; and imagine otherwise:

> The promise was so beautiful. It was there. We were not deceived about that. How could such a thing turn so completely into this other thing? [. . .] What can a person do with things that continue unsatisfied inside? Is their stifled cry not also life? (100)

In an everyday existence that requires him to accept as natural liberation turning into its opposite, the man instead holds that what 'continue[s] unsatisfied inside' is life itself: a stifled, but enduring, belief in the possibility of decolonisation. He is not passing detached judgement here from morally higher ground. Having 'loved ones' of his own, the man everyday wrestles with feeling like a disappointment to them. Unlike the reclusive character of Teacher, our protagonist, a civil servant, lives anchored within the society he sees so clearly. It is living daily with the struggle of resisting or acquiescing to its pressures that gives him knowledge of both its systemic workings, and how these penetrate his psyche.

There is a nuanced difference here between this and two conclusions critics have reached about Armah's approach to the self: that he either locates potential for change in the notion of the autonomous individual, or that he regards the individual as powerless. For Robert Fraser, Armah is 'concerned with the salvation of the people in toto, the reformation of the public will, rather than the redemption of the private soul or mind' (1980, xii). We could certainly make this claim for *Xala*; however, there is no incidence in Armah's novel of a positive example of collectivity as we find in Dakar's dispossessed farmers-turned-beggars. While the absence of such in *Beautyful Ones* does not discredit Fraser's interpretation, the easy separation he makes between 'the public will' and 'the private soul or mind' is something Armah, like Fanon, does not make. John Lutz more helpfully emphasises that Armah's attention to collectivity foregrounds how the appeal of acquisition stifles creative agency and distorts interpersonal relations, 'shrink[ing] the sphere of human activity to the exchanges of the marketplace and, in doing so, negat[ing] any singular or autonomous human activity struggling for articulation' (2003, 103). Codes that indicate class in neocolonial Ghana are propagated by individuals seeking self-assurance within the structures of a neocolonial or global capitalism, Armah emphasises. One moment in the novel particularly captures how these imperatives shape subjectivities. The protagonist's wife Oyo, who has assimilated the values and practices of the elite, suddenly changes her behaviour on their journey to Minister Koomson's home in the Upper Residential Area:

> Travelling, even a short ride in a taxi, had a very noticeable effect on Oyo [. . .] She would talk, bringing up the few rich things that had happened to her all her life, and some that had not really happened, some that had not even almost happened. (165)

Oyo compulsively performs a particular identity in terms of the agreed social code of neocolonial Ghana, hinting 'that in spirit, at least, they too belong to such areas' (165). Annoyed that her husband's familiarity with the driver is undermining a rare moment of class superiority, she responds with a performance. This produces the recognition she yearns for: the driver began 'to speak to her as if he now understood her greatness'. But the protagonist observes the whole exchange as 'some form of disease' (166), a practice that perpetuates the agreed codes of status in the post-independence nation-state.

Armah frames this false exchange as an effect and a reproduction of neocolonial capitalism. Koomson and his wife Estella also demonstrate this interpenetration. Once Oyo and the protagonist arrive at Koomson's, their visit turns into a dance of power and deference, negotiated through commodities like Estella's imported record player: '"What is that?" asked Oyo. At times she had the ability to make herself sound exactly like an admiring villager. A trick to please [. . .] Estella, as if this Sunday music had really moved her soul, closed her eyes, breathing deeply' (176). The self becomes constituted via the commodity, through which virtue- and wealth-signalling can take place. The man cannot bring himself to participate, but nor can he confront it outright, for he must continue living among them. But, as Jarrod Dunham observes, by 'existing apart from the dominant social pursuit, [the protagonist] is able to recognise its mechanisms at work' (2012, 288). These moments, I would suggest, do not stem from the personal ethics of the protagonist, somehow miraculously kept pure despite his conditions. In fact, 'impotent' is his frequently damning self-description (54). Non-participation may indeed be the next best thing when faced with the way things get done in the postcolony. It is a start, but *Beautyful Ones* does not confuse it with the collective work required for political, economic and social decolonisation.

Aligning with Fanon's dialectical view, Armah repeatedly asks where the psychic and societal alienation of standing apart can lead. 'Was there not something in the place and about the time that sought to make it painfully clear that there was too much of the unnatural in any man who imagined he could escape?' (55) the protagonist asks. A capacity to remain separate from society can be a self-preserving advantage when under pressure to conform, and it is precisely the protagonist's enduring capacities for imagining alternatives that cause him such inner turmoil. Nonetheless, at several moments in the novel, this is always in danger of fading into inconsequentiality on the societal scale. The man's micro-resistance is, however, imbued with the possibility of becoming perpetuated and amplified via everyday relations. In this productive irresolution may lie Fanon's more Existentialist pronouncements on 'the permanent tension of [their] freedom, [through which people] can create the ideal conditions of existence for a human world' (1952, 206). Armah, with his divided protagonist, is not turning from the promise of decolonisation to despair. *Beautyful Ones* narrates a process that Fanon, too, saw as necessary: the way in which anti-colonial struggle must also entail the self-negation of the (neo)colonial status of the subject. This negation can also be 'a founding activity, and an extremely radical terrain' (Samaddar 2009, 228).

A Man who Questions

What sets the protagonist's moral conscience apart is therefore not so much an outright, defiant refusal, but the fact that he remains conscious to the historical context in which he is immersed. Or, in the words of Fanon's closing *cri de coeur* in *Masks*, the inner turmoil provoked by his material circumstances have turned the protagonist into 'a man who questions' (1952, 206). When the coup exchanges one set of cronies for another, and the men in his office join the crowd outside 'in the same manner they had gone out in fear to hear the farts of Party men', the protagonist stalls. His thinking response, in the novel's dysfunctional society where 'suffering sleepers' (23) are the norm, cannot be insignificant.

> 'I know nothing about the men. Who will I be demonstrating for?'
> 'Look, contrey, if you don't want trouble, get out.'
> 'If two trains collide while I'm demonstrating, will you take the responsibility?'
> 'Oh, if it is the job, fine. But we won't tolerate any Nkrumahists now.'
> (186)

In the way the man performs fealty to his job, and in the way the union man performs acceptance of our protagonist's obviously political abstention from demonstrating as, instead, a seriousness towards his job, the native bourgeoisie's power as mere sign/symbol is rendered visible. I use sign/symbol in Achille Mbembe's sense when he seeks to define the 'postcolonised subject'. Mbembe argues that the ability to engage in 'apparently contradictory practices [that] ratify, de facto, the status of fetish that state power so forcefully claims by right . . . by that same token maintain[s], even while drawing upon officialese (signs, symbols), the possibility of altering the place and time of this ratification' (2001, 129). To obey here is not so much to follow a direct order (a simple power relationship) as to appear to fulfil the contradictory expectations and demands of a corrupt power structure. The result is ineffectual action or inaction – not clearly punishable, for not apparently oppositional. This retention of the right to disengagement in an almost impossible situation is Armah's investment in subjectivities informed by lived experience. It does not straightforwardly translate into the individual separating themselves from society, nor into the expression of a collective, political consciousness. Nonetheless, the protagonist refuses what Armah suggests may be the greatest of neocolonialism's victories: an unthinking, uncritical day-to-day existence that is reconciled to the arrest of decolonisation.

Being Fanon's 'man who questions' means that 'things continue unsatisfied inside' (Armah 100), making it perhaps the hardest way to choose to survive neocolonial power structures. It is difficult to differentiate the effects on the protagonist of this moment of covert refusal. However, in this scene, we do see the novel's conception of selfhood as that which simultaneously refuses to sever itself from the material reality that shapes it, and refuses to reconcile itself to it. The possibility of such a subjectivity rests on the fact that the protagonist's interiority is informed by his experiential understanding of the same reality as those he views so critically. It comes about only by experiencing the same temptations and hardships, not hovering at a partial remove. This complex sense of how subjectivities can, if they must, transform under and despite the pressures of neocolonial circumstances is finally borne out by Oyo and the man's unspoken reconciliation. In many ways more climactic than the confusion of the coup, the couple's passive-aggressive battle, where each has persisted throughout in what they believe to be the only way of surviving post-independence conditions, comes to an end when they both allow their own selves to be re-constituted. Upon seeing Koomson's fall from power, Oyo understands her husband's reasons for refusing to participate in Ghana's post-independence kleptocracy. 'Perhaps for the first time in their married life', the man felt, 'he could believe that [Oyo] was glad to have him the way he was. He returned the increasing pressure of her hand' (Armah 194). Seeing Koomson's state, Oyo feels 'tremendously disturbed' within (194). It is indeed a disturbing experience, for she must rearrange who does and does not deserve her respect upon confronting the fickle power structure she has (literally and figuratively) invested in. Yet it is also liberating, for this may translate into a potentially more harmonious future for them.

The Tension of Freedom

Beautyful Ones has been classed as part of a 'literature of disillusionment' in some respects (Lazarus 1990, 18), and considering its frequently fatalistic tone, its bitter condemnation of the native elite and uncertain conclusion, the observation is not unfounded. But when considered via the two particular devices discussed above – Armah's use of multiple temporality, and his protagonist's interiority – the novel is also deserving of Abiola Irele's description of it as 'the new realism' of its time and place (2001, 495). The loss of the illusion that independence would bring redistribution provokes a search for the causes and extent of the present decay. What emerges is that subjectivities themselves are at stake, and their constitution under neocolonial conditions signal bleak repercussions for society. In asserting that 'the future goodness may come eventually', but also asking 'where were the things in the present which would prepare the way for it?' (188), *Beautyful Ones* leaves its reader only with the certainty that remaking selves, and re-forming intersubjective relations, is needed. Decolonisation is only possible if one has experienced what decolonisation is not. Through such a confrontation with reality, Armah's protagonist wrestles daily with conditions that nudge him towards participating in the neocolonial economy. There is no societal congratulation for his grappling, but it sees Armah's protagonist through the belly of the beast – both literally (he and Koomson escape the authorities through a latrine hole) and figuratively (the protagonist neither hands Koomson over to claim a reward, nor does he accept anything in thanks). He is a conscious subject, which intolerable conditions turn, in the end, into a resistant one.

While both *Xala* and *Beautyful Ones* are concerned with the mass internalisation of a neocolonial capitalism that consolidated itself in West Africa in many new nation-states, this chapter has illustrated why they come at this problem from different angles. Armah's novel contains the themes and motifs that the above scholarship has pointed out, such as disgust and disillusionment, while keeping in sight how interiority itself can be a location of political dynamism. And although Sembène's film has rightly been celebrated as a parody of the African comprador bourgeoisies, it too emphasises that resistance must have a strongly psycho-political component if it is to counter the neocolonial commodification of life. As Fanon elucidates,

> only conflict and the risk it implies can make human reality, in-itself-for-itself, come true. This risk implies that I go beyond life toward an ideal which is the transformation of the subjective certainty of my own worth into a universally valid objective truth (1952, 193).

In other words, it is living within society, and therefore risking social censure and psychic malaise by choosing to daily experience its conditions, which enables what is systemic to be made visible through the vantage point of subjectivity.

Yet, transitions from colonial to neocolonial structures could be, and were, more violent than the conditions Sembène and Armah narrate. Post-independence years in much of Africa and Asia were turbulent to the degree where sheer survival often had to precede political action. The next chapter will explore how and why subjectivity is key to two texts that are situated within a significant subset of postcolonial film and literatures that narrate conflict. The Partition of India and the Nigerian Civil War are the contexts of, respectively, the Bengali director Ritwik Ghatak's 1960 film *The*

Cloud-Capped Star and the Nigerian writer Buchi Emecheta's 1982 novel *Destination Biafra*. In both, individual psychic suffering will serve to evidence a collective kind of nation-memory: one that challenges state-sanctioned historiographies, and allows subjective experience to count as testimony and witness to the obstruction of decolonisation.

4

History From Within: Violence and Subjective Experience in Ritwik Ghatak's *The Cloud-Capped Star* and Buchi Emecheta's *Destination Biafra*

Post-independence nation-states can create, or choose to perpetuate, certain narratives of history at the exclusion of others in order to justify their existence. Indian and Pakistani state-sanctioned historiographies of the 1947 Partition of the Subcontinent consistently treat it as inseparable from their own national births. Sometimes, it is framed as a necessary tragedy: a price that had to be paid for independence, which can also conveniently allow India to treat its Muslims 'as a diseased limb that had to be sacrificed for the health of the national body-politic' (Chatterji 1991, 168). Sometimes, it is remembered as the painful but historic birth-pangs of a nation, as was mobilised in Pakistan for a top-down Islamisation.[1] This instrumentalisation exists, too, in Nigerian state-sanctioned approaches to the historiography of the 1967–1970 Nigerian Civil War. Raisa Simola notes that 'the rather sparse official commemoration of the war has been left mainly to the military, which uses the opportunity to assure itself of its role as guarantor of national unity' (2000, 98). In bringing these two historical events together through its discussion of Bengali director Ritwik Ghatak's film *The Cloud-Capped Star* (1960) and Nigerian author Buchi Emecheta's novel *Destination Biafra* (1982), this chapter explores how both texts challenge such 'nation-histories' by developing a sustained and complex relationship between subjectivity and collective resistance in the context of mass violence.

In India, the need to maintain peaceful inter-community relations was cited by Jawaharlal Nehru as early as 1948 as a reason to censor cultural production about these events (Daiya 2002, 221). That the 'traumata resulting from the Partition are still not overcome and contain the potential for explosive conflicts in the future' (Hartnack 2012, 244) speaks to how collective memory,

---

[1] See also Ishtiaq Ahmed (2022) for a 75th anniversary overview of Partition memory in national contexts.

then and now, is something to be carefully managed.[2] The relatively belated public discourse on Partition does not necessarily mean state-sanctioned historiographies have been accepted by South Asians, however. The complex factors of post-Partition migration (internally and internationally), and cultural norms around the hiding and revealing of trauma, have been at play.[3] Cultural responses to the Nigerian Civil War, in contrast, came quickly. Non-fictional accounts by Nigerians of the 1967–1970 conflict emerged as early as Elechi Amadi's 1973 memoir *Sunset in Biafra*, and novels included Flora Nwapa's *Never Again* (1975) and Cyprian Ekwensi's *Survive the Peace* (1976). These and other similar works (Achebe 1975, 2013; Soyinka 1971, 1972) have been praised as providing the alternative to official military historiography. For Craig McLuckie, the civil war memoirs of Elechi Amadi, Wole Soyinka and Ken Saro-Wiwa 'challenge received notions' by 'depicting the effect [the war] had in real terms: human and subjective' (2001, 21), while for Ogaga Okuyade, poetry about the war is to be lauded for 'remaining focused on the widening circles of pain radiating from loss' (2012, 28). As these suggest, choosing to depict the subjective experience of conflict, as it was felt by civilians, refugees, bystanders and participants, carries both narrative power and political risk. Stories of the everyday (re)creation of sustenance, shelter, sanity and community out of constant and systematised scarcity during post-independence civil violence carried an affective charge that could, as fears like Nehru's suggest, have history repeating itself.

In Buchi Emecheta's novel *Destination Biafra*, war conditions are also represented via special attention to psychic effects. While rarely afforded as lengthy an analysis as *The Joys of Motherhood* (1979) or *Second-Class Citizen* (1974), *Destination* is a singular novel for the ways in which it seeks to gender the act of war historiography. Examining Emecheta's use of point-of-view and symbolism in particular, the second half of this chapter will discuss how this undertaking must be read beyond the idea of an addendum to existing literary responses to the Nigerian Civil War through the provision of a missing 'female perspective'.[4] Rather, *Destination* recuperates the emphasis on historicity and creative agency found in Fanon's conceptualisation of subjectivity in order to

---

[2] See also Gilmartin (2015) and Shani (2015) on how the interpretation of Partition resurfaced as a touchstone for narratives of the nation in the 2014 Indian general elections that resulted in a victory for Narendra Modi.

[3] The 1947 Partition Archive of oral history was launched in 2008, racing to record the memories of ageing survivors, while the Partition Museum at Amritsar opened as late as 2017.

[4] A term, as Polo B. Moji has noted (2014), found in much Emecheta scholarship without satisfactory definition.

render Nigerian women's points-of-view as the lens through which *all* facets of the war can be understood – even and especially its geopolitical stakes. The two texts of this chapter thus 'gradate between world and self, state and the psyche' (Young 2013, 20) to the effect of doing what Hannah Proctor (2018) has termed 'history from within'.

Landscapes of Loss

Although 'Partition' in scholarship came to primarily mean the division of Punjab in 1947 – the synecdochical 'site of rupture' (Harrington 2016, 2) – the creation of East Pakistan from Bengal was the formative event of Ghatak's life and work.[5] In the Subcontinent's post-independence decades, both partitions were often rendered 'inexplicable and unhistorical' as a period of 'communal madness', or transformed 'into a history of its causes and origins' (Pandey 2001, 45). Ghatak's film is rare as a story of life after arrival rather than the event itself. *Star* both challenges the psycho-social 'communal madness' nationalist narrative and claims that to tell of individual and collective psychic sufferings is to tell of the lasting material violence of impoverishment and dispossession under colonialism. Through close attention to the film's narrative and formal use of landscapes and interiors, this section will explore how *Star* treats psychic suffering as a mnemonic resource for understanding the socio-economic conditions, terror, poverty, violence and injustice that refugees continued to face after Partition itself. In this way, subjectivity emerges not as shorthand for individual disposition or personal attitude, but as subject to historical, political and social causations that 'take' (to return to Fanon's words) to 'inform the individual' to different degrees (Fanon 1952, 56).

Based on a story by Shaktipada Rajguru, Ghatak's most successful film is a narrative of the Partition of Bengal's long aftermath. It is concerned with the lives uprooted alongside the murders, lynchings, rapes and abductions that accompanied the 1947 migrations. Our protagonist Neeta, a young woman employed as a clerk, is the sole breadwinner of her household. She; her ageing parents; her beloved older brother Shankar, a promising musician; her restless younger brother Montu, an aspiring athlete; and her vivacious younger sister Geeta were once an urban petit-bourgeois family in Dhaka. Now they are penniless but educated refugees who live in the semi-rural environs of

---

[5] The Partition of Bengal and the later Bangladesh Liberation War of 1971 began to receive more consideration in comparative work on global partitions and Partition Studies in the past two decades (Feldman 1999; van Schendel 2001; Chatterji 1991, 2015; Harrington 2016).

Kolkata. Shankar, the elder brother, shuttles between long bouts of singing Tagore by the riverbank, dreaming of becoming a celebrated musician, and hounding Neeta for money. Neeta's boyfriend, Sanat, is a cerebral graduate student; he sees the disproportionate responsibility on Neeta's shoulders, but merely laments, 'it shouldn't be like this, but I'm powerless!' Her mother is over-burdened with domesticity,[6] and her ageing father and one-time schoolteacher, Taran 'Master', is unable to get work and later has a debilitating accident. Protected from immediate financial hardship and domestic labour by Neeta and her mother, Shankar is rewarded for his talents, leaving for Kolkata and returning a celebrated musician – just in time to comfort Neeta as she dies of tuberculosis. Succumbing to 'consumption', as it was then known, Neeta is consumed by her family in their desperation to escape the economic circumstances of post-independence refugeedom.

While Ghatak's politics and personal experiences made him suspicious of state-sanctioned versions of his country's past, place is of fundamental importance in *Star*. The film's natural landscapes work at the level of both narrative and form to simultaneously express psychic disorientation (the characters' loss of their home environment) and socio-economic dispossession (impoverished and de-classed by migration). The opening scene, featuring the solitary figure of Neeta as she walks to work, begins to establish that displacement, metaphorically and physically, looms over the story. Ghatak's extreme wide shots are remarkable in how much of the land and how little of the characters they frame; these often feature one dominant natural element, such as a river or tree, which takes on such proportions that it becomes the subject of the shot. The people who feature in these expansive shots are small and anonymous at first; it is unclear whether this expansive landscape fosters or alienates, embraces or overwhelms them into insignificance (Figure 4.1). This removes the land in a sense from the daily economic woes of the over-burdened characters, making it seem immutable or sacred: an almost mythological source for succour and inspiration.

Yet it is also a constant reminder of the characters' enforced physical distance from another land elsewhere. As this lends an expansive vision of 'the land' as that which *is* and *goes on* (perhaps pointedly beyond and broader than 'nation'), the landscape as a temporary solace makes no difference to the family's material hardship. This duality, wherein the land of arrival as a refuge exists in tension with the land of arrival as alienating, translates the

---

[6] 'Anyone who has seen conventional Bengali films of the 1940s and 1950s knows that inevitable courtyard with a long-suffering female in the middle of it,' Chidananda Dasgupta quips in one essay (1985, 260).

Figure 4.1 Landscapes of loss. *Meghe Dhaka Tara [The Cloud-Capped Star]*. Dir. Ritwik Ghatak, 1960.

psychic dissonance that accompanies Ghatak's characters' material conditions. Unlike Emecheta who, as Chidi Amuta (2007) and Ann Marie Adams (2001) have argued, was invested in the idea of unified nationhood as Nigeria's best chance against 'the neocolonial ploys of the British and the separatist drives of Nigerian males' (Adams 288), Ghatak's own interviews support the idea that 'if there is a strand uniting his diverse cinematic output, it is [a] strong current of anti-nationalism' (Raychaudhuri 2009, 469). People's sense of their home territory consists not merely of rivers, trees, buildings and streets; it encompasses their ancestry, social norms, moral codes, social interactions, local economies and community practices. These points of reference, belonging to lives lived elsewhere, are painfully absent in the silent grandeur of the characters' surroundings.

Landscapes in *Star* also provoke nostalgia in characters for their middle-class life before Partition, when the landscape may have evoked artistic sensibility. Jisha Menon points out that various sound effects 'rupture the sense of utopic nostalgia set up within the diegetic frame' (2013, 64), and the visual references work to similar effect. For example, in an early scene, Taran 'Master' exclaims to Neeta and Shankar as they walk through a rice paddy that 'to perceive this crop field's beauty costs no money!' The paddy looks excessively flooded, possibly ruined by too much rainfall. The shot includes the figure of what may be a farmer inspecting his crop in the background (Figure 4.2). Taran sees in the landscape an atemporality that invokes his anti-modern and anti-capitalist view of the field's value. Although rural depopulation in West

Figure 4.2 Taran's nostalgia. *Meghe Dhaka Tara [The Cloud-Capped Star]*. Dir. Ritwik Ghatak, 1960.

Bengal slowed in the 1970s as large urban manufacturing failed to take off, in the late 1950s, during which *Star* was shot, the wages of agriculture were rarely market clearing (Bagchi 1998, 2035) – living off the land was hardly a romantic affair. But as the pensive framing of the shot suggests, this is more about Taran attempting to come to terms with the loss of his schoolmaster job as a vital class indicator in his life. His use of John Keats to express his appreciation – 'Didn't Keats have a verse, "the poetry of the earth is never dead?"' – is an attempt to re-embody his middle-class subjectivity, reaching for what once assured him of his place in the world (such as aesthetic appreciation, mediated by the English literary canon). Ghatak takes seriously the loss of the formative intellectual and artistic pursuits of the family, but the landscape of the rice paddy here overlays Taran's escapism with the material struggle for survival.

In contrast, the landscapes that backdrop Shankar's ragas strike a harmonious note with his aesthetic pursuits, differentiating Shankar's musicality from his father's denial. That is not to say there is no classed and gendered element to Shankar's own talent: indeed, he tells Neeta it would be 'unseemly for an artiste' like himself to find a job. Although *bhadralok* himself, Ghatak had little admiration for his class, and his films (especially the 1962 *Subarnarekha*) often 'expose the arrogance of their casteism' (Asokan 2020, 2).[7] But Ghatak's typical ability to allow complexity without relativising the sources of social

---

[7] Bengali for the new class of 'gentlefolk' who rose during British rule in India in Bengal.

injustice is also illustrated where we see that Shankar's musicality, however 'unproductive', is a source of resilience for himself and Neeta. Performed either in open landscapes or indoors in dim light, Shankar's music is never cinematically rushed; the film's pace slows down instead, editing becomes minimal, and single light sources draw attention towards the performer. Moments that showcase his genuine skill with the sitar use wide aperture to isolate Shankar against a dramatically out-of-focus background. They present the otherwise immature character as a commanding presence, moved by and moving others through his music. Ghatak takes seriously that cultural moorings are valuable – though not in themselves enough – for ontological security in the face of loss.

The relation emerging here between material conditions and subjectivity is not passive and unidirectional. Shankar frustrates his family with his naivety, but through his method of survival he resists being 'merely here-and-now, sealed into thingness', in Fanon's psycho-political term (1952, 170). Ratik Asokan (2020) notes that Ghatak points to his characters' sources of resilience in their own living Bengali heritage (as in Shankar's renditions of Tagore's music). Landscape inspires Shankar to retain a creative fire that draws from the cultural reference points of his pre-Partition origins (no small feat considering the toll poverty can exact on the imagination). Yet *Star*'s treatment of the natural world is not romantic, which is a frequent refrain in scholarship that highlights Tagore's pastoral romanticism as the primary influence on Ghatak's cinema.[8] Partha Chatterjee offers a more convincing argument, proposing that, 'seen from a larger perspective, [Ghatak's films] are about the arbitrariness of political destiny in the twentieth century where people are forced to become citizens of new, hitherto unknown countries, build lives for themselves and rely on past memories for spiritual sustenance' (2012, 50). It is in the service of these social concerns that Ghatak deploys the Tagorean pastoral, a mode that generates the 'abiding psychological resonance' (Chatterjee 50) of his social stories. Ghatak's commitment to Bengali peasant and folk cultural forms dates back to his IPTA days.[9] The pastoral mode's 'layers of experience' (Chatterjee 50), in terms of intelligibility and effect on diverse audiences, would not have been lost on the group-theatre veteran.

In fact, often running alongside his pastoral mode for landscape are elements that speak to the socio-economic realities of post-Partition Bengal. For example, a recurring train that interrupts the aural and narrative continuity

---

[8] See Menon (2012) and Raychaudhuri (2009).
[9] See also Manishita Dass on Ghatak's keen interest in the 'epic form' of the indigenous folk traditions of performance like the *jatra* (2017, 83).

of several scenes situates Ghatak's landscapes historically. The sound of the train overwhelms dialogue and forces the actors (and likely the crew) to pause and wait for it to pass. Ghatak incorporates this uncontrollable environmental factor into his scenes as though it is a diegetic element. With all of the connotations of migration and violence trains carry in Partition historiography,[10] this situates the landscape from which Shankar draws inspiration inside historical events, even as his mental romanticisation of that landscape helps him survive. The trains reveal the family's 'arrival' location as one where resources pass through but never stop. Kolkata determines the spatial and economic contours of its semi-periphery, and their refugee settlement is a place oriented towards that which it never benefits from: post-independence urban industrialisation. Sayandeb Chowdhury (2015) notes the 'momentous visuality of dispossession' that was around Ghatak in the 1950s. 'Seething with the dislocated, it was only a matter of time before the city would inevitably become the locus of [Ghatak's] scopic drive', Chowdhury proposes (260). But the city in *Star* is not so much the locus as it is the entity dictating life around and near it. Kolkata keeps Neeta's family living as satellites to its economic activity, marking their lives with the people it claims.

Ghatak thus treats the landscape of West Bengal with a critical dualism. He represents the economic pressures of semi-peripherality that determine the characters' lives, as well as the psychic qualities of landscape that sustain Shankar. Manishita Dass has termed moves like these Ghatak's 'dynamic oscillation': a movement between 'humanist realism' and the 'affective transitions of melodrama' (2010, 244). It could be equally accurate to understand this as a layered but whole representational objective, rather than an oscillation between two distinct objectives. Ghatak's representation of the effects of Partition 'on the intimate and quotidian' is itself a representation of 'the foundational national trauma of the Indian subcontinent' (Dass 2010, 244). For him, nowhere else is this trauma most manifest, and therefore most able to jolt viewers, than in the everyday lives of its survivors. Emecheta's *Destination*, which will be discussed below, more obviously showcases 'oscillation' of the kind Dass ascribes to *Star*, in that Emecheta prefers a two-pronged narrative approach to retelling the civil war. Ghatak, however, never divorces the socio-economic specificities of the post-Partition landscape from character interiority, because the former are phenomena informing the latter. Cultural losses are a part of the material losses brought about by the seismic changes the region underwent in the period (the 1943 Bengal Famine, the 1946 Calcutta 'riots', and the migrations of 1947–1949). *Star*'s use of landscape skilfully inscribes onto 'the

---

[10] See also Navdip Kaur (2011).

apparently innocent spatiality of socio-economic life' (Chowdhury 2015, 256) those relations of power that dictate his characters' lives.

Terror Effects

Ghatak's expressionistic interiors are companions to this use of landscape. They channel the interpersonal terror effects of the family's forced migration, and how this is layered into the slow economic violence of their refugee-dom. Robert Young describes terror effects as the past experience of terror 'spreading into the violence of relationships, of people sealed within themselves' (2013, 324). Violence goes from that which is visited upon subjects by the state, to that which is re-created among subjects (in their interpersonal relationships) and within subjects (to themselves). It was almost impossible for any migrants from Bengal but the most well-off to reconstruct new lives across the border with little struggle. Middle-class, working-class and peasant refugees spent years in refugee camps, and most could not take up their past occupations (Raychaudhury 2009, 473). The vast majority of families like Neeta's were consigned to a slow economic death, becoming the collateral damage of nation-making. To suggest this entrapment, want, and a draining interpersonal dependency, *Star* makes use of high-contrast lighting, expressionistic angles, multiple depths-of-field (or a dull flatness) and tight angles in indoor scenes.

For example, whereas at the start of the film we had many glimpses of Neeta's personality, she grows more insular throughout the film, and Ghatak's frames grow darker. He shoots her from behind windows, metal bars, doorways, and in dim indoor light (Figure 4.3). In one moment of lucidity, Neeta's father sums Ghatak's suggestion here: 'Now that we are civilised, we educate the girl to wring her dry and ruin her future.' This is perhaps the most pointed difference in *Star*'s and *Destination*'s narratives, despite their shared representational focus on the gendered burdens of conflict. While solidarities between women will emerge in the latter, *Star* cautions that the Nehruvian state's insistence on education for women is also undeniably strategic, overlapping as it does with goals around capitalist development.[11] These limited ends to Indian women's education generated many setbacks for women's liberation after independence (with some turning from nationalist to revolutionary politics).[12] Neither the British Raj before independence nor the bourgeoisie in post-independence India had any real appetite to challenge caste, let alone

---

[11] On Nehru and women's empowerment, see also Tagra (1994).

[12] See also Ania Loomba on Indian women and communism in the twentieth century (2019).

Figure 4.3 Neeta's burden. *Meghe Dhaka Tara [The Cloud-Capped Star]*. Dir. Ritwik Ghatak, 1960.

patriarchy. As E. M. S. Namboodiripad writes, 'in India, many of the forms of exploitation of the pre-capitalist systems are continuing, some in the original and some in changed forms. There exists along with these a new system of exploitation as a result of capitalist development' (Prashad 2019, 89). Wage labour, itself exploitative, exploits Neeta further in a double-bind: honouring filial duty becomes honouring the demands of capital.

Ghatak's *Star* has therefore proven difficult for those looking to categorise Partition writing along gender lines, such as: 'women writers carve a subjecthood through memory, perception, recall and dream structures' whereas 'male narratives locate events at the centre of the story' (Jain 2006, 1657). Precisely the former representational pursuits have been attributed to Ghatak's film, leading some to designate his niche as 'the idea of womanhood, both idealised and ruthlessly exploited' (Chatterjee 2012, 49). More applicable is Jacob Levich's observation that there is a 'critique of the family-as-institution' (1997, 32) in *Star*, which lays bare how 'love and loyalty are conditioned by financial necessity' (32). Feminist and subaltern historiographies have unpacked the gendered dimensions of anti-colonial nationalist discourses in India at the time of Partition (although their focus on its sexual violence has tended to take precedence over the poverty left in its wake).[13] The former has been urgent and valuable work, but I would also draw attention here to the continuation

---

[13] See Daiya (2002) and Bhasin and Menon (1998).

of gendered violence in terms of economic oppression, and its asymmetrical psychological effects, on women Partition refugees. Ghatak's expressionistic camerawork and lighting are in this sense not abstractions, but affective techniques that reveal how familial bonds can recreate the psychic violence of displacement and loss.

Star's formal choices continue to evoke the question of cultural influence: are Ghatak's so-called melodramatic touches 'Indian' (a nod to the Bengali *jatra*) or 'Western' (a nod to Brecht)?[14] Eurocentric assumptions, as Moira Weigel (2008) cautions, do not allow 'melodrama' to be a value-free stylistic judgement. Ghatak's comparative lack of success in the West vis-à-vis Satyajit Ray, for instance, is not unrelated to persisting Western distaste towards, or fetishisation of, what it designates as 'Indian' aesthetics and tastes (exuberance, dynamism and sensory overload). Such expectations imply what an Indian realism can be – in other words, how much experimentation it is 'allowed' before it formally 'fits' melodrama instead. But what some have deemed melodrama, Ghatak has called his 'epic mode' for 'deal[ing] a straight knockout blow to the nose' (Ghatak 2000, 34) – to jolt his fellow *bhadralok* out of their class complacency. This neither calls for reading *Star* in isolation for its form, as Bonnie Fan does (2015), nor for fixating on Ghatak's anti-realist elements as obstacles to his social critique, as Chidananda Dasgupta argues (1985, 260).[15] To read Ghatak's form is not to read it over content; the former carries social heft, delivering a 'knockout blow' with the aid of a cinematic style that can represent both psychic experience and material conditions. Ghatak looked to Europe and found practices familiar to India, practices which Western audiences had to be 'built up' to, in terms of mental and cultural preparedness: 'Remember always that Brecht had to build up this "epic" attitude in the minds of men through his Alienation effect. In our community, this epic attitude is still a living tradition,' he argued (2000, 21–2). Here, Ghatak refuses to authorise a cultural mode historically present in South Asia (and therefore which preceded Bertolt Brecht) through reference to Europe. Instead, he gestures to *Verfremdungseffekt* as a close equivalent to what he does, while emphasising where his practice differs from what Brecht had to do ('build up' his audience to an 'epic attitude').

---

[14] *Jatra* is a popular folk-theatre form in Bengali-speaking regions of the Subcontinent, such as Odisha, West Bengal, Assam and Tripura in India as well as across Bangladesh.

[15] It is worth bearing in mind that the film's 'aural discontinuities' may also not be conscious formal choices, but down to the limited technical control available to Ghatak in semi-rural outdoor conditions with second-hand microphones, and uncontrollable peripheral noise like passing trains.

Weapons of the Weak

Anindya Raychaudhuri reads *Star*'s dark ending as a degree of 'alienation [that] provides the space from which [the characters] can begin to resist' (2009, 480), but this reading is difficult to locate in Ghatak's finale. The marginalisation Ghatak depicts, and the injustice of Neeta's death, is not figured as a form of resistance, despite her final protest. As Sugata Bose cautions, 'over-emphasis on the everyday processes of contest and compromise might obfuscate the reality of social dominance and leave a less than accurate impression of the "active" agency of labour resistance' (1993, 140). Marginalisation is the position from which resistance has to come, for it is the margins that those like Neeta's family now inhabit. But the weapons of the weak, so to speak, were rarely able to defend more than minimally defined norms and needs within the acutely unequal context of post-Partition India. Fanon reminds us that embodied experience *can* give rise to resistance – but not necessarily sustained resistance informed by knowledge of the powers structuring that experience. For instance, his chapter 'Colonial War and Mental Disorders' in *Wretched* examines various case studies that can all be considered experiences of marginalisation (1961, 200–50). The patients he describes include an Algerian peasant who turns homicidal himself after surviving a French rampage, and Algerian children who kill a white French playmate.[16] Some of the 'everyday processes of contest and compromise' (Sugata Bose 140) of the marginalised, as Fanon knew well, can be self-destructive rather than psychically transformational.

This may seem a despondent note for the film to end on, but there is also political power in *Star*'s long view. Gyanendra Pandey proposes we conceive of Partition as threefold: the first beginning with the Muslim League's insistence upon the establishment of Pakistan; the second being the splitting up of Punjab and Bengal; and the third the hundreds of thousands slaughtered, raped and displaced (2001, n.p.). This helps open up official Partition historiography to the experience of those who lived through its entire trajectory. To these three distinctions Ghatak's *Star* adds a fourth that is equally consequential: the experience of those who lived with Partition's decades-long aftermath of dispossession, displacement, forced urbanisation and destitution. In contrast, there are unmistakeable positions of agency for some of Buchi Emecheta's women refugees in *Destination Biafra*, which this chapter now turns to. But Emecheta's characters ultimately draw on a set of historical and contextual factors that seem absent in *Star*'s world. Refugeedom by post-independence

---

[16] See also Erica Burman (2019) on children in Fanon, analysed through his psychiatric, philosophical and political praxis.

conflict in *Destination* is more clearly traceable to the machinations of a capitalism in transition in 1960s Nigeria, and return after displacement is possible. This knowledge, available to Emecheta's characters in a way they are not to Ghatak's, leads to unexpected gender-based solidarities that cut across class, as *Destination* arrives at a more hopeful conclusion. Whereas Neeta is destroyed by the intersecting pressure of patriarchy, capitalist industrialisation and Partition dispossession, *Destination*'s women survive. It is not without cost, but Emecheta points to the effectiveness of collective practices of resilience among West African women who find themselves thrown together in wartime.

Shared Knowledge

In a 1986 speech at the Second African Writers' Conference in Stockholm, Emecheta draws attention to the work undertaken by African women to make their environments fit for collective psychic and social wellbeing.[17] 'Working and achieving to great heights is nothing new to the woman of Africa [. . .] But for the majority of African women, her real achievement – as I see it – is to make her immediate environment as happy as is possible under the circumstances' (1988, 179), she says. This work she configures as more than care-taking, going on to use an example of West African women's historic resistance to colonialism, the 'Women's War' in Aba (1929–1930). Turning oppressive circumstances around is, Emecheta proposes, nothing short of evidence that many African women daily 'achieve' in the face of great odds. This power is passed on, practised and known ('nothing new'), and it creates immediate, material changes in society.

Ariella Aïsha Azoulay describes how 'sealing certain deeds and actions in the past, imperial power secludes people, modes of life, and forms of action from themselves' (2019, 585), referring to what imperialism not only destroys but disavows having destroyed – by stamping that which it destroyed as always already ineffectual. Raising those 'modes of life and forms of action' available to women from their foremothers in a story about a neocolonial war, *Destination* intervenes not so much via the presentation of 'a female perspective' (Machiko 2008, 61), but through an account of several women and their means of agency and resilience in the present. Emecheta's novel pursues two representational tasks towards the above ends. One contextualises the war within its wider geopolitical stakes (confirming especially its neocolonial

---

[17] Delivered at the Scandinavian Institute of African Studies (now called the Nordic Africa Institute). See also K. H. Petersen (1988).

character), through a mixture of dialogue between characters with limited or localised knowledge and the delivering of general information in third-person omniscient narration (which takes the reader chronologically through events in Nigeria and London). The former device prioritises the observations of West African women experiencing the conflict simultaneously to their situating the war as neocolonial in character. The latter reveals to the reader pre- and intra-war political and economic developments, which confirm the predictions and interpretations offered by the novel's women before and after the fact. This section will first examine this interplay through moments in the novel where omniscient third-person narration is deployed to illustrate the neocolonial scramble for resources that undergirds the civil war, as well as how women demonstrate their existing knowledge of this.

The novel's other representational pursuit is that of affirming 'alternative terms of political affiliation' (Boehmer 15) with and beyond nationhood, through collective practices of survival. Sexual violence, refugeedom, the loss of children, the destruction of crops, hunger: all such war atrocities target things that reassure the very subjectivities of *Destination*'s women, who are often at one and the same time producers, workers, carers, mothers, sisters, cultivators, traders, healers, homemakers and sexual assault survivors. In scenes where women bear witness, negotiate safety and call upon the authority of the maternal (including but beyond biological motherhood) for self-defence, *Destination* frames women's resilience as organised resistance where possible, and as the collectivisation of psychic burdens, always. As we shall see, this not only provides a bulwark against the desubjectifying effects of the above atrocities – resonating in particular with Fanon's emphasis on creative agency, as described in Chapter 1 – but also enables the retelling of the civil war out of their conversations, testimonies and experiences.

'Was not the oil the reason for all this mess in the first place?'

As *Destination* recounts the war's many political and military manoeuvres in omniscient third person, its linear but diachronic timeline also follows Debbie Ogedengbe's journey from Lagos to the East. On a doomed mission to broker peace with Biafra's Colonel Chijioke Abosi, she is disguised as one of thousands of Igbo refugees heading in the same direction. *Destination* begins by establishing that independence was nominal through dramatising the motivations shaping Britain's exit. In the opening scene, a conversation between the last British Governor-General of Nigeria; an older statesman, Sir Fergus; and his officer son, Alan Grey, details two imperialist attitudes driving British strategy around Nigerian independence. Sir Fergus deploys the discourse of eugenics to equate West Africans with children: 'These people haven't even been given that paper yet and they behave as if they already own the whole world' (Emecheta 1982, 7).[18] For the younger Alan, the issue at hand is tapping the Hausa's mineral wealth and the Igbo's oil: 'Now we are to hand it over to these people, who've had all these minerals since Adam and not known what to do with them', he complains (8). But in then turning for geopolitical information to women who are absent from the decision-making itself, but subject to the lived effects of these decisions, Emecheta gets her reader to think about *where* they expect to find this evidence, and the potentially gendered nature of that expectation.

To do so, the novel first affirms the stakes of the capitalist world-system in a one and entire Nigeria, which must continue functioning as a petro-colony in neocolonial West Africa,[19] as known to Nigerian women. Debbie (the daughter of the inaugural finance minister who is later assassinated in the 1966 coup) situates Nigeria's 'resource curse' within the problem of postcolonial leadership, drawing attention to the economic bind that means any new leader will have to trade with the ex-coloniser: '[Abosi] made sure that through the way it was divided that the richest oil wells in the East fall into the hands of the non-Igbo-speaking people. In other words, he declared war' (115). This devolution of power away from 'Igbo-speaking-people' raises the highly politicised question of ethnicity after colonial rule (wherein the dominance of the Igbo as the majority ethnic group in East and South East Nigeria could also function to the detriment of minority ethnicities).[20]

Another example comes from one 'bold old woman who because of her age and fearlessness was becoming their leader' (177) during the harrowing lorry journey east that Debbie undertakes on her doomed mission to broker peace. Mrs Maduko demonstrates knowledge of the economic incentives behind the conflict when Debbie naïvely suggests that Abosi will surrender rather than let Biafrans starve. Mrs Maduko responds:

> Do you think those at the top will starve? No, they are probably there drinking champagne. And as for the businessmen, they don't want this war to end. You see that driver who brought us to the Benin-Agbor road? Well, he used to be an ordinary poor lorry driver, now he's a very wealthy man. (181)

---

[18] See also Angela Saini (2020) on the race pseudoscience that was widely subscribed to in the UK in the decades prior to and during *Destination*'s events.
[19] See Uche (2008) and Korieh (2012).
[20] See also Abdullahi Ayoade Ahmad (2015) on minorities and Nigerian policies, and Nwangwu et al. (2020) for a study of post-war Igbo nationalism.

She reminds Debbie that war is not only incidentally profitable, but that various players may escalate things precisely for its lucrative results. Several women echo her analysis in different ways. Debbie's friend Barbara observes how this war will accelerate a gendered asymmetry in the concentration of wealth: 'The woman and children who would be killed by bombs and guns would simply be statistics, war casualties. But for the soldier-politicians, the traders in arms, who only think of their personal gain, it would be the chance of a lifetime,' she says (114). Rarely openly stated by the male characters, the issue of control over natural resources – a key driver of the war – is presented by Emecheta as a known given for these women.

With its half-Itsekiri, half-Igbo protagonist in Debbie, the novel seems to reach for one multi-ethnic nation. But as Ann Marie Adams argues, 'Emecheta [also] realises that foreign and unmodified forms of government, when imposed on a colonised nation, will necessarily serve in the interests of colonial powers' (2001, 291). This is not only evidenced in moments like the above, which validate women's subjective impressions through geopolitical facts, but also in scenes in which Nigerian leaders fail to intervene for peace. Male leadership in *Destination* has echoes of Ousmane Sembène's *Xala*, in that, as explored in Chapter 3, the subjectivity crises of native elites have detrimental consequences for the wider populace. Their education, the narrator tells us, has rendered men like Abosi 'black white [men]', while exclusion from the same has others like Saka Momoh, the leader of the Nigerian forces who is 'hysterical' (109) with rage when challenged, hyper-sensitive to any real or imagined condescension. To recall Fanon in *Wretched* on how the conditions of independence in turn determine post-independence conditions: 'the very forms of organisation of the struggle [that will] suggest to [people] a different vocabulary' (1961, 36). This kind of organisational labour, and the social inter-dependency it fosters under circumstances of anti-colonial guerrilla struggle, was never experienced by this elite leadership.

Elina Eze, the wife of the Igbo MP Dr Eze, also understands long before her husband's arrest that the legacies of colonial education have combined with petty score-settling to escalate political tensions to the point of no return. 'Pity at the short-sightedness of her husband and his sex came over Elina. How could grown men make such blunders, and yet elevate themselves with such arrogance that one could not reach them to tell them the truth?' she wonders (240). As Dr Eze later collapses in fear, surrounded by the Nigerian army soldiers he never saw coming, 'he remembers his wife's voice saying, mere hours ago, "Was not the oil the reason for all this mess in the first place?" All women were witches – how did she know?' (241) That male leaders throughout arrive belatedly at what is either thought or said by *Destination*'s female characters also colours the tone of the omniscient third-person narration, suggesting that the narrator may be Emecheta's own voice. For example, we are told that Brigadier Onyemere, one of the instigators of the first coup,

> did not know what he had let himself in for. He thought that by praising the spirit of nationalism he would abolish tribalism, blunt the sharpness of imported religion [. . .] His false belief that he had been successful in his broadcast to the nation was fuelled by the praise the newspapers heaped upon him. (69)

This tone of narration – which lists metaphysical and material colonial legacies ('imported religion', 'tribalism') that no man could undo through good PR – echoes the mix of criticism and pity in Elina Eze's inner monologue. Underlining lack of foresight (Onyemere 'did not know'; Dr Eze was 'shortsighted') and the blindness that accompanies self-aggrandising ('his false belief'/'such arrogance'), the narrator confirms that these women – seemingly 'non-actors' in the events of 1966 – have insight via their own subject-positions.

Subjective experience, in the form of testimony, is another authoritative source in *Destination*. In scenes that centre women's and children's testimonies of localised violence, the novel illustrates how the act of narration provides re-integration into community, while the experiential information provided aids in collective decision-making. Prior to the declaration of Biafran secession, reports of violence against Igbos reach Colonel Abosi through witnesses, among whom Emecheta singles out a young mother and a teenage boy. Quoting these testimonies without interruption and in full staggers the forward thrust of the narrative with the introduction of violent imagery and fragmented sentences:

> One boy of about fifteen, who had long taken leave of his senses, rushed up to Ugoji and started to blubber, with saliva dripping from both corners of his mouth, 'My mother, my father . . . we were made to watch while they pounded them like yam with their clubs' [. . .] One of his brothers came and pulled him away, apologising and saying to Ugoji, 'He has been like this since the night of the incident.' Ugoji simply gaped. (84–5)

Delivering this information via testimony rather than third-person omniscient narrator lends it authority, as survivors become the reader's sole insight into the events of June to October 1966, when an estimated 80,000 to 100,000

Igbo were killed in pogroms in the north of Nigeria.[21] Another harrowing testimony, from a young woman, paints its lived experience:

> My husband was a chemist and we owned our own shop. As he was locking up, I heard the heavy footsteps of soldiers ... Our neighbours heard him calling for God's help, calling for his mother and me, but none of us could help. We all heard the firing, and I disobeyed him and ran out ... I was alone in the dirty muddy street where his bullet-ridden body, still warm, was left. (91)

Details like the 'body, still warm' and the 'heavy footsteps' render this young survivor's public testimony an act of narration: the bare facts of the night are brought to life via adjectives that describe the sensual experience of it. It is this latter quality that not only makes 'all the women present begin to cry', but also 'stir[s] the anger of those listening to fever point' (91), galvanising group feeling. Her testimony is socially powerful, which for all present, confirms its truth. That is to say, this unverifiable testimony facilitates political consensus not because its truth is confirmed by a third source but because it is confirmed as reality by others whose subjective experiences speak to the likelihood of these events.

Just as Ghatak resorts to highly spatial camerawork to capture the psychic suffering of his Partition refugees, it is helpful to think of this, too, in terms of spatialisation. Madhu Krishnan offers a definition of narrative spatialisation as that which 'draws on multiple scales and registers of social space [and] emphasises their interconnectedness as elements of a single, asymmetrically loaded system' (2018, 12). Pivoting between omniscient narration and women's points-of-view secures the authority of their lived experiences, and the knowledges deriving from their subjective observations, by echoing or confirming them through our omniscient narrator. This spatialising move situates women where they really were throughout the war: at the war front, because the war front was everywhere in East Nigeria.[22] *Destination*'s turn to women for the knowledge these circumstances impart is a historiographical intervention not because it presents these women's perspectives as addenda, but because it centres women's subjectivities in retelling the war.

---

[21] See also Heerten and Moses (2004) for a detailed historical account.
[22] See also Nnaemeka (1997, 238).

Socialising the Maternal

Having centred women in its narrativisation of the civil war, *Destination* then considers how they resist, transform their environment, and retain that Fanonian capacity to be 'actional' (or have creative agency) under various circumstances. As Christie Achebe's study (2010) of Igbo women in the civil war affirms, these foremost entailed the essential survival work of procuring food. To fight the food shortages, Igbo women used 'affia attack', a tactic of entering Nigerian-army occupied territories in disguise to buy food and fuel then smuggle these back across the line of fighting (805). This was both a survival tactic, and a reassertion of intersubjective relations. The blockade had at one and the same time stripped the majority of Igbo women of their agricultural work; their roles as providers and nurturers; and the community ties of market and field. Also rife was sexual violence and displacement, and Emecheta pays particular narrative attention to how their psychic and physical consequences are managed by women. She does so via implying a certain social power to the symbolisation of motherhood and the maternal, in senses including and beyond the biological. This becomes especially prevalent throughout the second half of the novel in scenes that weaponise (to deliberately use a term of combat) familial relations like mother, sister and son. Using them in moments that threaten to dehumanise women serves to remind men that certain socio-cultural codes are violated at great spiritual risk.

Elleke Boehmer's observation that Emecheta uses the symbolic – she singles out 'significant metaphors or defining images' in a manner interwoven with the 'day-to-day' (2005, 115) – manifests in *Destination*'s treatment of the maternal as a socially powerful symbol. For one, the novel gestures towards a *longue durée* of gender relations in pre-colonial and colonial West Africa, where – especially across Igbo, Yoruba, Fon, Lupe and Edo cultures – instances of women's authority over men exist, as part of cosmologies that conceive of the world as made up of a physical and a spiritual/ancestral half with their respective spheres of activity (Achebe et al. 2018). Although Emecheta never explicitly refers to these cosmologies, what we do know from the text is that characters are aware of a pre-colonial history that, in some contexts, had greater gender parity. In one scene, Debbie and her friend Barbara recall this past:

> 'But not a woman, we don't treat women like that.'
> Babs and Debbie laughed almost involuntarily and Teteku suspected he knew the reason. In the distant past in that part of Africa women were treated almost as men's equals, but with the arrival of colonialism their frail claim to equality had been taken away. (113)

This collectively known (albeit deemed 'taken away') authority manifests in several scenes where vulnerable women wrest some measure of power away from their wartime oppressors. For instance, when Nigerian soldiers stop a convoy of Igbo refugees and order the women to wait naked by the roadside, Mrs Maduko reminds the young soldiers of certain inviolable social inter-dependencies, such as that of child upon mother:

> One bold old woman went to the heap of clothes and took a lappa in which to wrap herself.
> 'What the hell are you doing? Stop or I'll shoot,' a soldier said savagely.
> 'Cover my nakedness, my son. The night is cold and this mother of yours is shivering,' she explained, as patiently as one would to a mentally sick child. The eager soldier thus addressed by her grumbled incoherently and looked away. (164)

Not only do Mrs Maduko's actions gain her agency in a situation of mortal danger, they assert a subjectivity at once ancestral mother and immediate relative ('this mother of yours') under conditions that dehumanise her. Its effectiveness gestures to a certain power that, as Emecheta has suggested in the exchange above between Debbie, Babs and Mr Teteku, has a social history. This stand-off between the women and soldiers momentarily exposes the civil war's construction of victims and perpetrators out of mothers and sons.

Debbie, whose high social class, singledom and Oxford education have thus far suggested her distance from motherhood, soon catches on to its social meaning. She manipulates the maternal into an emotive symbol in order to soften a tense exchange with a male stranger, securing herself safe passage eastwards: 'I am to go to my mother ... [she] is the only person I have,' she lies (156). The man who had attempted to waylay her then indicates his own longings through reference to his mother, a symbolic stand-in for psychic normalcy: 'He heaved a sigh and murmured, "Ah, our mothers. Mine is very old ... I want to be by her side"' (156). Both socialise the meaning of motherhood, turning it into a powerful proxy for what neither of them outwardly expresses: their desire for peace, no matter the victor. Even the novel's seemingly passive mother, the one-time privileged Stella Ogedengbe, steps into this social power when she must. Transforming from hapless trophy wife to pillar of strength after Debbie's rape, we are told '[Stella] had nursed, talked, prayed, then bullied, telling her daughter to put it all behind her ... this from a woman who for years had pretended to be so frail and dependent that tying her own headscarf was a big task' (150). Survival in gendered, neocolonial circumstances has had to take many forms, even for relatively comfortable women like Stella.

In these invocations of motherhood, *Destination* also demands recognition of secondary control mechanisms, which Christie Achebe defines as 'attempts to accommodate to objective conditions in order to affect a more satisfying fit with those conditions and control their psychological impact' (Achebe 2010, 789). Recalling Emecheta's comments about African women making the 'immediate environment as happy as is possible under the circumstances' (1988, 179), these mechanisms involve managing inter-dependency effectively under the detrimental effects of violence. When Debbie and her fellow refugees pass through an Igbo village that has been attacked, Mrs Maduko, we are told,

> listened sympathetically, then said with little preamble, 'Our men were useful, yes, very useful; but they have now been killed by other men . . . In the process of letting your husband provide for you, you have become dumb and passive. Go back to being yourself now. Get up, women, and let us bury the son of another sad woman.' (203–4)

She reminds the grieving mothers that survival does not mean acceptance; rather, anyone who has become 'dumb and passive' must take on the responsibility of being vocal and active in order for inter-dependency to work. Remembering the shared fact of their trauma is not a solution in itself to gendered violence, but it keeps isolation at bay until conditions change. The importance of this for the work of a decolonisation yet to come also emerged in Chapter 1's discussion of how Fanon grapples with the notion of 'freedom', especially in contexts where (neo-)colonialism seeks to divert resistance into mere reaction or individualism. That 'quality of being directed toward the future' (Clare 2013, 62), of being both agential and creative, is systematically blocked through tactics like 'divide and conquer'. In raising the shared responsibilities of motherhood over individual despair, Mrs Maduko's future-oriented action keeps in sight what Fanon calls 'the world I am heading for' (1952, 204).

It is important to note that images and metaphors of motherhood can frequently run the risk of biological essentialism; however, in the case of *Destination*, it is also clear that the above images are dissociated from the ideology of bourgeois domesticity, and even biological childbirth. There is a refusal in Emecheta's work to diminish the authority of the maternal to its carefully circumscribed power within the confines of the bourgeois family unit, or solely to responsibility over biological children.[23] It aligns instead with approaches

---

[23] Emecheta's treatment of motherhood often correlates with several African feminisms at once, including Womanism and Motherism, according to Onookome Okome (2017) and Susan Z. Andrade (2011), among others.

like that of Toni Morrison's to maternal images: as a complex trope of collective freedom and historical justice, without necessarily being contingent on, or emerging from, abilities of biological childbirth.[24] *Destination*'s characters claim agency and futurity by declaring themselves 'mother' to many 'children'.

History from Within

Such methods of resistance to, and management of, material and psychic suffering results not only in the above modes of bodily and narrative agency, but also in the breakdown of some class barriers. At first, Debbie had stood out among refugee women with her inability to handle physical labour: 'she walked down that dry road in the heat, with the weight of the child almost breaking her back. It struck her that African women her age carried babies like this all day and still farmed and cooked' (181). But her dearly acquired political consciousness is nonetheless significant. Living among Biafran refugee women, Debbie finds herself emplaced by the end of the novel within a network of mutual responsibility where her mental resilience is demanded by, and for, others; this in turn helps sustain it for herself. Deciding that 'no man, not even Abosi, was going to make a fool of her, a fool of all those unfortunate mothers who had lost their sons' (244), Debbie then rejects Alan Grey's offer of escape, instead staying in Nigeria so as to 'tell those orphans the story of how a few ambitious soldiers from Sandhurst tried to make their dream a reality' (245). Her refusal to leave for Britain is at once a commitment to use her class privilege to do historiographical work ('tell the story') and a confirmation of the civil war as neocolonial in character (with 'soldiers from Sandhurst' on both sides). This, in Barbara Harlow's conception of testimony and struggle, indicates in positive terms an unapologetic arrival at partisanship: of owning 'the active contribution that her narrative makes to the struggle' (73).

It also posits subjectivity as an unforgoable component of understanding (post)colonial conflict. Hannah Proctor argues that

> although interiorities may be obscure, difficult to analyse and inconsistently defined, subjectivity should not be subtracted from analyses of social injustice . . . Simply equating interiority with bourgeois individualism risks overlooking the generative ways in which an attentiveness to interiority might challenge a tendency to fetishise abstraction and generalisation (2018, n.p).

---

[24] See also Cobb-Moore and Billingsley (2017) on tropes of the maternal in Toni Morrison.

Agreeing with Proctor's caution, in this chapter I have sought to foreground how Ghatak's and Emecheta's treatments of subjectivity enable them to capture the material and psycho-social afterlives of Partition and the Nigerian Civil War respectively.

However, when there is no situation of outright conflict as in *Star* and *Destination*, but rather a more diffuse and gradual mass dispossession, 'resistance' can be harder to define. The post-independence re-structuring of the environments upon which people depended marked a key transition in several African and South Asian postcolonial nations, away from the more centralised nation-building approaches and internationalist politics of the immediate post-independence decades and towards integration into capitalist globalisation. Such spatial arrangements involved both Western finance capital, and buy-in from postcolonial governments. The next chapter investigates how and why this relates to subjectivity constitution as it considers the Indian writer Kamala Markandaya's 1954 novel *Nectar in a Sieve* and the Malian director Souleymane Cissé's 1978 film *Baara* (*Work*). Both follow characters who are at the mercy of their environment for their material survival and ontological security. The macro shifts towards capitalist globalisation that backdrop these two texts are 'slower' in their violence than mass migration or civil war, to borrow Rob Nixon's (2011) term. Considering what happens when 'here' no longer looks like the 'here' that used to help constitute one's subjectivity, Markandaya and Cissé attend to post-independence industrialisation's effects at the level of interiorities. These two texts' protagonists seek to sustain control over their modes of being in, and of, their spaces: the African urban factory in *Work*, and the South Asian rural village in *Nectar*, respectively. Their struggles render the relationship between subjectivity and place highly consequential to the future of decolonisation.

5

Emplacing the Self: Environment and Labour in Kamala Markandaya's *Nectar in a Sieve* and Souleymane Cissé's *Work*

The words 'space', 'place' and 'environment' traditionally encompass much of what geographers do and have done; in recent decades, the meanings attributed to these have become a crucial matter of debate in cultural and literary theory.[1] But anti-colonial thought has long recognised the need to fundamentally redefine the relationship between culture and the environments of postcolonial (nation-)spaces. For Aimé Césaire and Amílcar Cabral, such redefinition was part and parcel of liberation struggle. Cabral, the one-time agronomy student, writes that culture arises out of 'the physical reality of the environmental humus in which it develops, and it reflects the organic nature of society' (1974, 42). This also means situating colonialism's brutal human economy as the socio-environmental oppression that it also is. Césaire describes lucidly in *Discourse on Colonialism* (1950) that, when he talks about colonialism, he is also 'talking about natural *economies* that have been disrupted – harmonious and viable *economies* adapted to the indigenous population – about malnutrition permanently introduced, agricultural development oriented solely toward the benefit of metropolitan countries, the looting of products' (original emphasis) (2001, 43).[2] Within contemporary thought, Edouard Glissant's theory of Relations (1997), as well as the ecocritical interests of scholars including Arturo Escobar (1997), Ramachandra Guha and Juan Martínez-Alier (1997), and Graham Huggan and Helen Tiffin (2015), have all maintained that addressing history is integral to understanding literary representations of place and

---

[1] See also Carter et al. (1993); Huggan and Tiffin (2015); and DeLoughrey and Handley (2011).

[2] It could be said that a similar criticism, but with different political and aesthetic inflections, was levelled at colonialism via the poetics of *Négritude*, which often repurposed animistic beliefs as modes of self-emplacement in African environments. See Ahluwalia (2002), Garraway (2010) and Willoquet-Maricondi (1996) on *Négritude* and the natural world.

environment. This, they argue, particularly extends to how the latter's global crises has roots in the colonial order of things, wherein colonised places provided 'a primary source of raw materials and a site for state regulation on a scale massive enough to make the cherished Victorian notion of *laissez-faire* an ecological myth and an economic fantasy' (Mukherjee 2010, 18).

Working from this position – that it is impossible to understand history and geography, environment and culture without acknowledging their mutual interpenetration – this chapter considers a novel and film whose contexts and contents overlap upon the post-independence re-structuring of livelihoods and the environments these depended on. These transformations were often implemented by postcolonial governments for the avowed purposes of industrialisation and national sovereignty.[3] Set roughly two decades after the independences of India and Mali respectively, Markandaya's and Cissé's narratives of rural and urban post-independence change are backdropped by conditions where the transnational movement of capital has begun to re-route or co-opt these projects (already uneven in their domestic effects) in order to assimilate or openly coerce them into one world-system. These shifts happened at different paces and in different forms in India and Mali, the geopolitical, national, and economic reasons for which are beyond the scope of this chapter to analyse. But they included processes that strategically pursued, in Etienne Balibar's words, the 'realisation of space' for capitalist accumulation (Balibar and Wallerstein 1991, 89). While these major post-independence shifts in the organisation of global markets and labour power backdrop this section's texts, the chapter seeks to consider how, and why, environment comes to bear on the re-constitution of subjectivities in *Nectar* and *Work*.

First exploring how customary agricultural and social practices have constituted Markandaya's protagonist's subjectivity, the chapter will ask why these practices shape the protagonist's interpersonal relations and orient her life through a particular localism, in Arif Dirlik's meaning (1996). Moving on to discuss Cissé's film, it will then pursue the relation between subjectivity and labour in the film's representation of urban space. The chapter examines in

---

[3] This transition is of course more complex and varied than this summary can capture. Former colonies were already occupying economic positions crucial to the world-system, and found themselves at the dawn of independence largely holding the same systemic function and position. Nor were there sudden shifts but usually a steady assimilation of postcolonial national economies through privatisation, asymmetric contracts, loans, etc. However, it can be said that the already global flows of colonial capital shifted towards neocolonial modes and forms of accumulation and expansion from the late '70s onwards in particular.

both texts how places (with their colonial socio-economic histories), and the subjectivities of those emplaced within them, make possible what Arijit Sen and Lisa Silverman describe as 'embodied placemaking' (2014). Indicating an understanding of and engagement with physical place as a material product of human experience and memory of past events, alongside broad and local economic forces (2014, 13), embodied placemaking – despite its constriction under the 'realisation of space' (Balibar and Wallerstein 81) for capitalist accumulation – keeps the possibility of decolonisation alive in Markandaya's and Cissé's narratives. Fanon, Stefan Kipfer argues, often treats 'colonisation as spatial organization, and [views] decolonization in part as a form of transforming spatial relations in the colonial city and constructing nationwide socio-spatial alliances' (2005, 715). Emulating Fanon's emphasis on embodied subjectivity as a location of political potential, Markandaya's and Cissé's characters try to recuperate everyday forms of engagement with place that sustain the ability to resist, circumvent or confront dispossession.

The Body and Form of Consciousness

From post-independence India, *Nectar* looked unfashionably marked by a validation of peasant suffering and fortitude (Kumar 1996; Srivastava 1987), while in North America it was lauded as an Indian writer's 'translation' of 'authentic' India. Combined with Markandaya's privileged location and identity as an Anglicised, upper-class Brahmin writer living in London from 1948 onwards, the novel was 'tainted by the patronising tenor of the enthusiastic reception it received in the West at the time of first publication' (George 2009, 400), with *Nectar*'s village story somehow both unfashionably anti-modern and apolitically cosmopolitan. Narrating from her protagonist's point-of-view, Markandaya (much like R. K. Narayan with his fictional village of Malgudi) does not specify things the characters are themselves unself-conscious of – like language, dialect, caste and geographical location within India (the problems of these erasures will be returned to). The author's subsequent ten novels were little discussed, with her later 1970s and 1980s works decisively overshadowed by Indian writers like V. S. Naipaul and Salman Rushdie in the Anglophone literary sphere.

Under such circumstances, Rosemary Marangoly George points out, 'Markandaya's career, with its demonstrably spectacular beginning and dismal end, begs the question as to what kind of nationalist posture was tacitly or explicitly expected (by those in the Western and in the Indian literary, academic, and publishing worlds)' (2009, 401). Markandaya was no radical, but she explicitly stated her anti-colonialism, often expressed in the form of a Saidian kind of humanist universalism that did not equate to Eurocentrism.[4] In a 1963 biographical entry, she describes herself as 'anti-colonialist, anti-imperialist in politics' (Markandaya in George 2009, 405). In a later essay, she wrote, 'I am not, and have never been, a spokesperson for India – or an ambassador, as they lightheartedly put it' (1976, 27), seemingly in response to those expecting some 'nationalist posture' (George 401) of her. One reason as to these ambiguities is the narrow understanding of the national that is allowed by the model of national literary competition, a model detailed by Pascale Casanova (2004), which is not always conducive to reading the imaginaries of nation and nationhood within post-independence literatures. It falls short when, for example, the rejection of an inequitable nationalisation may be coming from a commitment to 'anti-colonialis[m], anti-imperialis[m]' (Markandaya in George 2009, 405), rather than to Western free-market liberalism. As Aamir Mufti argues, a 'national literature' can be the culmination of 'heterogeneous and dispersed bodies of writing assimilated onto the plane of equivalence and availability that is literature' (2010, 488), which encompasses work like *Nectar* – written for cosmopolitan audiences, but undeniably concerned with the politics of Indian nationhood as it affects labour, social relations and subjectivities.

A formative component of *Nectar*'s protagonist Rukmani's life is the rice paddy that she and her husband cultivate, and all the knowledges, experiences and social relations that accompany it. They live both at the mercy of natural forces, and at the mercy of their landlord. These natural and socio-economic forces have demands on Rukmani and Nathan beyond physical labour and the management of their meagre resources. To illustrate these, the novel follows how the characters must adapt to changes in harvest; how times of drought and plenty affect their personal psyches and their marital relationship; and how they interact with the nearby town – which provides them access to a market, but also eventually allows the market to dictate their lives. The bond between the character of Rukmani and this environment is sustained throughout *Nectar* by the recording of its incremental changes. These, in turn, provoke changes in Rukmani's memories, life perspective, social consciousness, sexual mores and economic relations. As such, in a Fanonian sense, they shape her subjectivity. To recall, Fanon's dialectic involving the self and the world holds an accumulation of history and the capacity for choice together as constituting of subjectivity: 'The past "takes" in quantity and, when solidly constructed,

---

[4] Articulated in Edward Said's thought, as Priyamvada Gopal interprets, as 'the human capacity for discovery, self-criticism and engaging in "a continuous process of self-understanding", [to mean] that no one is incapable of humanistic thinking and nothing is exempt from humanism's critical reach' (Gopal 2013, n.p).

informs the individual. He is the past in a changed value. But I can also revise [*reprendre*] my past, prize it, or condemn it, depending on what I choose' (1952, 202). The novel presents us with Rukmani's subjective and objective reality, foregrounding not only place but also her embodied experiences within it as mutually constituent elements of this environment.

For instance, through Rukmani's emotive responses to place, the reader understands both the practical demands of reproducing place, and the effects of place within herself: 'With each tender seedling that unfurled its small green leaf to my eager gaze, my excitement would rise and mount; winged, wondrous' (1956, 107). It is the first time she – the literate daughter of a village headman, who has never before touched a plough – cultivates a crop from seed to plant. Rukmani's everyday forms of engagement with her environment are described to the reader in ways that point to the production of what Paul Connerton calls 'place-memory . . . a combination of cognitive and habit-memory' (2009, 8), which produces and reproduces itself through habitualised social practices. These practices also sustain the material environment in which Rukmani is embedded. This reciprocity has parallels with Fanon's conception of the everyday, which for him is the only legitimate location for the making of 'new' people (1961, 239). That is, the remaking of material life itself after colonialism – especially modes of production and social reproduction – is also the means of transforming subjectivities.

To illustrate this, Markandaya's descriptions often contain both a natural phenomenon and its lived experience simultaneously, establishing how Rukmani's sensory observation of her environment is also creating place-memory: 'each time I paused I could hear sparrows twittering, and the thin, clear note of a mynah' (53); 'It rained so hard, so long and so incessantly that the thought of a period of no rain provoked a mild wonder. It was as if nothing had ever been but rain' (43); 'the purple brinjals and yellow pumpkins, the shiny green and red chillies' (27). These multi-sensory descriptions extend beyond knowledges of survival around sowing and reaping, demonstrating how her environment's visual, aural and sensual elements are orientating for the protagonist. Although they can read like romantic descriptions in isolation, the narrative weaves them into a whole that consists of both such sensory observations and of the economic necessities of rural life. In light of some strains of ecocritical feminism that elevate romantic textual representations of peasant women within a wider biological-essentialist tendency, what I mean by this constituting or orientating of subjectivity bears examining. The ecofeminist empirical claim, which examines the socio-political and economic structures that reduce many women's lives to poverty, ecological deprivation and economic powerlessness (Eaton and Lorentzen 2003, 2), is a valuable contribution to thought on the relationship between gender, environment and capitalism. Its conceptual work reveals how patriarchal ideologies work in intersection with these forces towards the domination of women and the exploitation of nature. But as South Asian critics including Ruvani Ranasinha (2016), Gayatri Spivak (1999) and Kumari Jayawardena (1986) have discussed in different contexts, its epistemological claims about the relationship between women and the natural environment often suggest a troublingly symbiotic relationship. For example, a claim like 'Woman-centred literature celebrates able, intelligent women as shapers of landscape . . . Rather than dominate or conquer land, they enjoy a cooperative, harmonious relationship with environment' (Zeleny 1997, 24) can translate easily into the notion of a first nature – the unknowable, essential, feminised Other – and a second nature, the knowing, male, doing self, which 'pacifies' nature to generate society.[5] These can prove all too useful in problematic constructions of land-as-woman in nationalist discourses, and the reduction of women to reproductive capacity.

That said, as Neelam Jabeen (2020) has proposed, rendering all ecofeminist claims of a woman–nature connection as essentialist would also dismiss the real, material connections between the oppression of women and the exploitation of land. When applied in literary criticism of postcolonial texts, any broad-brush charge like the former would be overlooking the fact that the culturally constructed woman–land association cannot merely be considered as symbolic in twentieth-century South Asian texts like *Nectar*.[6] Given that the 'female characters these texts present are actually treated as land' (Jabeen 1098) in many instances, probing this constructed association yields insights into the material forces determining postcolonial spaces, including environmental destruction, dispossession and privatisation (with all of their asymmetries along gender, caste and class lines). As such, while there is no symbiotic relationship between Markandaya's protagonist and her natural environment by virtue of her cisgendered, reproductive body, there is a relationship between Rukmani's embodied subjectivity and the land. It is one that suggests a conceptualisation of subjectivity that is neither the Enlightenment notion of the autonomous individual (tacitly classed, raced and gendered) nor

---

[5] 'First nature' itself is not neutral or ahistorical. It was originally produced in early modernity 'as something at odds with culture/society. In this phase, (white, Western) men and the "male" symbolic logic they represent are developing on the basis of their opposition to everything female that has consequentially been naturalised' (Flatschart 2018, 139).

[6] See also Kolondy (1975) and Howes (2005) for studies of the literary construction of feminised land.

a biological-essentialist one.[7] Rukmani's self-emplacement on the land comes from the 'fruitful work' of its cultivating, which 'gives body and form' to her 'consciousness' (Fanon 1961, 204).

The Self and the Market

As Vijay Prashad notes, the conversion of feudal landlords into capitalist landlords, and the conversion of tenant serfs into the agrarian proletariat, did not break the back of feudalism in post-independence India (2019, 89). Peasants experienced harsh pauperisation because of the overlay of the spatial configurations of neocolonial capitalism onto feudal relations. This was exacerbated by the unequal penetration of the two: *zamindars* re-invested little of their profits to modernise agriculture, though modernised industry had already arrived. Indeed, Paul Brass argues that the post-independence Indian government's agricultural production programmes sought rather 'to leave the prevailing patterns of rural control and dominance in the countryside intact to avoid precipitating rural class conflict', and to avoid 'diverting significant resources' away from urban zones (Brass 1990, 306). Markandaya's narrative establishes these systemic continuities between feudalism, colonialism and capitalism by highlighting the difference between competition for survival, and competition for profit.

Knowing when and where her environment must be conceded to is at the heart of competition for survival: 'Nature is like a wild animal that you have trained to work hard for you. So long as you are vigilant and walk warily with thought and care, so long will it give you its aid; but look away for an instant, be heedless or forgetful, and it has you by the throat,' Rukmani reflects (Markandaya 1954, 43). Represented here via the allegory of the trained (not tamed) animal is a 'cognitive mapping' of her locality, to raise Fredric Jameson's (1995) idea. It informs Rukmani's knowledge of herself as a part of, and reliant on, her surroundings. This tough but self-sustaining work also has consciousness-raising effects on Rukmani, who begins to appreciate a cultivator's life after she 'marries down'. It is work reminiscent of Fanon's distinction between that which is 'parachuted down' from postcolonial governments to the masses, and that which is 'the coherent, enlightened action of men and women' that 'assum[es] responsibility on the historical scale' (Fanon 1961, 165).

As the novel proceeds into its building action, her experience of rural labour will allow Markandaya to use the minute details of Rukmani's spatial

---

[7] See also Spivak (1999) on how the Enlightenment notion of the subject needs the 'differential example of the savage [. . .] a requirement of the thinking of autonomy itself and cannot therefore be cultivated out of the system' (Lloyd 2013, 93).

location, and the practices tied to her landscape, as 'a figurative machinery in which questions about the system and its control over the local ceaselessly rise and fall' (Jameson 1992, 5). When Rukmani encounters market forces, their disorienting and alienating effect is clearly discernible thanks to the sensory contrast the reader can now draw between the embodied experience of rural labour, as described so vividly above, and the new, mass production line:

> Not a month went by but somebody's land was swallowed up, another building appeared. Day and night the tanning went on. A never-ending line of carts brought the raw materials in – thousands of skins, goat, calf, lizard and snake skins – and took them away again tanned, dyed and finished. It seemed impossible that markets could be found for such quantities – or that so many animals existed – but so it was, incredibly. (51)

As the town begins to manufacture goods for national and perhaps global markets, the emphasis on volume and variety – 'never-ending', 'thousands', 'such quantities' – suggests a hitherto unknown scale of consumption. It is a state of things beyond the balance of give-and-take thus far verified by Rukmani's own empirical knowledge of the land. The tannery (owned by an absent, unnamed English man, in a nod to neocolonial dynamics) thus begins to force through changes at an economic and spatial level, but also at a subjective and intersubjective level. One Diwali, Rukmani remembers a neighbour who left when the tannery put their stall in town out of business: 'Last year Janaki had come with us, she and her children. This year who knew – or cared? The black thought momentarily doused the glow within me' (59). The sights, smells and sounds of communal celebration are haunted by her memory of a family whose livelihood was swallowed by the tannery. The interpersonal effects of this change are equally haunting. Now, 'nobody cared' so long as it was not them. This, Rukmani seems to foresee, will only compound the downturn in their material conditions: people, she observes, 'were reconciled . . . the readier to grasp the present' (33). It is not change itself that she resists, cyclicality being a fact of rural life, but easy reconciliation to the 'grasp[ing]' present.

This material and ontological distress problematises a frequent refrain within scholarship about this novel: that *Nectar* is a juxtaposition of the 'modern' and the 'traditional' (Misra 2001, 41) conceptualisation of the self. Malti Agrawal finds in the novel an embrace of 'the modern': 'had [Rukmani] been educated and self-sufficient, she [could] . . . struggle for her rights and eventually reach self-actualisation' (2007, 135), with little clarification as to what 'rights' and 'self-actualisation' would mean in 1950s rural India. Fawzia Afzal-Khan finds a celebration of 'the traditional', in that 'Markandaya establishes peasants as heroic figures of the mythic mode . . .' (1993, 100). Pravati Misra agrees with Agrawal, proposing that Rukmani's character conforms to 'the traditional image of women embodied in the mythical figures of Sita and Savitri, who silently bear all hardships' (2001, 41). The work of the Subalternists has somewhat contributed to reinforcing this juxtaposition, particularly after Ranajit Guha's work (1998) on the political psychology of peasants.[8]

It may be more accurate to say that *Nectar*'s characters act upon their changing circumstances, while allowing for some circumstances to act upon them. Neither do Rukmani and her husband 'bear all hardships' as one. Rukmani's literacy, and her knowledge of the customary domestic dynamics of multi-generational households, inform her consciousness differently. When their belongings are stolen in the city en route to their son, she thinks, 'the ease with which Nathan accepted the misfortune irritated me. Now I shall be wholly indebted to my daughter-in-law' (151). Additionally, Rukmani is clearly able to name the ecological and ontological oppressions wrought by the coming of the tannery:

> In the town there were the crowds, and streets battered down upon the earth, and the filth that men had put upon it, and one walked with care for what might lie beneath one's feet or threaten from before or behind. And in this preoccupation one forgot to look at the sun or the stars, or even to observe they had changed their setting in the sky: and knew nothing of the passage of time save in dry frenzy, by looking at the clock. But for us, who lived by the green, quiet fields, perilously close though these were to the town, nature still gave its muted message. (117)

This is not Markandaya 'idealis[ing] the countryside to call attention to its demise' (Zeleny 1997, 27); there is something less simplistic being explored in passages like these, which situate a Fanonian mode of embodied experience as key to reassuring one's subjectivity under the fluctuating social and economic conditions following independence. The view Rukmani demonstrates above is suggested in Sharda Jain's observation that Markandaya's protagonist 'voices the disgust of a thousand dispossessed families, saying, "while there was land, there was hope"' (2007, 153). The tannery has 'muted' those 'message[s]' from nature that Rukmani must be receptive to for her own survival. As Jain hints, the novel comments on the psychic experience ('disgust') of what Neil Lazarus (2018) calls the 'second moment' of the generalisation

---

[8] See also H. Singh (2002) and Vivek Chibber (2013) for responses.

of commodity production and wage labour, wherein the global peasantry becomes 'very much a part of the story of capitalist modernisation (Lazarus 2018, 165–73).

This 'second moment' (Lazarus 165) of capitalist modernisation is also about re-defining human value and social relations. In one scene, Rukmani's two elder sons Thambi and Arjun participate in a strike at the tannery, and this results in their deaths; their mother is told they died stealing. Two tannery representatives then warn Rukmani not to seek compensation for their deaths:

> 'He should not have struggled. In these circumstances you naturally have no claim on us.'
> 'Claim?' I said. 'I have made no claim. I do not understand you.'
> He made a gesture of impatience.
> 'You may think of it later, and try to get compensation. I warn you, it will not work.'
> Compensation, I thought. What compensation is there for death? (95)

The logic of industrialised capital is not only revealed to be unnatural ('what compensation is there for death?') – something the tannery's resource consumption had already told her – but also, in answering death with the tighter protection of property, it objectifies Rukmani's familial bonds. When she and Nathan then find out that their other, city-dwelling son left his young family to chase higher wages – not out of need, but in excess – they see this, too, as a failure to protect their own: 'We gave him life, we should have taught him better' (155). Passages like the above clearly suggest there is 'heroism' even in the midst of dispossession and poverty, but it has no 'mythic' dimensions (Afzal-Khan 1993, 100) – it is the sustenance of social inter-dependency under dehumanising conditions.

The reluctance of several critics to name the 'industrial values' and 'modern' forces they talk of as capitalism – and from there to read the historicity of the economic changes Markandaya is narrating – means that they also skip many scenes (like the two discussed above) that intertwine subjectivity, place and post-independence industrialisation.[9] When Rukmani laments the loss of their rural way of life, she is lamenting the destruction of a particular set of spatial relations and temporal orientations, as capital in 1950s India begins to forge 'a geographical landscape appropriate to its own dynamic of accumulation at a particular moment of its history, [which it will] destroy and rebuild to accommodate accumulation at a later date' (Harvey 2000, 59). When we do away

---

[9] See, for example, Zeleny (1997); Rogobete (2014); and Prasad (1984).

with the unstable categories of traditional and modern, we can instead specify that what the novel is doing is narrativising how neocolonialism is having to destroy the semi-feudal structural form that colonialism had operated through, so as to re-configure space to accommodate the capitalist globalisation into which India will be incorporated by the later twentieth century.[10] This spatial overhaul also marks the internalisation or the refusal of these re-configurations at the level of subjectivities.

Place-Memory and Resistance

Women's resistance to incorporation into the world-system has been and continues to be constituted by many activities. Although including organised resistance, these also entail forms that are too often relegated to the realms of the 'merely' social or interpersonal. As Kathryn B. Ward argues (1993), world-system theory has overlooked women's diverse resistance to those processes of incorporation that have inequitable socio-economic effects. Ward proposes that 'we need to redefine our notions of work, resistance, and incorporation to encompass the range of women's labours' (57). As gestured to in Chapter 4 through the 'secondary control mechanisms' (Achebe 2010, 789) used powerfully by women in Buchi Emecheta's *Destination Biafra* (1982), this redefinition must also extend to value judgements about resistance to the everyday subjective and interpersonal effects of this incorporation, versus organised political resistance. To that end, theories like the 'environmentalism of the poor' (Guha 2000) can be accompanied by an emphasis like Ward's (1993) on inequities along gender lines, and by the Fanonian conception of subjectivity that this book foregrounds.

The tannery in *Nectar* is an allegory that distils its world-systemic moment into a 'particular spatial or narrative model of the social totality' (Jameson 1995, 5) it paints. The allegory functions in ways that illustrate how Rukmani demystifies the sources of the economic and social turbulence in her environment:

> Because [the tannery] grew it got the power that money brings, so that to attempt to withstand it was like trying to stop the onward rush of the great juggernaut . . . There had been a time when we, too, had benefited, but we had lost more than we had gained or could ever regain. (135)

---

[10] See also Arturo Escobar (2010) on how this spatial re-configuration operates through developmentalism.

'The power that money brings' is nothing new to her, but the unprecedented scale of this kind of accumulation is also unstoppable by any means they know. This is crucial knowledge that helps Rukmani understand the latter's rewards as uneven and transient, and therefore not to be sought at risk to oneself: it 'benefits' at first, then takes away 'more than [they] could ever regain'. Her refusal to partake of this power that changes the 'face' of a place, and follows up any meagre benefit with insurmountable loss, couches political knowledge within the effects she has experienced.

Indeed, this proves vital knowledge for bringing about Rukmani's resilience in the face of destitution. When Rukmani and Nathan's hopes of living with their son in the city crumble, the elderly couple shelter in a temple. There,

> with each passing day [their] longing for the land grew; brown earth and green fields and the rustling rice paddy, not, curiously, as they were, but as [they] had first known them . . . Keeping pace with these longings, [their] distaste for the city grew and grew and became a sweeping, pervasive hatred (169).

The nature of the resistance they choose is both an ontological and a material one: it comprehends the affinity between rejecting economic participation in the new world-system and reaffirming pre-existing inter-dependencies with place. However, they must temporarily participate in the hyper-exploitative spaces of the city to earn enough to return. Guided by a streetwise orphan named Puli, Rukmani and Nathan break rocks at a stone quarry to save funds to return home. There, they feel solidarity with strangers in an otherwise ruthless situation: 'The man behind me kept prodding me with his baskets until at last I turned around in irritation. Then I saw he was a very old man, and the load he carried kept slipping. My irritation vanished' (174). Rukmani and Nathan also trust that co-dependence will sustain them better: 'We had become dependent on the boy, respecting his independent spirit as much as his considerable knowledge of the city and its many kinds of people' (178). Their temporary family unit works out of trust in one another's respective knowledges of different environments. They cannot stop the juggernaut of capitalist expansion, but they in a sense emerge victorious by recognising their solidarity with urban labourers, and by 'saving' one of the future generation.

While resistance can therefore be read in this novel through the ontological refusal of forced re-emplacement, there are some limits to interpreting these dynamics in *Nectar*. Caste, for example, is one evasion Markandaya makes in order to affirm social inter-dependency. Rukmani never mentions the castes of Puli, the quarry workers, or others she meets in the city, which presumably would not have the social homogeneity of her village. The latter may have been imagined as belonging to a region less impacted than the Punjab or Bengal regions by post-Partition migration (such as Markandaya's native state of Karnataka). But this evasion is still a marked difference from earlier Anglo-Indian writing that worked with juxtapositions of village and city, like Raja Rao's *Kanthapura* (1938). In Rao, the contentious relationship between the two is mapped onto Gandhian ideology's rejection of strictures against caste pollution, which is 'seen by some to be the word from the city, to be either lionised or repudiated as such' (Gopal 2009, 48). Either *Nectar*'s fictional city has (incredibly) wholly embraced this Gandhian call; Rukmani has lived too sheltered a life to understand caste difference when she sees it; or in the 'any Indian village' vein of R. K. Narayan's fictional Malgudi, this is Markandaya's own representational choice.

This does not, however, dismiss the validity of the relationship the novel draws between subjectivity and environment in the context of post-independence rural transformation. Markandaya's protagonist cannot be read as a 'natural' ecologist. As Ramachandra Guha and Juan Martínez-Alier (1997) and Rob Nixon (2011) among others have stressed, the green commitments of the most dispossessed 'are seamed through with other economic and cultural causes, as they experience environmental threat not as a planetary abstraction but as a set of inhabited risks, some imminent, others obscurely long term' (Nixon 2011, 4). But Rukmani does return to her home village where her daughter, son and grandson await her, having resisted both permanent displacement and internalising the transactional social relations brought about by the tannery. It is not a return to a past idyll. The hard labour of the quarry has killed Nathan; her daughter Ira can never marry, having borne from sex work a child with albinism; and her remaining son is unemployed until the local medical centre is built. But in having refused at a subjective and interpersonal level what she can of both capitalist industrialisation and feudal patriarchy, Rukmani is able to re-emplace herself in the environment that once constituted her subjectivity. The changes her experiences have wrought upon her, and the changes the world-system is wreaking upon her village, remain. But she nonetheless 'looked about [her] at the land, and it was life to [her] starving spirit' (188).

A Web of Contradictions

Despite the two-decade gap and the geographical distance between the two, *Nectar*'s political and ontological emphases map onto the shifts in consciousness and the spaces of struggle depicted in Souleymane Cissé's 1978 film *Work*. France left behind a particular media landscape in Senegal, Mali, Mauritania and Côte d'Ivoire. Paris-controlled in an economic sense more than an artistic one, Manthia Diawara's apt term for this is 'technological paternalism' (1987, 61). The French Ministry of Cooperation's *Bureau du Cinéma* provided technical assistance to 185 shorts and features made between 1963 and 1975 by Francophone Africans, making up 80 per cent of all Black African film production (Andrade-Watkins 1996, 112). This often conceived the latter along French norms of *auteur*-led Second Cinema. Programmes of French aid for culture, meanwhile, 'existed independently from the commercial distribution system in Francophone Africa, which was under the joint monopoly of French companies SECMA and COMACICO, who excluded African films from African commercial screens' (Armes 1986, 233). Thus the French system of distribution and film aid was able to sustain two equally profitable practices. On the one hand, they could nurture then introduce West African filmmakers to metropolitan audiences; on the other, they could distribute commercial French and American films in West Africa, a large new market that could help cover mainstream Western cinema's high overhead costs.[11]

Ousmane Sembène describes the impossible bind the above set-up placed upon West Africa's first filmmakers:

> We are enclosed in a web of contradictions . . . If an African country had proposed a budget to me I would have accepted with joy . . . But I will not wait, sitting on a chair, for my country to take in hand all its political and economic destinies [before making a film]' (Sembène in Busch and Annas 2008, 10–11).

Both he and Cissé learned their craft in the Soviet Union; Cissé's training at the VGIK film school in Moscow in the 1960s 'allowed him to bring a critical gaze shaped by Marxist concepts of class analysis to his first three feature-length studies of contemporary Mali' (Armes 2006, 78). The 'web of contradictions' Sembène describes runs strongly throughout Cissé's *Work*, where an abundance of French commodities are utilised by the Malian elite – while goods produced for the domestic market hint at neocolonial manoeuvres. Depicting an urban locale where Western capital cheapens African labour (with the tacit assent of post-independence governments), the film pauses on

---

[11] An important exception to such a West African cinema was the development of cinemas in Angola and Guinea-Bissau, which were directly born of armed revolutionary movements. Centring documentaries linked to struggles for independence, its early examples looked to Brazilian and Cuban Third Cinema. More on this from Hoefert de Turégano (2003).

the psycho-political potential in the everyday.[12] It follows two young men whose fates are intertwined by their distant kinship: Balla Traoré, a manager at a textile factory, and Diarra, a good-natured but oftentimes naïve porter who keeps getting harassed off the streets by the police. Balla is instructed by his boss Sissoko, an old nationalist of the independence generation (whose father made his wealth by stealing public funds), to lay off his workers to cover the factory's 200-million-Franc debt. He secretly disobeys. Balla also pays Diarra's bail and gives him a job at the factory. But when he facilitates a workers' meeting on conditions, wages and hours, Sissoko has his lackeys lure Balla away from the meeting and murder him. Sissoko then returns home to find his much-younger wife Djeneba with a lover, and strangles her. As the incensed workers carry Balla's body home, they waylay Sissoko long enough for the police to arrive and arrest him for femicide. As with Markandaya's *Nectar*, Cissé's film uses its environment as a container for its themes, propelling its story through formal choices around framing, sequencing, architecture, space and place.

Spatial Strategies

The French colonial imaginary conceived of space as external to the self: a domain upon which one could act, the better to administer the populations that inhabited it. One 'lived "in" space; one did not create space by interaction with it. It was an inert realm which could be remodelled, not a realm which was in process' (Langford 2005, 103). Its configuration as such helped facilitate not only the oppression of the indigenous inhabitants of a place and their ontologies about it, but also the re-inscribing of its non-human elements as raw material awaiting 'use'. Such 'spatial strategies', in Henri Lefebvre's term (1991, 112), not only unfold in space but are also about space. They are designed to support and maintain relations of power or of resistance, and can be seen as 'articulating the physical-material and mental-imaginative aspects of social space' (Deshpande 1998, 250). Cissé introduces Bamako's spatial order as one that makes use of the material aspects, as well as the lived experience, of social environments to compel these spaces to produce for, and integrate into, the neocolonial routes of global capital.

---

[12] This interpenetration of place and subjectivity has also been examined – though with less attention to its cinematic representation – in the 'spatial turn' in postcolonial scholarship (Upstone 2009; Soja 2011; Krishnan 2017; Quayson 2020), and in work within Urban Studies that attends to the production of everyday life for urban majorities in the Global South, such as AbdouMaliq Simone's scholarship (2018).

Figure 5.1 The inspection. *Baara [Work]*. Dir. Souleymane Cissé, 1978.

The film first explores these strategies at work in the textile factory, depicting how it is experienced by differently classed characters. For example, the viewer learns of the educated, idealistic character of Balla through his bodily movements within and across the factory space. When Balla walks among the workers and attempts to talk to them over the noise of the machinery, Cissé's choice of a tracking shot (the camera following alongside the subject at a consistent distance) to chart Balla's progress along the factory floor gives the viewer a sense of his transience (Figure 5.1). Although a character conscious of his station, Balla is seen as uneasy with the class demarcations reproduced by the spatial configuration of his workplace. He attempts to get 'stuck in', but ends up inconveniencing the workers as they move to let their manager through. In the character of Balla, we can see a particular class and generation of Malians caught between a socially committed politics (Balla's friend later fails, for instance, to convince him to join the private sector) and the political realities of a neocolonial state. *Work*'s spatial dynamics thus begin to communicate some of the contradictions that characterise a post-independence generation of educated youth, who are neither workers themselves nor comprador bourgeoisie (which Balla's boss, Sissoko, represents instead).[13]

As sympathetic as Balla's portrayal is, it is the embodied experiences of those of Diarra's class that Cissé's lens prioritises. Just as ceaseless production

---

[13] A demographic that Cissé will politicise more explicitly in his next film, *The Wind* (1982).

is shown to directly affect the natural environment in *Nectar*, in *Work* it is shown to sap the energies of those subject to its machinations, minimising the possibility of political organising. When Balla tells the workers to try to be at the meeting, Diarra, covered in dye and sweat, responds with 'I'm too tired'. The difference in their experiences of the same space is unmistakeable thanks to the intense physicality of this scene. Diarra's naked torso is glistening with sweat and inky black dye as Balla stands unruffled in a crisp shirt. In the film's space of production (the factory), which is also Balla's space of class anxiety, we can observe the 'development of underdevelopment' that marks the continuity of those spatial precepts to French colonialism (Warwick Research Collective 2015, 13). To that end, Cissé's camera initiates intimate close-ups of the unnamed labourers and their labours. The viewer's attention is directed to and held by sequences featuring the faces, hands and creations of the welders, dye makers, assemblers, weavers, printmakers, cotton spinners and machinists at Sissoko's factory (Figure 5.2). Walter Benjamin (1969), Béla Balázs (2010) and Gilles Deleuze (2013) among others have all described the affective power of the close-up, usually utilised to reveal hidden meaning, disclose a character's inner state, or encourage the viewer to look on an object or subject in a new light. However, Cissé's extreme close-ups (forehead to chin) work in ways closer to what Laura Marks has termed 'haptic visuality' (2000), where the eye functions as a faculty of touch. The physicality of the workers' labours is foregrounded in these close-ups, where the sweat on their faces, the fumes of the machinery, hair texture, and red street dust on skin is discernible.

Figure 5.2 Bodily labours. *Baara [Work]*. Dir. Souleymane Cissé, 1978.

This technique is still spatial in nature: it constrains the cinematic frame on a face, which in turn eliminates its capacities of recording environment, context and even temporal movement. Cissé is here almost demanding a kind of ground zero of mutual recognition from the viewer. We see the cotton being spun and the textiles being dyed in a flurry of dirty, agile hands; young men at the local mosque fidgeting with their *tasbīh*; and the *griots* using hand gestures to emphasise their oral storytelling. Such embodied modes of being in place both challenge and co-exist with the production line of neocolonial capitalism. In fact, the socio-spatial nature of these activities and their locations are visually alluded to alongside the humanising close-ups. Does the street or the *griot* come first? Would the mosque courtyard be a mosque courtyard if the local men did not congregate there? In *Work*, people neither uniformly internalise nor reject the activities associated with production, that is, with neocolonial capitalism's 'realisation of space' (Balibar 1991, 89) for accumulation. Their actions always criss-cross with other logics that are delineating these social spaces. In some of them, like the factory, *Work* shows 'the tendency of capital to invest itself in fixed spaces through which spatial practices are ordered, oriented towards the maximisation of profit and the (re)production of its own logic' (Krishnan 2018, 63). Others, it has not entirely penetrated, like the five daily instances of ceasing 'productivity' for Islamic prayer.

Architectures of Independence

These representational strategies also influence *Work*'s engagement with the built urban environment. The significance of urban architecture in *Work* is set against the context of half a century of French colonial spatial models and education. As Rachael Langford argues, it was not enough to know that spatial distinctions existed in the colonial city, but 'they had to be seen patently to exist in concrete space and time, and to give rise to a "correct", desired form of spatial practice, which could be taught' (2005, 96). In practice, however, the sharply segregated 'dual city' of the kind Fanon describes (Algiers) in *Wretched* was relatively uncommon in colonial Africa (Bissell 2011). Later, post-independence spatial configurations were not all straightforwardly inclusionary where colonial ones had been exclusionary, either. After their independences, an African Modernist architectural aesthetic grew popular in Mali, Côte d'Ivoire, Ghana and Senegal.[14] The often daring designs of these parliament

---

[14] 'Modernism' here describes this architecture in reference to Modernist aesthetic style, some characteristics of which include the reduction of design to essential forms and colours; simple horizontal and vertical elements; and an emphasis on functionality that

buildings, universities, central banks, independence memorials and stadiums are frequently held up as indication of a forward-looking spirit, but they also evidence the contradictions and dilemmas experienced within pan-African organising and the nation-building processes of the time.[15] Indeed, after independence, cultural urban projects such as the Musée National du Mali could in fact continue 'to adhere to fixed delineations of identities rooted in colonial interpretations, which failed to adhere to the changing notions of identities and belonging in the postcolonial nation-state' (Mew 2015, 186). For instance, in a series of scenes where Balla enters an African Modernist building upon being summoned to his boss Sissoko's office, height, distance and shape work with and through cinematic spatial phenomena such as negative space, panning and framing to imbue his meeting with political significance. As the camera pans over the futuristic lines and boxy shapes of the building's exterior, we occasionally lose sight of Balla, as the camera's movement ceases to be prompted by the subject of its frame (Figure 5.3). Fading into insignificance, our 'bright young thing' Balla is visually swallowed up by a building full of bureaucrats. Architecture in this scene serves to shroud factory owner Sissoko in layers of protective concrete and corporate impunity. As the camera glides aimlessly over the building's surfaces rather than follow Balla's progress inside in real-time, the viewer is kept locked outside, along with the people Sissoko professes to serve.

These independence architectures could also be charged, however, as sites of political resistance in this era. In Fanon's 'historical geography' (Kipfer 2005, 715), decolonisation must entail the transformation of colonial spatial organisation, because the realisation of space is ultimately a collective activity. One of the ways in which people are induced to be 'actional', and therefore transformed in their ways of relating to themselves and to others, is the spatial exercising of popular agency. 'Creating new structures, such as stadiums, to make room for dialectical relationships between bodies, cities, and the world' (Adalet 2021, 4) carries the potential to challenge colonial boundaries and separations – with 'creating' here understood not just as having a hand in designing and constructing a structure, but the aforementioned 'embodied

---

often emerged from utopian and socialist visions. See also Robert Klanten and Sofia Borges (2016).

[15] For one, their aesthetic boldness did not necessarily extend to a radical re-imagining of the powers they housed, or the societies they served. Some economic growth (in GDP terms) following independence from colonialism in West Africa did coincide with this radical architectural aesthetic, but know-how did not. Building designs and architects were often imported from outside the continent, with only a handful of the latter being African, like the Senegalese architects Cheikh N'Gom and Pierre Goudiaby Atepa.

Figure 5.3 Architectures of independence. *Baara [Work]*. Dir. Souleymane Cissé, 1978.

placemaking' (Sen and Silverman 2014). As 'new structures create the possibility of a different regime of movement' (Adalet 4), some spaces become environments of political education when 'hijacked' by citizens, as Diawara recalls Alpha O. Konaré doing in 1969 when he stood up to sing the national anthem in protest against privatisation at the Stade Omnisport Modibo Keïta, completed in 1965.

Such collective place-memories, to recall Paul Connerton's (2009) term, exist in tension with the neocolonial goings on inside other buildings in *Work*, such as Sissoko's office. This contradiction generates broader questions about modernisation, particularly vis-à-vis its historically particular – namely, imperialist – formation. Modernisation never was, nor is, entirely what various meta-narratives have designated it to be, as an array of scholarship has shown.[16] *Work*'s African Modernist spaces evoke, on the one hand, a meta-narrative of modernisation, with its tendency to oppress the local and erase differences of location and history; on the other, they underline that *Work*'s spaces, and

[16] I use 'modernisation' to refer to processes of the liberalisation of markets and their incorporation into Euro-American capitalism, and its attendant epistemological assumptions of Eurocentrism, manifest in colonial narratives of 'progress' upon a linear civilisational timeline. I understand 'modernity', concurring with Arif Dirlik, as 'not a thing but a relationship', which is nevertheless 'a single modernity, of which there is a multiplicity of expressions and articulations' (Dirlik 2003, 289). See also Parry (2002); Dirlik (1997) and Ingham and Warren (2003).

the subjectivities they engender, exist in tension with the operations of one world-system. Given that 'a preoccupation with the local that leaves the global outside of its line of vision is vulnerable to manipulation at the hands of global capital' (Dirlik 1997, 467), reading the local as object of the operations of capital is a component of any inquiry into the sources and consequences of neocolonialism. That is not to say that *Work* configures its characters' environments as straightforwardly allegorical distillations of world-systemic currents or events. But the film's representation of the built environment does reinforce the relationship between itself and the subjectivities of those who experience it – with all the place-memories these may evoke of the kinds of decolonisation envisioned but not realised.

The Materiality of Identity

As the film progresses, textiles, and the way they materially and symbolically function, further relate these world-systemic processes to the formation of subjectivities. The period saw General Traoré hurl a particular accusation at the national factories for 'draining the resources of the peasants, inducing drought, famine, and corruption' (Diawara 2003, 70). The cotton factory was thus a fraught terrain of national politics. At one and the same time, *Work*'s textile factory provides local people with their livelihoods, absorbs them into parts of the global economy, and literally reproduces the nation and its national(ist) myths. For instance, Mali's traditional cotton fabric *Bògòlanfini* is hand-dyed with fermented mud. But the final product under Balla's supervision at the factory is a mass-produced and chemically dyed commemorative cloth. It features a man who resembles Jacques Foccart, superimposed upon a map of Africa where Mali is distinguished in green. Foccart founded the *Service d'Action Civique*, a Gaullist militia operating in West Africa as part of France's sphere of influence over its former colonies from the 1960s to the 1980s.[17] As this striking detail suggests, the factory, in printing global and national events considered important indicators of the progress of nation-time, is a space that reproduces multiple and contrasting ideologies (Figure 5.4). The cloth is depicted interspersed via a cut-reverse-cut technique with the dangerous and dirty process of its making. The structure of production is such that the workers' labours in the national factories may actually be sustaining the nation's economic bondage to France. Monsieur Foccart, one of the masterminds

---

[17] The SAC's members were accused of almost every crime imaginable between 1968 and 1981, and they reported directly to de Gaulle via Foccart. See also Kaye Whiteman (1997).

Figure 5.4 Françafrique. *Baara [Work]*. Dir. Souleymane Cissé, 1978.

of this bondage, is honoured with a portrait. Such material details link the film's productive spaces to the reproduction of capitalism occurring at a world-systemic scale.

But the psycho-political is not divorced from these processes. Clothing is the realm of the intimately local: of self-fashioning, self-presentation, socio-economic belonging and identity signalling. This relation is strengthened by what clothes designate more broadly in *Work*. In moments throughout the film, it functions as a tool for performing identity in, and according to, the requirements of neocolonial spatial logics (something Ousmane Sembène also explores in *Xala*, as discussed in Chapter 3). Factory owner Sissoko is always shown in traditional *agbada*, but Cissé's script suggests there is no correlation between such displays of indigeneity and the subjectivities of the post-independence elite. The son of an independence-era civil servant who laundered stolen public funds by setting up the factory, Sissoko's values, we have been told, begin and end with: 'it's always best to clear one's debts with the government in order to work with a free hand'.

Balla, on the other hand, chooses his clothes according to his environment and his anticipated class interactions: an *agbada* to see his boss Sissoko; a shirt and bell-bottomed jeans at home and the factory. Balla's sartorial choices again illustrate links between the 'world-ing' of Bamako's spaces and the subjectivities these spaces inform. The Malian generation that came of age a decade after independence had grown up seeing much of the independence-era elite turn into opportunists dressed in the garb of tradition. While many African countries were socialist leaning during this period, very few adopted the Soviet or Chinese Communist model wholesale, though John Hazard points out that Mali's Modibo Keïta was the only African president who, during the 1960s, tried 'to introduce orthodox Marxism-Leninism' into his society (1969, 1). The difficulty of access to the sounds and styles of a global seventies counter-culture; the comparatively more prosperous economies of neighbouring Senegal and Côte d'Ivoire; and an austere social life grated on the youth of Keïta's Mali. 'I definitely did not like the neighbourhood policing, the curfews, and the imposition of Russian and Chinese in our school curriculum,' Diawara recalls (2003, 70). However, this generation had also 'unconsciously absorbed the elements of independence as an everyday fact' (Diawara 70), and therefore did not welcome the military coup that deposed Keïta in 1968, either. General Traoré faced student protests from the late 1970s onwards, as Cissé's *The Wind* (1982) immortalises. Balla's sartorial choices suggest a generation straddling both this local Malian context and a 'global long sixties' (Klimke and Nolan 2018) youth counter-culture.

Much of the film's emphasis on sartorial devices is also about the social performances they enable. Cissé is reluctant to visually prioritise any one character in ways that could suggest they are the subject of the story. However, through the materiality of his settings (especially their textiles and clothing), Cissé does come down against the native elite class as a whole, demonstrating not only that they have betrayed the redistributive promises of decolonisation, but also that they have fostered a culture of class aspiration and status-signalling via commodities. For example, when Balla and his wife M'Batoma dine with boss Sissoko and his wife Djeneba, they change to traditional dress, but find that the objects of Sissoko and Djeneba's bourgeois life are those of Western consumer markets – with a touch of symbolic 'Africa' thrown in. Sissoko and Djeneba's *boubous* are cut from imported cloth; their uniformed cooks, nannies and drivers flit in and out of sight; and *fufu* and *jollof* rice are paired with French wines. In yet another scene at a public restaurant, where Balla's friend gets drunk and rants at the bureaucrats in attendance, the elites' imported cloth is once again a loaded shorthand for deceit. 'Sitting there with your elegant clothes and your bald heads, acting like you own the world. It'll all come out soon in court!' he shouts. *Work* teases out how the contradictions upon which post-independence neocolonialism rests – foreign debt with nationalist hardlining, resource wealth with mass poverty – are clothed over with empty culturalisms, like Sissoko's sartorial choices. However, the contradictions of this situation can also foster political consciousness, as the film's ending will suggest.

Publicising the Private, Politicising the Public

Work constructs its last and perhaps most compelling relation between place and the constitution of subjectivities in its climax. A series of cuts to and from two spaces that are explicitly political and explicitly gendered occur: the street and the bedroom. During the workers' meeting that sets *Work*'s climax in motion, Sissoko's informants lure Balla to his private office and strangle him. Indicating temporal simultaneity, we then cut to Sissoko, who is being taken home in his chauffeur-driven car; and then to Sissoko's wife Djeneba, who is at that moment in bed with a lover. Sissoko comes home; the lover flees; and the couple have an argument. In the meantime, Balla's wife M'Batoma calls at Sissoko's mansion (presumably to see if Balla is there). Inside, the argument gets heated, with Djeneba holding the upper hand. She speaks what is to be her last truth to power in a striking, static mid-shot, where Cissé positions the camera slightly above her eye level. The technique uncomfortably places the audience in Sissoko's position, standing at the foot of the bed and looking down on a vulnerable but accusatory Djeneba. 'I know how you made your fortune. Your father misused public funds, and you dare brag about it,' are her final words; Sissoko chokes her. The physicality of the murder, the prominence of Djeneba's body in its vulnerability, and the surrounding imported luxury goods (Marlboro cigarettes, Johnnie Walker whiskey) make this 'private' crime profoundly public, given her last words. Whereas the domestic setting of the murder could have enclosed Sissoko's act within the private sphere, he murders her not immediately upon discovering the affair, but at her boldly voicing what everyone knows: that his political power is bought, his wealth stolen. Given what an integral role public and private spaces have together always played in constituting the gendered body,[18] for Djeneba to thus politicise the bedroom speaks to how 'women face a form of hyper-exploitation under patriarchal, neoliberal capitalism' (Krishnan 2018, 120).

This is one of the two distinct but parallel-running exposés in the climax of *Work*, which until then had only hinted at the gendered foundations of the neocolonial spaces it uncovered. Indeed, Djeneba initially appeared to be a character defined through the bourgeois private spaces she moved through with an attitude of bored entitlement. Her reproductive responsibilities fulfilled (the three children off-loaded to domestic help), the global commodities adorning her home had exuded the impression of mobility. Yet the very systems of labour and subjection that bring into her home these luxury commodities is also revealed to have murdered Balla, widowed M'Batoma, and

---

[18] See also Elizabeth Grosz (1995).

transformed Djeneba first into trophy wife, then corpse. The governing systems (and with it, the spatial strategies) of post-independence Mali function through the violence of Western capital in collusion with the neocolonial state, which is always, in either case, also a patriarchal violence. Given that 'the city is one of the crucial factors in the social production of (sexed) corporeality' (Grosz 1995, 104), for Djeneba to use her last words to politicise the bedroom as an extension of the hypocrisy and violence of the neocolonial city crowns the critique Cissé has been building, literally and figuratively.

This idea is visually cemented after the climactic moment of the murder, in a scene in which the factory workers carry Balla's dead body onto the street and M'Batoma collapses at the sight. From protesting their conditions when given the space to do so, the workers now take away space from their subjugator: they form a human barrier to Sissoko's car as he tries to escape the police. Sissoko is indeed half-saved, half-caught when he is arrested for the murder of Djeneba (only). In the end, despite some form of justice being served, Cissé returns for his final shots to haptic close-ups of Diarra and his fellow factory workers, who are now on the streets awaiting casual employment. Despite this ambiguous ending, there is an unmistakeable frustration to *Work*'s climax that women (including elite African women like Djeneba) and workers suffer the brunt of the consequences of speaking truth to power. The film peels away the alleged distinctions of postcolonial urban environments – private/public, factory/street – to reveal that spatial strategies of neocolonialism are total but varied along class and gender lines. At the same time (and this is what makes Cissé a dialectical filmmaker indeed), in pursuing total spatial penetration, neocolonial capital lays itself open to the risk of cultivating political consciousness through its contradictions. Balla does not die in vain, if what he had hoped for in suggesting the workers' meeting was consciousness-raising.

Work cinematically maps an environment marked by accumulation and divestment, production and reproduction, offering a way in which we can understand the relation between spaces and subjectivities in a postcolonial context. It demands recognition of the textile workers' individual interiorities through extreme close-ups, while establishing a link between their collective labours and the subjectivities those labours help form and reform. In its particular attention to the material commodities that these spaces and labours create, *Work* illustrates the economic hypocrisy of the supposedly socialist elite; meanwhile, via the architecture of Bamako, it hints at the alternative futures that once presented themselves in the independence era. Adding to this the classed sexual politics of/in private spaces with Sissoko's second, spontaneous act of murder, Cissé's film configures the post-independence urban landscape as a space of entanglements constituted by capital, but underpinned by what makes capital, in turn, possible: raw materials, manufactured into commodities by human labour. The productive and social reproductive labours that turn the public and private spaces of this city into a nodal point within the world-system also generate consciousness of that system's flows.

Discussing two texts that foreground questions of place and space in this final chapter has been a choice intended to highlight how internal colonialism remained a feature of post-independence life. This is, in many ways, where the post-independence decades had brought Africa and South Asia by the mid-1980s. Markandaya's 1950s India and Cissé's 1970s Mali both see 'global and local capital, acting through nation-states in most cases, [encroach] ever more deeply into areas of the world still available as natural and human resources' (Loomba 2015, 255), as demonstrated by the symbolism of raw materials (animal skins in *Nectar* and cotton in *Work*) within these two narratives. The field of postcolonial literary criticism, in its increasing intersection with eco-critical thought (James and Morel 2018), has come to understand and excavate not only how people were often regarded as part of this 'raw material', but also how they were coerced over time into viewing their environments, and their subjective and group relationships to it, through the same. The field has not often turned to post-independence literary and cinematic texts in comparison, however, to trace the representation of these forces at work. *Nectar* was an anomaly in Markandaya's writing, in that she never wrote a rural Indian setting again. *Work* was overshadowed in film festival circuits by *Yeelen* (1987), Cissé's later, and altogether stylistically different, film. These and other differences cannot be flattened, but both texts speak to the mid-to-late twentieth-century transition of postcolonial spaces into the global(ised) space of one world-system. Presenting their audiences with stories that foreground how environments shape, and are shaped, by subjectivities with place-memories, their narratives affirm that, contrary to Césaire's hopes, 'decolonisation' in the forms it took after flag independences had questionable aftermaths. But, so long as the land survives (*Nectar*), and collective, vigilante justice is there for the taking (*Work*), there is no end to the struggle for 'a good decolonisation' (Césaire 1959, 126) instead.

Conclusion

In *The Psychic Life of Power*, Judith Butler considers how 'power that at first appears as external, pressed upon the subject, pressing the subject into subordination, assumes a psychic form that constitutes the subject's self-identity' (1997, 3). Here, Ankhi Mukherjee writes, Butler's words suggest that 'subordination is that which is forced on a subject yet forms a subject' (2022, 19). Agency here emerges from and in answer to this oppressive power, rendering that which is being forced into subordination a subject when it answers this force with something – as opposed to, we can assume, an object that is not transformed by this force. There is something here of Fanon's assertion that the '"thing" which has been colonized becomes man during the same process by which it frees itself' (Fanon 1961, 37). But as Mukherjee points out, Butler is talking about the norms and normalisation of the psyche in relation to stable societies and healthy selves. 'What if the subject was rendered impossible through its need for affirmation from "categories, terms, and names" not of its own making, and which pronounced it as a non-being, as nothing, as garbage?', Mukherjee asks (19). What of the self, in other words, in an 'environment of the colonial type' (Fanon 1961, 181)?

Although Mukherjee problematises Butler here in the context of 'the subject [who] is not entitled to any sociality and remains unattached to the social' (19), namely the racialised poor in contemporary urban life, her question resonates with long-standing struggles against imperialism and colonialism in Africa and South Asia. A materialist approach to subjectivity – elucidated in this book particularly through the thought of Fanon, itself having seen much engagement from various fields and approaches – helps us understand this query, which continues to matter so long as our world is still inequitable along colonial lines. As Sabelo J. Ndlovu-Gatsheni writes, the current international political economy is built upon a 'real existing empire' (2018, 18), since imperialism never ended but merely transformed and continues to 'impose, reproduce and maintain Euro-American hegemony over the world' (24). For Ndlovu-Gatsheni, this especially constrains epistemic freedom – 'the right to think, theorise, interpret the world, develop own methodologies and write from where one is located and unencumbered by Eurocentrism' (17). But it is also important to recall that such colonial assumptions around knowing are scaffolded by colonial assumptions around being. And while many arguments do exist for grouping Marxian concepts among those Eurocentric 'ideas of history' that reproduce 'silences as an imperial/colonial technology of dismemberment' (Ndlovu-Gatsheni 17), some more convincing than others, thinking about being in a manner 'unencumbered by Eurocentrism' must necessarily involve thinking about being 'through and out' (Hook 2004, 91) of a present-day neocolonialism: of the exploitation of labour, the theft of collective wealth, and ecological destruction. Subjectivity remains a politically urgent consideration for any materialist interrogation of colonialism's formative influence on our world, which is 'shaped by the wars it propagated and the migrations that followed' (Boehmer 2020). In his dialectics between self and world that 'stretches Marxism' (1961, 40), Fanon's psycho-politics continues to be a point of reference bent towards decolonisation as an unfinished project.

By understanding colonialism as both a systemic structuring of the world and a discursive regime that has invented social categories like race (to be internalised in service of that structure), Chapter 1 has drawn from recent scholarship across fields to consider how Fanon elucidates this dialectical relation between the self and the world. Delineating the key contours along which subjectivities and their material conditions remain mutually effectual and co-constitutive – through their historicity, corporeality and creative agency – Fanon grapples with identifying what colonialism does to the three, and why they are key factors in any work of 'decolonising the mind' (Ngũgĩ 1986). This task was expressed with differences in inflection, but consistently linked the creation of a new economy and society with the transformation of people's ways of being and relating to others. For the revolutionary Burkinabè leader Thomas Sankara, this meant the cultivation of self-worth and integrity, in conjunction with fully internalising the dignity of oneself and others. 'We have to recondition our people to accept themselves as they are, to not be ashamed of their real situation, to be satisfied with it, to glory in it, even,' Sankara (1988) identified. Efforts towards liberation had to consider ways through and out of how domination had produced, and everyday continued to produce, subjectivities. In other words, the agency that is first reclaimed by reacting to the coloniser's violence with violence has to then turn creative. This refashioning is no substitute for the redistributive promise of decolonisation: that is, an end to the theft of the wealth generated by the labours of the formerly colonised, alongside the 'shattering', in Sankara's words again (Murrey 82), of administrative apparatuses in former colonies that facilitate it. But this psychic 'reconditioning' is nonetheless part of the political, social, cultural and economic processes that decolonisation promised.

For some, like Amílcar Cabral, this meant the more time-consuming method of taking no political action without the legitimising force of this psychic transformation en masse. As Basil Davidson recounts from first-hand observations (1981, 18), armed resistance began almost a decade after PAIGC was founded in Bissau in 1956, because Cabral and its fellow founders maintained that people (in this context, the multi-ethnic peasantry of Guinea-Bissau and Cape Verde) must themselves come to decide on the necessity of militant anti-colonial resistance. Cabral believed, as several of the narratives explored in this book demonstrate, that a liberation 'parachuted down' (Fanon 1961, 165) was too easy to terminate, redirect or reverse in post-independence decades. For the young Chinua Achebe, meanwhile, anti-colonial political energies in pre-independence Nigeria felt like a 'mental revolution' that 'reconciled [one] to [oneself]' (1975, 145). His recollection reaches beyond its immediate relevance to Nigerians of his generation. As Chapter 1 concluded, neither Fanon nor any of the above and other anti-colonial thinkers provide any prescriptive plan for what this psycho-political transformation must look like or entail, because many of them – and Fanon especially – urges beginning with, and always referring back to, the 'concrete conditions' (1952, 4) at hand in every confrontation with colonial structures. This insistence on situational consciousness, bodily dignity, and agency – being historical, embodied, and actional selves – makes possible, but does not guarantee, resisting the 'internalisation' of 'the economic' (1952, 4).[1] For Fanon, who variously refers to this psycho-political process as 'disalienation' and the overcoming of 'inferiority complexes', the process itself is one of becoming human. This is not because his so-called *damnés* are not already human, or that anyone should have to overcome colonisation to be recognised as human. It is because this system of dispossession, accumulation and exploitation is also sustained through the debilitating psychic effects we have seen play out throughout the four novels and four films studied, including social isolation, inertia, fear, nostalgia, emasculation, disorientation and misdirected anger.

The range of themes, narratives, political energies and social contexts found in the post-independence works considered in this book are all concerned

---

[1] By 'bodily dignity', I am thinking with Pramod K. Nayar's convincing argument that 'Fanon clearly aligns the dignity of the human with the integrity of the human form – and it is this integrity that colonialism's biopolitical regime takes apart' (2019, 219).

with these debilitating psychic legacies. They explore just how material the consequences of such effects could be, including consequences at a national scale. Although Ranjana Khanna proposes the addition of 'melancholia' to the above effects – a 'melancholia' that stems from the 'inability to introject the lost ideal of nation-statehood' (2003, 29), perhaps most prevalent in Armah's *The Beautyful Ones Are Not Yet Born* – as early as the 1950s and 1960s, African and South Asian literary and cinematic narratives were also suggesting that confrontation with (neo-)colonialism includes, but extends well beyond, what the independent nation-state may have promised. To that end, while this form of melancholia is certainly present in some of the texts here considered, Chapters 2 to 5 have sought to bring into view that the mutually effectual relationship between the two large concepts in this book's title – subjectivity and decolonisation – more often than not makes possible consciousness, resistance, justified anger, and creative action in response to the failures of the postcolonial nation-state in delivering decolonisation.

Arising from different contexts but situated with a twentieth-century period of historical and political transition that shared this disappointment, post-independence narratives thus hold on to hope for 'a good decolonisation' (Césaire 1959) yet to come, through iterating and reiterating that structural decolonisation and the 'decolonising of minds' (Ngũgĩ 1986) are concurrent and inter-related processes. So long as the embodied experience of everyday struggle fosters unexpected moments of political consciousness (as it does for Bimala in *Home and the World* and Rukmani in *Nectar in a Sieve*), and the psychic weight of struggle is collectivised rather than serving to further alienate (as it transpires for Gikonyo in *A Grain of Wheat* and Debbie in *Destination Biafra*), subjectivities can be re-constituted through and out of the colonialism that once produced them. As such, post-independence novels such as those of Armah, Emecheta, Markandaya and the early works of Ngũgĩ do so much more than form a 'literature of combat' that is politically engaged for the price of being 'mimetically naïve' (Sorensen 2014). Post-independence films, too, offer complex considerations of the above dilemmas – considerations not straightforwardly expected from a militant Third Cinema, nor from World Cinema (a category that, as Mazierska and Kristensen [2020] contend, is a product of global capitalist circuits of film production, distribution and exhibition).

Instead, these texts' excavations of everyday life under the various social conditions attendant upon the early years of nation-statehood speak to one another across space and time. They diverge on many points and are united by questions raised at the juncture of flag independence and the unfulfilled promises of decolonisation. This brings together even those novels that critical approaches tend to place furthest from one another – such as the Britain-based, bourgeois Markandaya's almost naturalistic ode to the Indian countryside, *Nectar in a Sieve*, versus Ngũgĩ's broadly revolutionary vision for a 'nationalitarian' (Lazarus 1993) Kenya, *A Grain of Wheat*. It similarly unites two films almost never studied together for their focus on those that independence internally displaced: that celebrated piece of *cinéma engagé*, Ousmane Sembène's *Xala* (1975), and the less-known Ritwik Ghatak's stylistically daring Partition drama, *The Cloud-Capped Star* (1960). None of these or the other four texts discussed in this book are motivated purely by either the prospect of politicising their audiences or analysing the individual psyches of their characters. Grappling as they are with the conditions of a world that is now no longer ostensibly colonial, yet far from decolonised, what they seek to examine from different places and through different stories is what 'decolonising the mind' can look like in everyday life, with all of its stops and starts. Drawing attention to subjectivity as that which has social and historical location, these narratives all affirm the psycho-political nature of the quotidian experiences they represent.

Ray's protagonist in *Home and the World*, for instance, enters a love triangle that irrevocably changes her marriage, but the gradual transformation of her political consciousness is what reveals the ongoing linkages between colonial capital, patriarchy and Indian nationalism in her particular time and place. Bimala's subjectivity, informed even if unconsciously by the everyday material surroundings of her upper-caste Bengali household, is neither the politically blank slate her husband assumes nor the ideal (in the Hegelian sense) realm of 'feminine intuition' that her love interest Sandip thinks it to be. Ray's cinematic techniques for collapsing the gendered and gendering home/world binary underscores and enriches these plot dynamics, going beyond his Tagorean source material. This irresolution around gender surfaces also in Ngũgĩ's *A Grain of Wheat*, where women's subjectivities remain unincorporated into the novel's dialectical relationship between political consciousness and history. This provides a conceptual and narrative tension that, when examined as it was in Chapter 2, gestures towards two important questions for the novel's post-independence context (and indeed beyond): whether the experience of anti-colonial struggle truly did transform its participants towards the revolutionary consciousness needed to build society anew, and to what extent this same struggle was invested in the notion of restoring a particular kind of masculinity.

Subjectivity as that which is shaped by social and historical location is also of key interest to the critical work of Armah's *Beautyful Ones* and Sembène's *Xala*, but with greater emphasis on the unjust material consequences that this relation

– one that is in crisis among the native elites in these texts – begets en masse. In *Beautyful Ones*, the transformation of Nkrumahism within the space of a few short years from a revolutionary promise to a cumbersome bureaucracy weighs heavy on the protagonist's sense of time and self.[2] *Xala* is markedly different in tone, using satire to construct the central allegory of the film – the native elite as complicit against and/or unable to spearhead national decolonisation. But it, too, yields a structural analysis of the relationship between problems of subjectivity constitution and arrested decolonisation, illustrated especially via three overlapping themes: self-fashioning, language, and land. These two West African texts explored in Chapter 3 assert, without illusions but with a deep attachment to the stakes, that only embodied subjectivities daily grappling with the affective powers of neocolonial capitalism can turn people from 'suffering sleepers' (Armah 13) into resistant subjects.

The knowledges that arise from grappling with these affective powers can also be objectively true – and sometimes they help people survive incredibly violent conditions, as in the two major post-independence conflicts discussed in Chapter 4: the 1947 atrocities that followed the Partition of India and the 1967–1970 Nigerian Civil War. Through its focus on the subjective experiences and collective knowledges of West African women, Emecheta's *Destination* affirms the gendered effects of the civil war as the lens through which *all* facets of the war can be understood – even and especially the latter's macro causes in petro-capitalism. Meanwhile, Ghatak's *Cloud-Capped Star*, a snapshot of 'life after arrival', narrativises Partition's violent effects on inter-subjective relations. Despite having the darkest ending of perhaps all the texts here, the film asserts that to tell of individual and collective psychic sufferings is to tell of the lasting material violence of impoverishment and dispossession under colonialism and nation-formation. In both texts, the proximity of various kinds of violence (from the immediate sexual violence of civil war to the slow economic violence of refugeedom) brings into sharp focus how (neo-)colonial conditions can turn interiority itself into a source of knowledge on its structural workings.

The contexts and contents of *Nectar in a Sieve* and *Work*, meanwhile, overlap upon the post-independence re-structuring of livelihoods, and the environments they depended on, to serve global market demands. As Chapter 5 has explored, the relation between place and labour in the postcolonial nation-state's rural and urban spaces of production is an important vector in understanding the relationship between subjectivity and decolonisation. The bond

---

[2] See also Ama Biney (2008) on an evaluation of Nkrumah's legacy in terms of the controversies surrounding him as a political figure and his vision for Pan-Africanism.

between the character of Rukmani and her environment in Markandaya's novel is given form through its disruption, as the customary agricultural and social practices that help constitute the protagonist's subjectivity are transformed upon the penetration of her local economy by global market forces. The novel's spatio-subjective narrative methods include representing the psychic and interpersonal effects that the coming of an industrial tannery has on the protagonist and her social world. These reveal for the reader the contours of an emerging world-system where ecological destruction is technologically accelerated and national industrialisation comes to mean dispossession for many. *Work*, too, maps a post-independence environment marked by accumulation and divestment, production and social reproduction, offering a way in which we can understand the relation between spaces and subjectivities in its particular context of urban Mali. In his attention to the material wealth that these spaces create, Cissé illustrates the dependence of an emergent globalisation upon the labours of the same West African classes that French imperialism depended upon throughout what Amílcar Cabral called 'classical' (Davidson 1981) colonialism. But in also representing the political potential of African women speaking truth to power, and of labour organising – possibly aided by politically conscious, educated youth (as exemplified by the character of Balla) – *Work* understands private and public space as ripe for dissent, and full of means of resistance to post-independence exploitation.

The historical reasons throughout the twentieth and twenty-first centuries for the arrest of decolonisation include factors that are beyond the scope and aims of this book to analyse, but which an array of scholarship has identified in, among other things, the forces of US imperialism, Cold War politics, European neocolonialism, civil wars, comprador postcolonial governments and the cultivation of economic dependency through the policies of the IMF and World Bank.[3] Of immediate interest to the post-independence novel and film in particular have been the effects of these forces as they are lived and experienced by people. Subjectivity, understood through a psycho-political lens that draws on Fanon's insights and the work that has been done on his thought (in Fanon Studies, Liberation Psychology, Africana Philosophy and beyond), continues to open up important routes of inquiry when used as a thematic framework in Comparative Literature and Film Studies. It is, indeed, a crucial vector to consider for any literary or film criticism interested in the representation of postcolonial life – given that the latter is to be understood as 'living with the

---

[3] See, for example, the still relevant edited volume *World Bank Literature* (Kumar 2002) on an interrogation of World Bank hegemony in postcolonial literatures, as well as in other forms of cultural production.

legacies of' (Shohat 1992, 108) colonialism, in its economic, socio-cultural and psycho-political dimensions.

This latter dimension, variously understood as 'mental colonisation' (Sankara in Murrey 2018), 'inferiority complexes' (Fanon 1952) and a lack of 'reconciliation with oneself' (Achebe 1975, 145), is always taken seriously in the post-independence novel and film. The psycho-political dimension is interrogated alongside the historical reasons for the failure of the independences to deliver in the postcolonial world the redistributive promises of decolonisation. This interrogation is not intended to place blame at the feet of the colonised for the continuation of their own exploitation and subjugation, but to serve as a reminder that colonialism is 'innocent of none of the wounds inflicted upon body and consciousness' (Fanon 1959, 118) that may have outlived its official end. Fiction continues to wield the ability to draw on those 'things that continue unsatisfied inside' (Armah 1969, 100) in order to imagine the kind of world that is desired instead. For, as Aimé Césaire argues when he says that 'people know better than anyone what they need, they know it from within, and they know that all creation, because it is creative, is participation in a combat for liberation' (Césaire 1959, 127), the creation of narrative, too, is an act that draws out what is 'known' from 'within'. When subjectivity itself is a terrain of and for decolonisation, engaging with its constitution and re-constitution becomes a matter of political import. When it is constituted through embodied, creative struggle against the 'real existing empire' (Ndlovu-Gatsheni 18) of our time, it becomes a resource for resistance in the search for a justice that decolonisation once promised.

Bibliography

Achebe et al. '11: Women and Authority in West African History'. *History Textbook: West African Senior School Certificate Examination*, 2018, <wassce historytextbook.com> (accessed 24 November 2023).
Achebe, Chinua. *Morning Yet on Creation Day: Essays*. Anchor Press, 1975.
——. *There Was a Country: A Memoir*. Penguin Books, 2013.
Achebe, Christie. 'Igbo Women in the Nigerian-Biafran War 1967–1970: An Interplay of Control'. *Journal of Black Studies*, vol. 40, no. 5, 2010, pp. 785–811.
Adalet, Begüm. 'Infrastructures of Decolonization: Scales of Worldmaking in the Writings of Frantz Fanon'. *Political Theory*, vol. 50, no. 1, 2022, pp. 5–31.
Adams, Ann Marie. 'It's a Woman's War: Engendering Conflict in Buchi Emecheta's *Destination Biafra*'. *Callaloo*, vol. 24, no. 1, 2001, pp. 287–300.
The Afro-Asian Networks Research Collective. 'Manifesto: Networks of Decolonization in Asia and Africa'. *Radical History Review*, vol. 131, 2018, pp. 176–82.
Afzal-Khan, Fawzia. *Cultural Imperialism and the Indo-English Novel: Genre and Ideology in R. K. Narayan, Anita Desai, Kamala Markandaya, and Salman Rushdie*. Pennsylvania State University Press, 1993.
Agathangelou, Anna M. 'Fanon on Decolonization and Revolution: Bodies and Dialectics'. *Globalizations*, vol. 13, no. 1, 2016, pp. 110–28.
Agrawal, Malti. 'Portrayal of Womanhood in Post-Colonial Indian English Fiction'. *New Perspectives in Indian Writing in English*, edited by Malti Agrawal. Atlantic Publishers, 2007.
Agrawal, Shivam. 'Education and Its Influence on the Nation-Building Process: A Reflection on Ambedkar's Views in Colonial India'. *Contemporary Voice of Dalit*, vol. 13, no. 2, 2021, pp. 132–40.

Ahluwalia, Pal. 'Négritude and Nativism'. *Politics and Post-Colonial Theory: African Inflections*. Taylor & Francis, 2002.

Ahmad, Abdullahi Ayoade. 'The Position of Minority Identity in Nigeria and its Effect on Governmental Policies'. *International Journal of Research in Social Sciences*, vol. 5, no. 4, 2015, pp. 89–103.

Ahmed, Ishtiaq. 'The partition memory and the Pakistan nation-state project, 75 years on'. *The Round Table*, vol. 111, no. 6, 2022, pp. 685–98.

Ahmed, Sara. *Queer Phenomenology*. Duke University Press, 2006.

Althusser, Louis. 'Ideology and Ideological State Apparatuses (Notes towards an investigation)'. *Lenin and Philosophy and Other Essays*, translated by Ben Brewster. Monthly Review Press, 1971, pp. 142–7.

Amuta, Chidi. 'Marxist Aesthetics: An Open-Ended Legacy'. *African Literature: An Anthology of Criticism and Theory*, edited by Tejumola Olaniyan and Ato Quayson. Wiley-Blackwell, 2007.

Anderson, Benedict. [1983]. *Imagined Communities: Reflections on the Origin and Spread of Nationalism*. Verso, 2016.

Anderson, Warwick et al. *Unconscious Dominions: Psychoanalysis, Colonial Trauma, and Global Sovereignties*. Duke University Press, 2011.

Andrade, Susan Z. *The Nation Writ Small: African Fictions and Feminisms, 1958–1988*. Duke University Press, 2011.

Andrade-Watkins, Claire. 'France's Bureau of Cinema: Financial and Technical Assistance Between 1961 and 1977'. *African Experiences of Cinema*, edited by Mbye B. Cham and Ishaq Imruh Bakari. BFI Publishing, 1996, pp. 112–27.

Andrews, Kehinde. *The New Age of Empire: How Colonialism and Racism Still Rule the World*. Allen Lane, 2021.

Appadurai, Arjun. *Modernity At Large: Cultural Dimensions of Globalization*. University of Minnesota Press, 1996.

Appiah, Kwame Anthony. *Cosmopolitanism: Ethics in a World of Strangers*. Penguin, 2007.

Armah, Ayi Kwei. *The Beautyful Ones Are Not Yet Born*. London: Heinemann, 1969.

Armes, Roy. *Patterns of Realism*. Garland, 1986.

——. *Third World Film Making and the West*. Berkeley: University of California Press, 1987.

——. *African Filmmaking: North and South of the Sahara*. Indiana University Press, 2006.

Asokan, Ratik. 'A New Look At Ritwik Ghatak's *Bengal*'. *The New York Review of Books*, 25 January 2020, <https://www.nybooks.com/daily/2020/01/25/a-new-look-at-ritwik-ghataks-bengal/?printpage=true> (accessed 24 November 2023).

Ayuk, G. Ojong. 'The Lust for Material Well-Being in *The Beautyful Ones Are Not Yet Born* and *Fragments* by Ayi Kwei Armah'. *Présence Africaine*, vol. 132, 1984, pp. 33–43.

Azoulay, Ariella Aïsha. *Potential History: Unlearning Imperialism*. Verso, 2019.

Batchelor, Kathryn and Sue-Ann Harding. *Translating Frantz Fanon Across Continents and Languages: Frantz Fanon Across Continents and Languages*, edited by Kathryn Batchelor and Sue-Ann Harding. Routledge, 2017.

Bagchi, Amiya Kumar. 'Studies on the Economy of West Bengal since Independence'. *Economic and Political Weekly*, vol. 33, no. 47/48, 1998, pp. 2973–78.

——. 'Rabindranath Tagore and the Human Condition'. *Economic and Political Weekly*, vol. 49, no. 12, 2014, pp. 38–46.

Balázs, Béla. *Early Film Theory: Visible Man and the Spirit of Film*. Berghahn Books, 2010.

Balibar, Etienne and Immanuel Wallerstein. *Race, Nation, Class: Ambiguous Identities*. Verso, 1991.

Banerjee, Prathama. *Elementary Aspects of the Political: Histories from the Global South*. Duke University Press, 2020.

Barrington, Lowell. *After Independence: Making and Protecting the Nation in Postcolonial & Postcommunist States*. University of Michigan Press, 2006.

Bartolovich, Crystal. 'Introduction'. *Marxism, Modernity and Postcolonial Studies*, edited by Bartolovich et al. Cambridge University Press, 2002.

Bâ, Mariama. *So Long a Letter*, translated by Bodé-Thomas Modupé. Heinemann, 1997.

Beckett, Paul A. 'Frantz Fanon and Sub-Saharan Africa: Notes on the Contemporary Significance of His Thought'. *Africa Today*, vol. 19, no. 2, 1972, pp. 59–72.

——. 'Algeria vs. Fanon: The Theory of Revolutionary Decolonization, and the Algerian Experience'. *The Western Political Quarterly*, vol. 26, no. 1, 1973.

Benjamin, Walter. 'The Work of Art in the Age of Mechanical Reproduction', translated by Harry Zohn. In *Illuminations*, edited by Hannah Arendt. Schocken Books, 1969.

Bernard, Anna. 'Reading for the Nation: "Third-World Literature" and Israel/Palestine'. *New Formations*, vol. 73, 2011, pp. 78–89.

Bernasconi, Robert. 'Identity and Agency in Frantz Fanon'. *Sartre Studies International*, vol. 10, no. 2, 2004, pp. 106–9.

Berthomé, Jean-Pierre. 'Ousmane Sembène 1923–2007: L'héroïsme au quotidien'. *Positif*, vol. 559, 2007, pp. 65–6.

Bertoldi, Andreas. 'Oedipus in (South) Africa?: Psychoanalysis and the Politics of Difference'. *American Imago*, vol. 55, no. 1, 1998, pp. 101–34.

Beshara, Robert K. *Freud and Said: Contrapuntal Psychoanalysis as Liberation Praxis*. Palgrave Macmillan, 2020.

Bevins, Vincent. *The Jakarta Method: Washington's Anticommunist Crusade and the Mass Murder Program That Shaped Our World*. PublicAffairs, 2020.

Bhabha, Homi K. 'Sly Civility'. *October*, vol. 34, 1985, pp. 71–80.

——. *The Location of Culture*. Routledge, 1994.

Bhambra, Gurminder. 'Decoloniality'. *Global Social Theory*, 2 August 2016, <globalsocialtheory.org/topics/decoloniality> (accessed 23 November 2023).

Bhasin, Kamla and Ritu Menon. *Borders & Boundaries: Women in India's Partition*. Rutgers University Press, 1998.

Biccum, April R. 'Development and the "New" Imperialism: A Reinvention of Colonial Discourse in DFID Promotional Literature'. *Third World Quarterly*, vol. 26, no. 6, 2005, pp. 1005–20.

Biney, Ama. 'The Legacy of Kwame Nkrumah in Retrospect'. *Journal of Pan African Studies*, vol. 2, no. 3, 2008, pp. 129–59. *Gale Academic OneFile*, <https://www.jpanafrican.org/docs/vol2no3/LegacyOfKwameNkrumah.pdf> (accessed 29 November 2023).

Bissell, William Cunningham. 'Between Fixity and Fantasy: Assessing the Spatial Impact of Colonial Urban Dualism'. *Journal of Urban History*, vol. 37, no. 2, 2011, pp. 208–29.

Biswas, Moinak. *Apu and After: Re-visiting Ray's Cinema*. Seagull Books, 2005.

Boehmer, Elleke. *Stories of Women: Gender and Narrative in the Postcolonial Nation*. Manchester University Press, 2005.

——. *Postcolonial Poetics: 21st-Century Critical Readings*. Palgrave Macmillan, 2018.

——. 'The Duel: Are Empires Always Bad?' *Prospect Magazine*. December 2020, <reader.exacteditions.com/issues/90626/page/18> (accessed 29 November 2023).

Boone, Catherine. 'The Making of a Rentier Class: Wealth Accumulation and Political Control in Senegal'. *The Journal of Development Studies*, vol. 26, no. 3, 1990, pp. 425–49.

Boone, Catherine, Fibian Lukalo and Sandra F. Joireman. 'Promised Land: Settlement Schemes in Kenya, 1962 to 2016'. *Political Geography*, vol. 89, 2021, pp. 1–13.

Bose, Anuja. 'Frantz Fanon and the Politicization of the Third World as a Collective Subject'. *Interventions*, vol. 21, no. 5, 2019, pp. 671–89.

Bose, Sugata. *Peasant Labour and Colonial Capital: Rural Bengal since 1770*. Foundation Books, 1993.

Bourdieu, Pierre. *Political Interventions*, translated by David Fernbach and edited by Franck Poupeau and Thierry Discepolo. Verso, 2008.

Bourdieu, Pierre and Loïc Wacquant. *An Invitation to Reflexive Sociology*. University of Chicago Press, 1992.

Brass, Paul Richard. *The Politics of India since Independence*. Cambridge University Press, 1990.

Breidlid, Anders. 'Culture, Indigenous Knowledge Systems and Sustainable Development: A Critical View of Education in an African Context'. *International Journal of Educational Development*, vol. 29, 2009, pp. 140–8.

Brennan, Timothy. *Salman Rushdie and the Third World: Myths of the Nation*. Palgrave Macmillan, 1989.

——. 'The National Longing for Form'. *Nation and Narration*, edited by Homi K. Bhabha. Routledge, 1990.

——. 'Fanon for the Present'. *College Literature*, vol. 45, no. 1, 2018, pp. 10–17.

Brody, Richard. '"Baara": A Must-See Film of Patriarchal Abuse, at the New York African Film Festival'. *The New Yorker*, 3 June 2019, <www.newyorker.com/culture/the-front-row/baara-a-must-see-film-of-patriarchal-abuse-at-the-new-york-african-film-festival> (accessed 24 November 2023).

Brown, Matthew H. 'Bringing the Rain Indoors: Rereading the National Allegory in Ousmane Sembène's *Xala*'. *Ousmane Sembène and the Politics of Culture*, edited by Lifongo Vetinde and Amadou Fofana. London: Lexington Books, 2015, pp. 67–83.

Brown, Nicholas. *Utopian Generations: The Political Horizon of Twentieth-Century Literature*. Princeton University Press, 2009.

Bruce-Lockhart, Katherine. 'Unsound Minds and Broken Bodies: the Detention of "Hardcore" Mau Mau women at Kamiti and Gitamayu Detention Camps in Kenya, 1954–1960'. *Journal of Eastern African Studies*, vol. 8, no. 4, 2014, pp. 590–608.

Buck-Morss, Susan. 'Hegel and Haiti'. *Critical Inquiry*, vol. 26, no. 4, 2000, pp. 821–65.

Burman, Erica. *Fanon, Education, Action: Child as Method*. Routledge, 2019.

Busch, Annett and Max Annas, eds. *Ousmane Sembène: Interviews*. University of Mississippi Press, 2008.

Butler, Judith. *The Psychic Life of Power: Theories in Subjection*. Stanford University Press, 1997.

Cabral, Amílcar. 'The Weapon of Theory'. *The First Tricontinental Conference of the Peoples of Asia, Africa and Latin America*, January 1966, Havana. Speech. Available at <https://www.marxists.org/subject/africa/cabral/1966/weapon-theory.htm> (accessed 24 November 2023).

——. 'National Liberation and Culture'. *Transition*, no. 45, 1974, pp. 12–17. JSTOR, <www.jstor.org/stable/2935020> (accessed 22 December 2020).

———. *Return to the Source; Selected Speeches*. Monthly Review Press, 1974.
———. *Decolonisation and Resistance*, trans. Dan Wood. Rowman and Littlefield, 2016.
Callinicos, Alex. 'Race and Class'. *International Socialism*, vol. 2, no. 55, 1992, pp. 3–39.
Cardullo, Ben. *Out of Asia: The Films of Akira Kurosawa, Satyajit Ray, Abbas Kiarostami and Zhang Yimou*. New York: Praeger, 2008.
Carter, Erica, James Donald and Judith Squires. *Space and Place: Theories of Identity and Location*. Lawrence and Wishart, 1993.
Casanova, Pascale. *The World Republic of Letters*, translated by M. B. Debevoise. Harvard University Press, 2004.
Casci, Simonetta. 'Nationalism and Gender Ideology in Bengali Literature'. *Il Politico*, vol. 64, no. 2 (189), 1999, pp. 277–91.
Césaire, Aimé. 'The Man of Culture and his Responsibilities'. *Présence Africaine*, nos. 24–5, 1959, pp. 125–32.
———. *Discourse on Colonialism*. Monthly Review Press, 2001.
———. *Toussaint Louverture: La révolution française et le problème colonial*. Éditions Présence Africaine, 2009.
———. *Cahier D'un Retour Au Pays Natal*. Éditions Présence Africaine, 2016.
Chakravarti, Sudeshna. 'Rabindranath and the Bengal Partition of 1905'. *Tagore: At Home in the World*, edited by Sanjukta Dasgupta and Chinmoy Guha. SAGE India, 2013.
Chamley, Santorri. 'The Triumph of Skill over Adversity'. *Index on Censorship*, issue 3, 1991, p. 20.
Chatterjee, Partha. *Nationalist Thought and the Colonial World: A Derivative Discourse*. University of Minnesota Press, 1993.
———. 'Indian Cinema: Then and Now'. *India International Centre Quarterly*, vol. 39, no. 2, 2012, pp. 45–53.
Chatterji, Joya. 'The Making of a Borderline: The Radcliffe Award for Bengal'. *Region and Partition: Bengal, Punjab and the Partition of the Subcontinent*, edited by I. Talbot and G. Singh. Oxford University Press, 1991.
Chaudhuri, Amit. *Clearing a Space: Reflections on India, Literature and Culture*. Peter Lang, 2008.
Chaudhary, Zahid R. 'Subjects in Difference: Walter Benjamin, Frantz Fanon, and Postcolonial Theory'. *differences: A Journal of Feminist Cultural Studies*, vol. 23, no. 1, 2012, pp. 151–83.
Cherki, Alice. *Frantz Fanon: Portrait*. Éditions Points, 2016.
Chibber, Vivek. *Postcolonial Theory and the Specter of Capital*. Verso, 2013.
Choudhuri, Supriya. 'Dangerous Liaisons'. *Thinking on Thresholds: The Poetics of Transitive Spaces*, edited by Subha Mukherji. Anthem Press, 2013.

Chowdhury, Sayandeb. 'The Indian Partition and the Making of a New Scopic Regime in Bengali Cinema'. *European Journal of English Studies*, vol. 19, no. 3, 2015, pp. 255–70.

Chrisman, Laura. 'Inventing Post-Colonial Theory: Polemical Observations'. *Pretexts: Studies in Writing and Culture*, vol. 5, no. 1, 1995, pp. 205–12.

——. *Postcolonial Contraventions: Cultural Readings of Race, Imperialism, and Transnationalism*. Manchester University Press, 2003.

Cissé, Souleymane, and Jean-François Senga. 'Interview De Souleymane Cissé Par Jean-François Senga'. *Présence Africaine*, no. 144, 1987, pp. 133–8. JSTOR, <www.jstor.org/stable/24351508> (accessed 22 December 2020).

Clare, Stephanie. 'Geopower: The Politics of Life and Land in Frantz Fanon's Writing'. *Diacritics*, vol. 4, no. 4, 2013, pp. 60–80.

Cobb-Moore, Geneva and Andrew Billingsley. *Maternal Metaphors of Power in African American Women's Literature: From Phillis Wheatley to Toni Morrison*. University of South Carolina Press, 2017.

Colpani, Gianmaria. 'Crossfire: Postcolonial Theory Between Marxist and Decolonial Critiques'. *Postcolonial Studies*, vol. 25, no. 1, 2022, pp. 54–72.

Connerton, Paul. *How Modernity Forgets*. Cambridge University Press, 2009.

Cooper, Darius. *The Cinema of Satyajit Ray: Between Tradition and Modernity*. New York: Cambridge University Press, 2000.

Cooppan, Vilashini. *Worlds Within: National Narratives and Global Connections in Postcolonial Writing*. Stanford University Press, 2009.

Craggs, Ruth and Claire Wintle, eds. *Cultures of Decolonisation: Transnational Productions and Practices, 1945–70*. Manchester University Press, 2015.

Croombs, Matthew. 'In the Wake of Militant Cinema: Challenges for Film Studies'. *Discourse*, vol. 40, no. 1, 2019, pp. 68–89.

Cross, Hannah. 'Labour and Underdevelopment? Migration, Dispossession and Accumulation in West Africa and Europe'. *Review of African Political Economy*, vol. 40, no. 136, 2013, pp. 202–18.

Curtis, Richard. 'Fanon, Hegel and the Materialist Theory of History'. *Frantz Fanon and Emancipatory Social Theory*, edited by Dustin J. Byrd and Seyed Javad Miri. Brill, 2019, pp. 95–100.

Daiya, Kavita. '"Honorable Resolutions": Gendered Violence, Ethnicity, and the Nation'. *Alternatives: Global, Local, Political*, vol. 27, no. 2, 2002, pp. 219–47.

Danto, Elizabeth Ann. *Freud's Free Clinics: Psychoanalysis and Social Justice, 1918–1938*. Columbia University Press, 2007.

Dasgupta, Chidananda. 'Cinema, Marxism, and the Mother Goddess'. *India International Centre Quarterly*, vol. 12, no. 3, 1985, pp. 249–64.

Dasgupta, Sanjukta, Sudeshna Chakravarti and Mary Mathew, eds. *Radical Rabindranath: Nation, Family and Gender in Tagore's Fiction and Films*. New Delhi: Orient BlackSwan, 2013.

Dass, Manishita. 'The Cloud-Capped Star: Ritwik Ghatak on the Horizon of Global Art Cinema'. *Global Art Cinema: New Theories and Histories*, edited by Rosalind Galt and Karl Schoonover. Oxford University Press, 2010.

——. 'Unsettling Images: Cinematic Theatricality in the Cinema of Ritwik Ghatak'. *Screen*, vol. 58, no. 1, 2017, pp. 82–9.

Davidson, Basil. 'Remembering Cabral'. *Review of African Political Economy*, no. 58, 1993, pp. 78–85.

——. [1981]. *No Fist Is Big Enough to Hide the Sky: The Liberation of Guinea-Bissau and Cape Verde, 1963–74*. Zed Books, 2017.

Davis, Muriam Haleh. 'The US Academy and the Provincialization of Fanon'. *The Los Angeles Review of Books*, 9 November 2022, <https://lareviewof books.org/article/the-us-academy-and-the-provincialization-of-fanon>.

Deleuze, Gilles. *Cinema I: The Movement-Image*. Bloomsbury Publishing, 2013.

DeLoughrey, Elizabeth M. and George B. Handley. *Postcolonial Ecologies Literatures of the Environment*. Oxford University Press, 2011.

Deshpande, Anirudh. *Class, Power and Consciousness in Indian Cinema and Television*. Primus Books, 2009.

Deshpande, Satish. 'Hegemonic Spatial Strategies: The Nation-Space and Hindu Communalism in Twentieth-Century India'. *Public Culture*, vol. 10, no. 2, 1998, pp. 249–83.

Devi, Surama and Nabarupa Bhattacharjee. *Life After Ritwik Ghatak*. Photojaanic, 2016.

Diawara, Manthia. 'Sub-Saharan African Film Production: Technological Paternalism'. *Jump Cut: A Review of Contemporary Media*, no. 31, 1987, pp. 61–5.

——. *African Cinema: Politics & Culture*. Indiana University Press, 1992.

——. 'Toward A Regional Imaginary in Africa'. *World Bank Literature*, edited by Amitava Kumar. University of Minnesota Press, 2003.

Dirlik, Arif. 'The Global in the Local'. *Global/Local: Cultural Production and the Transnational Imaginary*, edited by Wimal Dissanayake and Rob Wilson. Duke University Press, 1996.

——. *The Postcolonial Aura: Third World Criticism in the Age of Global Capitalism*. Routledge, 1997.

——. 'Global Modernity? Modernity in an Age of Global Capitalism'. *European Journal of Social Theory*, vol. 6, no 3, 2003, pp. 275–92.

Dovey, Lindiwe. 'Listening Between the Images: African Filmmakers' Take on the Soviet Union, Soviet Filmmakers' Take on Africa'. *The Oxford Handbook of Communist Visual Cultures*, edited by Aga Skrodzka, Xiaoning Lu and Katarzyna Marciniak. Oxford University Press, 2020.

Drabinski, John. 'Frantz Fanon'. *Stanford Encyclopedia of Philosophy*, Stanford University. 14 March 2019, <plato.stanford.edu/entries/frantz-fanon> (accessed 24 November 2023).

Dunham, Jarrod. 'The Fanonian Dialectic: Masters and Slaves in Ayi Kwei Armah's *The Beautyful Ones Are Not Yet Born*'. *The Journal of Commonwealth Literature*, vol. 47, no. 2, 2012, pp. 281–94.

Dupré, Colin. *Le Fespaco, une affaire d'Etat(s): Festival Panafricain de Cinéma et de Télévision de Ouagadougou*. L'Harmattan, 2012.

Eaton, H. and L. A. Lorentzen, *Ecofeminism and Globalization: Exploring Culture, Context, and Religion*. Rowman & Littlefield, 2003.

El Alaoui, Khadija. 'An Afro-Asian Tune without Lyrics'. *Meanings of Bandung: Postcolonial Orders and Decolonial Visions*, edited by Robbie Shilliam and Quynh N. Pham. Rowman & Littlefield, 2016.

Emecheta, Buchi. *Destination Biafra*. Heinemann, 1982.

——. 'Feminism with a Small 'f!' *Criticism and Ideology: Second African Writers' Conference*, edited by Kirsten Holst Petersen. Scandinavian Institute of African Studies, 1988. pp. 173–85.

Escobar, Arturo. *Encountering Development: The Making and Unmaking of the Third World*. Princeton University Press, 1997.

Eze, Emmanuel Chukwudi. *Race and the Enlightenment: A Reader*. Wiley-Blackwell, 1997.

——. *On Reason: Rationality in a World of Cultural Conflict and Racism*. Duke University Press, 2008.

Fan, Bonnie. 'Lights, Camera, Melodrama: The Role of Lighting in The Cloud Capped Star'. *Senses of Cinema*, 30 June 2015, <www.sensesofcinema.com/2014/feature-articles/lights-camera-melodrama-the-role-of-lighting-in-the-cloud-capped-star> (accessed 24 November 2023).

Fanon, Frantz. [1959]. *A Dying Colonialism*. Translated by Haakon Chevalier. S.l.: Grove Press, 1982.

——. *Peau noire, masques blancs*. Éditions du Seuil, 1952.

——. [1952]. *Black Skin, White Masks*. Translated by Richard Philcox. Grove Press, 2008.

——. *Les damnés de la terre*. Éditions du Seuil, 1961.

——. [1961]. *The Wretched of the Earth*. Translated by Richard Philcox. Grove Press, 2004.

——. [1964]. *Toward the African Revolution: Political Essays*. Translated by Haakon Chevalier. Grove, 2004.

——. *Alienation and Freedom*. Translated by Steven Corcoran, edited by Jean Khalfa and Robert J. C. Young. Bloomsbury, 2018.

Feldman, Shelley. 'Feminist Interruptions'. *Interventions*, vol. 1, no. 2, 1999, pp. 167–82.

Flatschart, Elmar. 'Crisis, Energy, and the Value Form of Gender: Towards a Gender-Sensitive Materialist Understanding of Society-Nature Relations'. *Materialism and the Critique of Energy*, edited by Brent Ryan Bellamy and Jeff Diamanti. MCM Publishing, 2018, pp. 121–58.

Fofana, Amadou. *The Films of Ousmane Sembène: Discourse, Politics, and Culture*. Amherst: Cambria Press, 2012.

Foley, Barbara. *Marxist Literary Criticism Today*. London: Pluto Press, 2019.

Fraser, Bashabi. *Bengal Partition Stories: An Unclosed Chapter*. Anthem Press, 2008.

Fraser, Robert. *The Novels of Ayi Kwei Armah: A Study in Polemical Fiction*. Heinemann, 1980.

Freire, Paolo. *Pedagogy of the Oppressed*. Penguin, 2017.

Gabriel, Teshome H. '*Xala*: A Cinema of Wax and Gold'. *Jump Cut: A Review of Contemporary Media*, vol. 27, 1980, pp. 31–3.

Gadjigo, Samba. 'Art for Man's Sake: A Tribute to Ousmane Sembène'. *Framework*, vol. 49, no. 1, 2008, pp. 30–4.

Ganguly, Keya. *Cinema, Emergence, and the Films of Satyajit Ray*. University of California Press, 2010.

Garraway, Doris L. '"What Is Mine": Césairean Negritude between the Particular and the Universal'. *Research in African Literatures*, vol. 41, no. 1, 2010, pp. 71–86.

Gaztambide, Daniel José. *A People's History of Psychoanalysis: From Freud to Liberation Psychology*. Rowman and Littlefield, 2019.

George, Rosemary Marangoly. 'Where in the World Did Kamala Markandaya Go?' *NOVEL: A Forum on Fiction*, vol. 42, no. 3, 2009, pp. 400–9.

Gerard, Emmanuel and Kuklick, Bruce. *Death in the Congo: Murdering Patrice Lumumba*. Harvard University Press, 2015.

Getachew, Adom. *Worldmaking after Empire: The Rise and Fall of Self-Determination*. Princeton University Press, 2019.

Ghatak, Ritwik. *Rows and Rows of Fences: Ritwik Ghatak on Cinema*. Seagull Books, 2000.

Ghosh, Deepanjan. 'In Bengal, the bond of Rakhi once symbolised eternal protection – between Hindus and Muslims'. *Scroll.in*, 7 August 2017, <https://scroll.in/magazine/846275/in-bengal-the-bond-of-rakhi-once-symbolised-eternal-protection-between-hindus-and-muslims> (accessed 24 November 2023).

Gibson, Nigel. *Fanon: The Postcolonial Imagination*. Wiley, 2003.

——. 'Relative Opacity: A New Translation of Fanon's *Wretched of the Earth* – Mission Betrayed or Fulfilled?' *Social Identities*, vol. 13, no. 1, 2007, pp. 69–95.
Gikandi, Simon. *Ngũgĩ Wa Thiong'o*. Cambridge University Press, 2000.
Gilmartin, David. 'The Historiography of India's Partition: Between Civilization and Modernity'. *The Journal of Asian Studies*, vol. 74, no. 1, 2015, pp. 23–41.
Gilroy, Paul. *The Black Atlantic: Modernity and Double Consciousness*. Harvard University Press, 1993.
Glissant, Édouard. *Poetics of Relation*. Translated by Betsy Wing, University of Michigan Press, 1997.
Goerg, Odile. *Tropical Dream Palaces: Cinema in Colonial West Africa*. Oxford University Press, 2010.
——. *Tropical Dream Palaces: Cinema in Colonial West Africa*. Hurst, 2020
Goldblatt, Cullen. *Beyond Collective Memory: Structural Complicity and Future Freedoms in Senegalese and South African Narratives*. Routledge, 2020.
Gopal, Priyamvada. *The Indian English Novel: Nation, History, and Narration*. Oxford University Press, 2009.
——. *Literary Radicalism in India: Gender, Nation and the Transition to Independence*. Routledge, 2012.
——. 'Humanism for a globalised world'. *New Humanist*, 2 December 2013, <https://newhumanist.org.uk/articles/4458/humanism-for-a-globalised-world> (accessed 24 November 2023).
Gopalan, Lalitha. 'World Cinema'. *The Cambridge World History*, edited by J. R. McNeill. Cambridge University Press, 2015.
Gordon, Lewis. *What Fanon Said*. Fordham University Press, 2015.
——. *Fear of Black Consciousness*. Allen Lane, 2022.
Grosz, Elizabeth. *Space, Time, and Perversion*. Routledge, 1995.
Gugler, Josef and Omar Cherif Diop. 'Ousmane Sembène's *Xala*: The Novel, the Film, and their Audiences'. *Research in African Literatures*, vol. 29, no. 2, 1998, pp. 147–58.
Guha, Ramachandra and Juan Martínez-Alier. *Varieties of Environmentalism: Essays North and South*. Earthscan Publications, 1997.
Guha, Ramachandra. *Environmentalism: A Global History*. Longman, 2000.
Guha, Ranajit. *Dominance without Hegemony: History and Power in Colonial India*. Harvard University Press, 1998.
Guneratne, Anthony and Wimal Dissanayake. *Rethinking Third Cinema*. Routledge, 2003.
Hagan, George. 'Nkrumah's Cultural Policy' in *Dilemmas of Culture in African Schools: Youth, Nationalism, and the Transformation of Knowledge*, edited by Cati Coe. Chicago: University of Chicago Press, 2005, p. 61.

Hallam, Julia. 'Civic Visions: Mapping the "City" Film 1900–1960'. *Culture, Theory and Critique*, vol. 53, no. 1, 2012, pp. 37–58.

Hammond, Andrew. 'Ngũgĩ wa Thiong'o & the Crisis of Kenyan Masculinity'. *Men in African Film & Fiction*, edited by Lahoucine Ouzgane. James Currey, 2011.

Hamouchene, Hamza. 'Fanon's Revolutionary Culture and Nationalism'. *Voices of Liberation: Frantz Fanon*, edited by Leo Zeiling. Haymarket Books, 2016.

Harfouch, Ali S. 'Hegel, Fanon, and the Problem of Recognition'. *Frantz Fanon and Emancipatory Social Theory*, edited by Dustin J. Byrd and Seyed Javad Miri. Brill, 2019, pp. 139–51.

Harlow, Barbara. *Resistance Literature*. Methuen, 1987.

——. *After Lives: Legacies of Revolutionary Writing*. Verso, 1996.

Harman, Chris. 'The State and Capitalism Today'. *International Socialism*, vol. 2, no. 51, 1991, pp. 3–54.

Harrington, Louise. '"Fragmentary Evidence": The Struggle to Narrate Partition'. *South Asian Review*, vol. 31, no. 1, 2011, pp. 262–76.

——. '"Fragmentary evidence": the struggle to narrate Partition'. *South Asian Review*, vol. 31, no. 1, 2011, pp. 262–76.

Harrow, Kenneth. 'Sembène Ousmane's *Xala*: The Use of Film and Novel as Revolutionary Weapon'. *Studies in Twentieth Century Literature*, vol. 4, no. 2, 1980, pp. 177–88.

——. 'Ngũgĩ Wa Thiong'o's "A Grain of Wheat': Season of Irony"'. *Research in African Literatures*, vol. 16, no. 2, 1985, pp. 243–63.

Hartnack, Christine. 'Roots and Routes: The Partition of British India in Indian Social Memories'. *Journal of Historical Sociology*, vol. 25, 2012, pp. 244–60.

Harvey, David. *Spaces of Hope*. University of California Press, 2000.

Hazard, John. 'Marxian Socialism in Africa: The Case of Mali'. *Comparative Politics*, vol. 2, no. 1, 1969, pp. 1–15.

Heerten, Lasse and A. Dirk Moses. 'The Nigeria–Biafra War: Postcolonial Conflict and the Question of Genocide'. *Journal of Genocide Research*, vol. 16, no. 2–3, 2004, pp. 169–203.

Hegel, Georg Wilhelm Friedrich. [1807]. *The Phenomenology of Spirit*, translated by Peter Fuss and John Dobbins. University of Notre Dame Press, 2019.

Hennessey, Rosemary and Chrys Ingraham. *Materialist Feminism: A Reader in Class, Difference, and Women's Lives*. Psychology Press, 1997.

Herbert, Daniel. 'Globality without Totality in Art Cinema'. *Postmodern Culture*, 2010, <www.pomoculture.org/2013/09/03/globality-without-totality-in-art-cinema> (accessed 24 November 2023).

Hodges, Hugh. 'Writing Biafra: Adichie, Emecheta and the Dilemmas of Biafran War Fiction'. *Postcolonial Text*, vol. 5, no. 1, 2009, <https://www.postcolonial.org/index.php/pct/article/view/898> (accessed 24 November 2023).

Hoefert de Turégano, Teresa. 'African Cinemas'. *World Literature Today*, vol. 8, no. 13, 2003, pp. 14–18.

Holst, John D. 'The Pedagogy of Ernesto Che Guevara'. *International Journal of Lifelong Education*, vol. 28, no. 2, 2009, pp. 149–73.

Hook, Derek. 'Frantz Fanon, Steve Biko, "Psychopolitcs" and Critical Psychology'. *Critical Psychology*, edited by Derek Hook. Juta Academic Publishing, 2004, pp. 84–114.

Howes, David. 'Skinscapes: Embodiment, Culture and Environment'. *The Book of Touch*, edited by C. Classen and D. Howes. Berg Publishers, 2005, pp. 27–39.

Hudis, Peter. *Frantz Fanon: Philosopher of the Barricades*. Pluto Books, 2015.

Huggan, Graham and Helen Tiffin. *Postcolonial Ecocriticism: Literature, Animals, Environment*. Routledge, 2015.

Ingham, Patrice Claire and Michelle R. Warren. *Postcolonial Moves: Medieval through Modern*. Palgrave, 2003.

Irele, Abiola. *The African Imagination: Literature in Africa and the Black Diaspora*. Oxford University Press, 2001.

Isabella, Brigitta. 'Rewriting Solidarities in Juxtaposition'. *Interventions*, vol. 24, no. 7, 2022, pp. 1089–105.

Jabeen, Neelam. 'Women, Land, Embodiment: A Case of Postcolonial Ecofeminism'. *Interventions*, vol. 22, no. 8, 2020, pp. 1095–109.

Jahan, Rahmant. '"Nectar in a Sieve": A Tale of Hunger, Starvation and Death'. *Indian Literature*, vol. 53, no. 5, 2009, pp. 199–210.

Jain, Jasbir. 'Daughters of Mother India in Search of a Nation: Women's Narratives about the Nation'. *Economic and Political Weekly*, vol. 41, no. 17, 2006, pp. 1654–60.

Jain, Sharda. 'Kamala Markandaya's *Nectar in a Sieve*'. *New Perspectives in Indian Writing in English*, edited by Malti Agrawal. Atlantic Publishers, 2007.

Jaji, Tsitsi Ella. *Africa in Stereo: Modernism, Music, and Pan-African Solidarity*. Oxford University Press, 2014.

James, Erin and Eric Morel. 'Ecocriticism and Narrative Theory: An Introduction'. *English Studies*, vol. 99, no. 4, 2018, pp. 355–65.

Jameson, Fredric. *The Political Unconscious: Narrative as a Socially Symbolic Act*. Cornell University Press, 1982.

——. 'Third-World Literature in the Era of Multinational Capitalism'. *Social Text*, vol. 15, 1986.

——. *The Geopolitical Aesthetic: Cinema and Space in the World System*. Indiana University Press, 1995.
Jayawardena, Kumari. *Feminism and Nationalism in the Third World*. Zed Books, 1986.
——. *Feminism and Nationalism in the Third World*. Verso, 2016.
Jeyifo, Biodun. 'The Nature of Things: Arrested Decolonization and Critical Theory'. *Research in African Literatures*, vol. 21, no. 1, 1990, pp. 33–48.
——. 'An African Cultural Modernity: Achebe, Fanon, Cabral, and the Philosophy of Decolonization', *Socialism and Democracy*, vol. 21, no. 3, 2007, pp. 125–41.
Juan, E. San. 'The Limits of Postcolonial Criticism: The Discourse of Edward Said'. *Against the Current*, 1998, <againstthecurrent.org/atc077/p1781> (accessed 24 November 2023).
Kakraba, Alexander Dakubo. 'Ayi Kwei Armah's Vulgar Language in *The Beautyful Ones Are Not Yet Born*: A Therapeutic Tool'. *Current Research Journal of Social Sciences*, vol. 3, no. 4, 2011, pp. 306–13.
Kalter, Christoper. 'A Shared Space of Imagination, Communication, and Action Perspectives on the History of the Third World'. *The Third World in the Global 1960s*, edited by Samantha Christiansen and Zachary A. Scarlett. Berghahn Books, 2013.
Kaur, Navdip. 'Violence and Migration: a Study of Killing in the Trains During the Partition of Punjab in 1947'. *Proceedings of the Indian History Congress*, vol. 72, 2011, pp. 947–54.
Kebede, Messay. 'The Rehabilitation of Violence and the Violence of Rehabilitation: Fanon and Colonialism'. *Journal of Black Studies*, vol. 31, no. 5, 2001, pp. 539–62.
Kedourie, Elie, ed. *Nationalism in Asia and Africa*. The World Publishing Co., 1970.
Kesteloot, Lilyan, and Ellen Conroy Kennedy. 'Senghor, Negritude and Francophonie on the Threshold of the Twenty-First Century'. *Research in African Literatures*, vol. 21, no. 3, 1990, pp. 51–7. JSTOR, <http://www.jstor.org/stable/3819633> (accessed 22 November 2023).
Khanna, Neetu. *The Visceral Logics of Decolonization*. Duke University Press, 2020.
Khanna, Ranjana. *Dark Continents: Psychoanalysis and Colonialism*. Duke University Press, 2003.
Kilian, Cassis. 'Glimmering Utopias: 50 years of African Film'. *Africa Spectrum*, vol. 45, no. 3, 2010, pp. 147–59.
Kipfer, Stefan. 'Fanon and Space: Colonization, Urbanization, and Liberation from the Colonial to the Global City'. *Environment and Planning D: Society and Space*, vol. 25, no. 4, 2007, pp. 701–26.

Klanten, Robert and Sofia Borges. *The Tale of Tomorrow: Utopian Architecture in the Modernist Realm*. Gestalten, 2016.

Klimke, Martin and Mary Nolan. 'Introduction'. *The Routledge Handbook of the Global Sixties: Between Protest and Nation-Building*, edited by Chen Jian et al. Routledge, 2018, pp. 1–11.

Kolondy, Annette. *The Lay of the Land: Metaphor as Experience and History in American Life and Letters*. University of North Carolina Press, 1975.

Korieh, Chima. *The Nigeria-Biafra War: Genocide and the Politics of Memory*. Amherst: Cambria, 2012.

Krebs, Andreas. 'The Transcendent and the Postcolonial: Violence in Derrida and Fanon'. *Human Architecture: Journal of the Sociology of Self-Knowledge*, vol. 5, 2007, pp. 89–99.

Krishnan, Madhu. 'From Empire to Independence: Colonial Space in the Writing of Tutuola, Ekwensi, Beti, and Kane'. *Comparative Literature Studies*, vol. 54, no. 2, 2017, pp. 329–57.

——. *Writing Spatiality in West Africa: Colonial Legacies in the Anglophone/Francophone Novel*. Boydell & Brewer, 2018.

Kumar, A. V. Suresh. *Six Indian Novelists: Mulk Raj Anand, Raja Rao, R. K. Narayan, Balachandran Rajan, Kamala Markandaya, Anita Desai*. Creative Books, 1996.

Kumar, K. 'Partition in School Textbooks: A Comparative Look at India and Pakistan'. *Pangs of Partition: The Human Dimension*, edited by S. Settar and I. B. Gupta. Indian Council of Historical Research and Manohar, 2002.

Lambert, Laurie L. *Comrade Sister: Caribbean Feminist Revisions of the Grenada Revolution*. University of Virginia Press, 2020.

Landy, Marcia. 'Political Allegory and "Engaged Cinema": Sembène's "Xala"'. *Cinema Journal*, vol. 23, no. 3, 1984, pp. 31–46.

Langford, Rachael. 'Locating Colonisation and Globalisation in Francophone African Film and Literature Spatial Relations in *Borom Sarret* (1963), *La Noire de . . .* (1965) and *Cinéma* (1997)'. *French Cultural Studies*, vol. 16, no. 1, 2005, pp. 91–104.

Lazarus, Neil. 'Pessimism of the Intellect, Optimism of the Will: A Reading of Ayi Kwei Armah's *The Beautyful Ones Are Not Yet Born*'. *Research in African Literatures*, vol. 18, no. 2, 1987, pp. 94–111.

——. *Resistance in Postcolonial African Fiction*. Yale University Press, 1990.

——. 'Disavowing Decolonization: Fanon, Nationalism, and the Problematic of Representation in Current Theories of Colonial Discourse'. *Research in African Literatures*, vol. 24, no. 4, 1993, pp. 69–98.

——. 'Disavowing Decolonization: Nationalism, Intellectuals, and the Question of Representation in Postcolonial Theory', *Nationalism and*

Cultural Practice in the Postcolonial World. Cambridge University Press, 1999.
——. *The Postcolonial Unconscious*. Cambridge University Press, 2011.
——. 'The Novel and Consciousness of Labour'. *The Cambridge Companion to World Literature*, edited by Ben Etherington and Jarad Zimbler. Cambridge University Press, 2018.
Lee, Christopher J. *Making a World After Empire: The Bandung Moment and Its Political Afterlives*. Johns Hopkins University Press, 2010.
Lefebvre, Henri. *The Production of Space*. Translated by Donald Nicholson-Smith. Wiley-Blackwell, 1991.
——. *Critique of Everyday Life, Vol. 1.* Translated by John Moore. Verso, 2008.
Lenin, V. I. [1917]. *Imperialism, the Highest Stage of Capitalism*. Penguin, 2010.
Levich, Jacob. 'Subcontinental DIVIDE: The Undiscovered ART of Ritwik Ghatak'. *Film Comment*, vol. 33, no. 2, 1997, pp. 30–5.
Levieux, Michèle. 2004. 'Camarade Sembène, l'aîné des anciens Sembène Ousmane'. *L'Humanité*, <https://www.humanite.fr/culture-et-savoir/cannes-2003-et-2004/camarade-sembene-laine-des-anciens-sembene-ousmane> (accessed 29 November 2023).
Lindner, Kolja. *Marx, Marxism and the Question of Eurocentrism*. Springer, 2022.
Lindo, Karen. 'Ousmane Sembène's *Hall of Men*: (En)Gendering Everyday Heroism'. *Research in African Literatures*, vol. 41, no. 4, 2010, pp. 109–21.
Lloyd, David. 'The Pathological Sublime: Pleasure and Pain in the Colonial Context'. *The Postcolonial Enlightenment: Eighteenth-Century Colonialism and Postcolonial Theory*, edited by Daniel Carey and Lynn Festa. Oxford University Press, 2013.
——. *Under Representation: The Racial Regime of Aesthetics*. Fordham University Press, 2018.
Lockwood, David. 'The Indian Emergency in Economic Context'. *Proceedings of the Indian History Congress*, vol. 76, 2015, pp. 865–74.
Loomba, Ania. *Colonialism/Postcolonialism*. Third edition. Routledge, 2015.
——. *Revolutionary Desires: Women, Communism, and Feminism in India*. Routledge, Taylor & Francis Group, 2019.
Lugones, Maria. 'The Coloniality of Gender'. *Worlds and Knowledges Otherwise*, Spring 2008, pp. 1–17.
Lukács, György. [1938]. 'Realism in the Balance'. *The Norton Anthology of Theory and Criticism*, first edition, edited by Vincent B. Leitch. W. W. Norton & Co, 2011, pp. 1033–58.
Lutz, John. 'Pessimism, Autonomy, and Commodity Fetishism in Ayi Kwei Armah's *The Beautyful Ones Are Not Yet Born*'. *Research in African Literatures* vol. 34, no. 2, 2003, pp. 94–111.

Lynch, Kevin. *The Image of the City*. MIT Press, 1960.
Lynn, Thomas J. 'Community, Carnival, and the Colonial Legacy in Ousmane Sembène's *Xala*'. *Cincinnati Romance Review*, vol. 23, 2004, pp. 60–74.
Macaulay, Thomas Babington and G. M. Young, [1835]. 'Minute by the Hon'ble T. B. Macaulay'. *Speeches by Lord Macaulay, with his Minute on Indian education*. AMS Press, 1979.
Macey, David. *Frantz Fanon: A Biography*. Picador, 2000.
Machiko, Oike. 'Becoming a Feminist Writer: Representation of the Subaltern in Buchi Emecheta's *Destination Biafra*'. *War in African Literature Today*, edited by E. Emenyonu. Boydell & Brewer, 2008.
Mahler, Anne Garland. *From the Tricontinental to the Global South: Race, Radicalism, and Transnational Solidarity*. Duke University Press, 2018.
Maiers, Wolfgang and Charles W. Tolman. 'Critical Psychology as Subject-Science'. *Psychology and Society: Radical Theory and Practice*, edited by Ian Parker and Russell Spears. Pluto, 1996.
Maldonado-Torres, Nelson. 'Frantz Fanon and the Decolonial Turn in Psychology: From Modern/Colonial Methods to the Decolonial Attitude'. *South African Journal of Psychology*, vol. 47, no. 4, 2017, pp. 432–41.
Manji, Firoze and Bill Fletcher Jr, eds. *Claim No Easy Victories: The Legacy of Amílcar Cabral*. Codesria and Daraja Press, 2013.
Markandaya, Kamala. *'One Pair of Eyes'*. *The Commonwealth Writer Overseas: Themes of Exile and Expatriation*, edited by Alastair Niven. Brussels: Librairie M. Didier, 1976, pp. 23–32.
Markandaya, Kamala. [1954]. *Nectar in a Sieve*. Signet Books, 1995.
Marks, Laura. *The Skin of the Film: Intercultural Cinema, Embodiment, and the Senses*. Duke University Press, 2000.
Marriott, David. 'Whither Fanon?' *Textual Practice*, vol. 25, no. 1, 2011, pp. 33–69.
———. *Whither Fanon?: Studies in the Blackness of Being*. Stanford University Press, 2018.
Martín-Baró, Ignacio. *Writings for a Liberation Psychology*, edited by Adrianne Aron and Shawn Corne. Harvard University Press, 1994.
Marx, Karl. [1847]. *The Poverty of Philosophy*. International Publishers, 1963.
Marx, Karl and Friedrich Engels. [1932]. *The German Ideology*, translated by C. J. Arthur. Electric Book Co., 2001.
Marx, Karl. *Economic and Philosophic Manuscripts of 1844*, translated and edited by Martin Milligan. Dover Publications, 2007.
Mazierska, Ewa and Lars Kristensen. *Third Cinema, World Cinema and Marxism*. Bloomsbury Academic, 2020.

Mbembe, Achille. 'Provisional Notes on the Postcolony'. *Africa: Journal of the International African Institute*, vol. 62, no. 1, 1992, pp. 3–37.
——. *On the Postcolony*. University of California Press, 2001.
——. *Critique of Black Reason*. Duke University Press, 2017.
Mbũgua wa Mũngai. *Remembering Kenya: Identity, Culture, Freedom*, Vol. 1, edited by Mbũgua wa Mũngai and George Gona. Twaweza Communications, 2010.
McCann, Gerard. 'Where was the "Afro" in Afro-Asian Solidarity? Africa's "Bandung Moment" in 1950s Asia'. *Journal of World History*, vol. 30, no. 1/2, 2019, pp. 89–123.
McCulloch, Jock. *Black Soul, White Artefact: Fanon's Clinical Psychology and Social Theory*. Cambridge University Press, 1983.
McGowan, Abigail. 'Khadi Curtains and Swadeshi Bed Covers: Textiles and the Changing Possibilities of Home in Western India, 1900–1960'. *Modern Asian Studies*, vol. 50, no. 2, 2016, pp. 518–63.
McLuckie, Craig W. 'Literary Memoirs of the Nigerian Civil War'. *Matatu*, vol. 23, no. 1, 2001, pp. 29–37.
Memmi, Albert. [1957]. *The Coloniser and the Colonised*. Routledge, 2013
Menon, Jisha. *The Performance of Nationalism: India, Pakistan, and the Memory of Partition*. Cambridge University Press, 2013.
Merivirta, Raita. *The Emergency and the Indian English Novel: Memory, Culture and Politics*. Routledge India, 2019.
Merleau-Ponty, Maurice. *Phenomenology of Perception*, translated by Colin Smith. Routledge, 1962.
Messier, Vartan. 'Decolonizing National Consciousness Redux: Ousmane Sembène's *Xala* as Transhistorical Critique'. *Postcolonial Text*, vol. 6, no. 4, 2011, pp. 2–22.
Mestman, Mariano. 'Third Cinema/Militant Cinema: At the Origins of the Argentinian Experience (1968–1971)'. *Third Text*, vol. 25, no. 1, 2011, pp. 29–40.
Mew, Sophie. 'Managing the cultural past in the newly independent states of Mali and Ghana' in *Cultures of Decolonisation: Transnational Productions and Practices*, edited by Ruth Craggs and Claire Wintle, pp. 1945–70. Manchester University Press, 2015.
Mignolo, Walter. 'The Geopolitics of Knowledge and the Colonial Difference'. *South Atlantic Quarterly*, no. 101, 2000, pp. 57–96.
Mills, Charles W. *The Racial Contract*. Cornell University Press, 1997.
Minh-Ha, Trinh T. *Woman, Native, Other: Writing Postcoloniality and Feminism*. Indiana University Press, 1989.
Misra, Pravati. *Class Consciousness in the Novels of Kamala Markandaya*. Atlantic Publishers & Dist, 2001.

Mitra, Indrani. '"I Will Make Bimala One With My Country": Gender and Nationalism in Tagore's *Home and the World*'. *Modern Fiction Studies*, vol. 41, no. 2, 1995, pp. 243–64.

Mohanty, Chandra Talpade. 'Under Western Eyes: Feminist Scholarship and Colonial Discourses'. *Feminist Review*, vol. 30, 1988, pp. 61–88.

Mohanty, Satya P. *Literary Theory and the Claims of History: Postmodernism, Objectivity, Multicultural Politics*. Cornell University Press, 1997.

Moji, Polo B. 'Gender-based Genre Conventions and the Critical Reception of Buchi Emecheta's *Destination Biafra*'. *Literator*, vol. 35, no. 1, 2014, <https://literator.org.za/index.php/literator/article/view/420/1497> (accessed 24 November 2023).

Mudimbe, V. Y. *The Invention of Africa*. Indiana University Press, 1988.

Mueller, Gustav E. 'The Hegel Legend of "Thesis-Antithesis-Synthesis"'. *Journal of the History of Ideas*, vol. 19, no. 3, 1958, pp. 411–14.

Mufti, Aamir. 'Orientalism and the Institution of World Literatures'. *Critical Inquiry*, vol. 36, no. 3, 2010, pp. 458–93.

Mukherjee, Ankhi. *Unseen City: The Psychic Lives of the Urban Poor*. Cambridge University Press, 2022.

Mukherjee, Upamanyu. *Postcolonial Environments: Nature, Culture and the Contemporary Indian Novel in English*. Palgrave, 2010.

Mungwini, Pascah. *African Philosophy: Emancipation and Practice*. Bloomsbury, 2022.

Murphy, David. 'An African Brecht: The Cinema of Ousmane Sembene'. *New Left Review*, vol. 16, 2002, pp. 115–29.

Murphy, David. 'Culture, Development, and the African Renaissance: Osumane Sembène and Léopold Senghor at the World Festival of Negro Arts (Dakar 1966)'. *Ousmane Sembène and the Politics of Culture*, edited by Lifongo Vetinde and Amadou Fofana. London: Lexington Books, 2015, pp. 1–16.

Murray-Román, Jeannine. 'Walking with Fanon: Towards Decolonized Embodiments'. *Interventions*, 2023. doi: 10.1080/1369801X.2023.2191862

Murrey, Amber, et al. *A Certain Amount of Madness: The Life, Politics and Legacies of Thomas Sankara*. Pluto Press, 2018.

Mushengyezi, Aaron. 'Reimagining Gender and African Tradition: Ousmane Sembène's *Xala* revisited'. *Africa Today*, vol. 51, no. 1, 2004, pp. 47–62.

Mwangi, Evan. *Africa Writes Back to Self: Metafiction, Gender, Sexuality*. SUNY Press, 2009.

Mwikisa, Peter W. 'Politics and the Religious Unconscious in Ngũgĩ Wa Thiongo's *A Grain of Wheat* and His Other Works'. *Scriptura*, vol. 92, no. 2, 2006, pp. 248–64.

Nadaswaran, Shalini. 'The Legacy of Buchi Emecheta in Nigerian Women's Fiction'. *International Journal of Social Science and Humanity*, vol. 2, no. 2, 2012, pp. 146–50.

Nagib, Lucia. 'Towards a positive definition of World Cinema' in *Remapping World Cinema: Identity, Culture and Politics in Film*, edited by Stephanie Dennison and Song Hwee Lim. Wallflower Press, 2006, pp. 26–33.

Nandy, Ashis. *The Illegitimacy of Nationalism: Rabindranath Tagore and the Politics of Self*. Oxford India Paperbacks, 1994.

——. *The Intimate Enemy: Loss and Recovery of Self under Colonialism*. Oxford University Press, 2009.

Nayar, Pramod K. 'Fanon and Biopolitics'. *Frantz Fanon and Emancipatory Social Theory*, edited by Dustin J. Byrd and Seyed Javad Miri. Brill, 2019, pp. 217–30.

Ndlovu-Gatsheni, Sabelo J. *Epistemic Freedom in Africa: Deprovincialization and Decolonization*. Routledge, 2018.

Ndong, Louis. 'The Use of Languages as Linguistic Militancy in Ousmane Sembène's Films: Between Film Aesthetics and Cinematographic Reception'. *African Renaissance*, vol. 14, no. 3, 2017, pp. 51–64.

Nehru, Jawaharlal. 'A Tryst with Destiny: Speech on the Granting of Indian Independence, August 14, 1947'. *Internet History Sourcebooks: Modern History*, <sourcebooks.fordham.edu/mod/1947nehru1.asp> (accessed 19 September 2023).

Ngũgĩ wa Thiong'o. [1967]. *A Grain of Wheat*. Penguin Modern Classics, 2002.

Ngũgĩ wa Thiong'o. *Homecoming: Essays on African and Caribbean Literature, Culture and Politics*. Heinemann, 1972.

——. *Writers in Politics: Essays*. East African Publishers, 1981.

——. *Moving the Centre: The Struggle for Cultural Freedoms*. James Currey, 2004.

——. [1986] *Decolonising the Mind: The Politics of Language in African Literature*. James Currey, 2011.

Niang, Sada, et al. 'Interview with Ousmane Sembène'. *Research in African Literatures*, vol. 26, no. 3, 1995, pp. 174–8.

Niang, Sada, Gadjigo, Samba, and Sembène, Ousmane. 'Interview with Ousmane Sembene'. *Research in African Literatures*, vol. 26, no. 3, 1995, pp. 174–8.

Nicholls, Brendon. *Ngũgĩ wa Thiong'o, Gender, and the Ethics of Postcolonial Reading*. Ashgate, 2010.

Niemi, Minna. 'Challenging Moral Corruption in the Postcolony: Ayi Kwei Armah's *The Beautyful Ones Are Not Yet Born* and Hannah Arendt's *Notion of Individual Responsibility*'. *Postcolonial Studies*, vol. 20, no. 2, 2017, pp. 217–36.

Nixon, Rob. *Slow Violence and the Environmentalism of the Poor*. Harvard University Press, 2011.
Nnaemeka, Obioma. 'Fighting on All Fronts: Gendered Spaces, Ethnic Boundaries, and the Nigerian Civil War'. *Dialectical Anthropology*, vol. 22, no. 3–4, 1997, pp. 235–63.
Nnolim, Charles. 'Structure and Theme in Ngũgĩ wa Thiong'o's *A Grain of Wheat*'. *Critical Perspectives on Ngũgĩ wa Thiong'o*, edited by G. D. Killam. Three Continents Press, 1984.
Nwahunanya, Chinyere. 'The Aesthetics Of Nigerian War Fiction'. *Modern Fiction Studies*, vol. 37, no. 3, 1991, pp. 427–43.
Nwangwu, Chikodiri, et al. 'The Political Economy of Biafra Separatism and Post-war Igbo Nationalism in Nigeria'. *African Affairs*, vol. 119, no. 477, 2020, pp. 526–51.
Nwoye, Augustine. *African Psychology: The Emergence of a Tradition*. Oxford University Press, 2022.
O'Brien, Donal Cruise. 'The Shadow-Politics of Wolofisation'. *The Journal of Modern African Studies*, vol. 36, no. 1, 1998, pp. 25–46.
Ogot, B. A. and W. R. Ochieng. *Decolonisation and Independence in Kenya 1940–1993*. James Currey, 1995.
Ogot, Bethwell A. *My Footprints on the Sands of Time: An Autobiography*. Trafford Publishing, 2003.
Ogunyemi, Chikwenye Okonjo. 'Womanism: The Dynamics of the Contemporary Black Female Novel in English'. *Signs*, vol. 11, no. 1, 1985, pp. 63–80.
Okome, Onookome. 'Obituary: Buchi Emecheta (1944–2017)'. *The Journal of Commonwealth Literature*, vol. 52, no. 2, June 2017, pp. 401–8.
Okuyade, Ogaga. 'How Does Violence Mean? Understanding Nigerian Civil War Poetry'. *Commonwealth: Essays and Studies*, vol. 34, no. 2, 2012, pp. 19–29.
Olaniyan, Tejumola. 'Africa: Varied Colonial Legacies'. *A Companion to Postcolonial Studies*, edited by Henry Schwarz and Sangeeta Ray. John Wiley & Sons, 2008.
Opondo, Sam Okoth. 'Cinema is our "night school": Appropriation, Falsification, and Dissensus in the Art of Ousmane Sembène'. *African Identities*, vol. 13, no. 1, 2015. pp. 34–48.
Orrells, David and Pierre-Philippe Fraiture. *The Mudimbe Reader*. Virginia University Press, 2016.
Pandey, Gyanendra. *Remembering Partition: Violence, Nationalism, and History in India*. Cambridge University Press, 2001.
Pape, Marion. 'Nigerian War Literature by Women: From Civil War to Gender War'. *Body, Sexuality, and Gender: Versions and Subversions in African*

Literatures, edited by Flora Veit-Wild and Dirk Naguschewski. Editions Rodopi, 2005.
Parry, Benita. 'Liberation Theory: Variations on Themes of Marxism and Modernity'. *Marxism, Modernity and Postcolonial Studies*, edited by Bartolovich et al. Cambridge University Press, 2002.
——. *Postcolonial Studies: A Materialist Critique*. Routledge, 2004.
Peacock, Sunita. 'The Nationalist Question and the Bengali Heroine In Rabindranath Tagore's *Ghare Baire or the Home and the World*'. *Pakistan Journal of Women's Studies: Alam-e-Niswan*, vol. 18, no. 2, 2011, pp. 23–36.
Peterson, Brian J. *Thomas Sankara: A Revolutionary in Cold War Africa*. Indiana University Press, 2021.
Petersen, K. H., ed. *Criticism and Ideology: Second African Writers' Conference*. Nordic Africa Institute, 1988, pp. 173–85.
Prasad, Hari Mohan. 'The Fictional Epic on Indian Life – A Study on Theme and Technique in *Nectar in a Sieve*'. *Perspectives on Kamala Markandaya*, edited by Madhusudan Prasad. Vimal Prakashan, 1984.
Prashad, Vijay. *Red Star Over the Third World*. Pluto Press, 2019.
Proctor, Hannah. 'History from Within'. *Historical Materialism*, 2018, <www.historicalmaterialism.org/articles/history-from-within> (accessed 24 November 2023).
Quayson, Ato. *Strategic Transformations in Nigerian Writing*. Indiana University Press, 1997.
——. 'Colonial space-making and hybridizing history, or "Are the Indians of East Africa Africans or Indians?"' *Diasporas: Concepts, Intersections, Identities*, edited by Kim Knott and Seán McLoughlin. Zed Books, 2010.
——. 'Introduction: Postcolonial Spatialities'. *Interventions*, vol. 22, no. 8, 2020, pp. 967–76.
——. *Tragedy and Postcolonial Literature*. Cambridge University Press, 2021.
Quigley, Lakshmi. 'Bengali Art House Cinema, Women's Subjectivity, and History: Satyajit Ray's use of Silence in *Charulata* (1964) and *Devi* (1960)'. *Journal of International Women's Studies*, vol. 19, no. 1, 2018, pp. 50–62.
Quijano, Aníbal. 'Coloniality and Modernity/Rationality'. *Cultural Studies*, vol. 21, no. 2, 2007, pp. 168–78.
Radhakrishnan, R. 'Postcoloniality and the Boundaries of Identity'. *Callaloo*, vol. 16, no. 4, 1993, pp. 750–71.
Radithalo, Sam. 'Kenyan Sheroes: Women and Nationalism in Ngũgĩ's novels'. *English Studies in Africa*, vol. 44, no. 1, 2001, pp. 1–11.
Ranasinha, Ruvani. *Contemporary Diasporic South Asian Women's Fiction: Gender, Narration and Globalisation*. Palgrave Macmillan UK, 2016.

Ratele, Kopano. *The World Looks Like This from Here: Thoughts on African Psychology*. Wits University Press, 2019.

Ray, Sangeeta. *En-Gendering India: Woman and Nation in Colonial and Postcolonial Narratives*. Duke University Press, 2000.

Raychaudhuri, Anindya. 'Resisting the Resistible: Re-Writing Myths of Partition in the Works of Ritwik Ghatak'. *Social Semiotics*, vol. 19, no. 4, 2009, pp. 469–81.

Read, Jason. *The Production of Subjectivity: Marx and Philosophy*. Brill, 2022.

Reed, Edward S. 'The Challenge of Historical Materialist Epistemology'. *Psychology and Society: Radical Theory and Practice*, edited by Ian Parker and Russell Spears. Pluto, 1996.

Rillon, Ophélie. 'Rebellious Bodies: Urban Youth Fashion in the Sixties and Seventies in Mali'. *The Routledge Handbook of the Global Sixties*, edited by Chen Jian et al. Routledge, 2018, pp. 135–46.

Rogobete, Daniela. 'A Mother's Plight – Fear and Hope in Kamala Markandaya's *Nectar In A Sieve*'. *Romanian Journal of English Studies*, vol. 11, no. 1, 2014.

Rosen, Philip. 'Nation, inter-nation and narration in Ousmane Sembène's films'. *A Call to Action: The Films of Ousmane Sembène*, edited by Sheila Petty. Praeger, 1996.

——. 'Notes on Art Cinema and the Emergence of Sub-Saharan Film'. *Global Art Cinema: New Theories and Histories*, edited by Rosalind Galt and Karl Schoonover. Oxford University Press, 2010, pp. 252–63.

Rovine, Victoria L. 'Pith and Power: Colonial Style in France and French West Africa'. *Journal of Material Culture*, vol. 27, no. 3, 2022, 280–312.

Roy, Alexis. 'Peasant Struggles in Mali: From Defending Cotton Producers' Interests to Becoming Part of the Malian Power Structures'. *Review of African Political Economy*, vol. 37, no. 125, 2010, pp. 299–314.

Roy, Srila. *Remembering Revolution: Gender, Violence and Subjectivity in India's Naxalbari Movement*. Oxford University Press, 2014.

Said, Edward. *Culture and Imperialism*. Vintage Books, 1993.

——. 'Yeats and Decolonization'. *The Edward Said Reader*, edited by Moustafa Bayoumi and Andrew Rubin. Granta, 2000.

Saini, Angela. *Superior: The Return of Race Science*. 4th Estate, 2020.

Salamon, Gayle. '"The Place Where Life Hides Away": Merleau-Ponty, Fanon, and the Location of Bodily Being'. *differences: A Journal of Feminist Cultural Studies*, vol. 17, no. 2, 2006, pp. 96–112.

Salem, Sara. '"Stretching" Marxism in the Postcolonial World: Egyptian Decolonisation and the Contradictions of National Sovereignty'. *Historical Materialism*, vol. 27, no. 4, 2019, pp. 3–28.

Samaddar, Ranabir. *Emergence of the Political Subject*. SAGE Publications India, 2009.

Sankara, Thomas. *Thomas Sankara Speaks: The Burkina Faso Revolution 1983–1987*, edited by Michel Prairie. Pathfinder Press, 1988.

Sarkar, Sumit. '"Middle-class" Consciousness and Patriotic Literature in South Asia'. *A Companion to Postcolonial Studies*, edited by Henry Schwarz and Sangeeta Ray, 2000, pp. 252–68.

Sarkar, Tanika. 'Many Faces of Love: Country, Woman, and God'. *R. Tagore's The Home and the World, A Critical Companion*, edited by Pradip Kumar Datta. Anthem Press, 2005.

Sartre, Jean-Paul and Senghor Léopold Sédar. *Anthologie de la Nouvelle poésie nègre et Malgache de Langue française / Orphée Noir*. Presses Universitaires de France, 1998.

Schwarz, Henry and Sangeeta Ray. *A Companion to Postcolonial Studies*. Wiley & Sons, 2008.

Sekyi-Otu, Ato. *Fanon's Dialectic of Experience*. Harvard University Press, 1997.

Sen, Arijit and Lisa Silverman. *Making Place: Space and Embodiment in the City*. Indiana University Press, 2014.

Sengoopta, Chandak. 'The Contours of Affinity: Satyajit Ray and the Tagorean Legacy'. *South Asia: Journal of South Asian Studies*, vol. 35, no. 1, pp. 143–61.

Sengupta, Jayita. 'Ray's Narrative Vision and Synaesthetic Appreciation of Tagore in *Ghare Baire*'. *Filming Fiction: Tagore, Premchand, and Ray*, edited by Mohd Asaduddin and Anuradha Ghosh. Oxford University Press, 2012.

Shani, Giorgio. 'Spectres of Partition: Religious Nationalism in Post-Colonial South Asia'. *Asian Nationalisms Reconsidered*, edited by Jeff Kingston. Routledge, 2015.

Sharma, Brij Kishore. 'Jawaharlal Nehru's Model Of Development'. *Proceedings of the Indian History Congress*, vol. 73, 2012, pp. 1292–302, <www.jstor.org/stable/44156330> (accessed 22 December 2020).

Sharma, Devika and Tygstrup, Frederik. *Structures of Feeling: Affectivity and the Study of Culture*. Walter de Gruyter GmbH & Co KG, 2015.

Sharma, Govind Narain. 'Ngũgĩ's Christian Vision: Theme and Pattern in *A Grain of Wheat*'. *Critical Perspectives on Ngũgĩ wa Thiong'o*, edited by G. D. Killam. Three Continents Press, 1984.

Sharifi, Majid and Chabot, Sean. 'Fanon's New Humanism as Antidote to Today's Colonial Violence'. *Frantz Fanon and Emancipatory Social Theory*, edited by Dustin J. Byrd and Seyed Javad Miri. Brill, 2019, pp. 251–71.

Shohat, Ella. 'Notes on the "Post-Colonial"'. *Social Text*, vol. 1, no. 31/32, 1992, pp. 99–113.
Simola, Raisa. 'Time and Identity: The Legacy of Biafra to the Igbo in Diaspora'. *Nordic Journal of African Studies*, vol. 9, no. 1, 2000, pp. 98–117.
Simone, AbdouMaliq. *Improvised Lives: Rhythms of Endurance in an Urban South*. Polity, 2018.
Singh, H. 'Caste, Class and Peasant Agency in Subaltern Studies Discourse: Revisionist Historiography, Elite Ideology'. *The Journal of Peasant Studies*, vol. 30, 2002, pp. 134–91.
Smiet, Katrine. 'Rethinking or Delinking? Said and Mignolo on Humanism and the Question of the Human'. *Postcolonial Studies*, vol. 25, no. 1, 2022, pp. 73–88.
Smith, Étienne. 'La Nationalisation Par Le Bas: Un Nationalisme Banal? Le cas de la wolofisation au Sénégal'. *Raisons Politiques*, vol. 37, 2010, pp. 65–77.
Solanas, Fernando and Octavio Getino. 'Toward A Third Cinema'. *Cinéaste*, vol. 4, no. 3, 1969, pp. 1–10. JSTOR, <www.jstor.org/stable/41685716> (accessed 22 December 2020).
Soja, Edward W. 2011. 'Foreword'. *Postcolonial Spaces: The Politics of Place in Contemporary Culture*, edited by Andrew Teverson and Sara Upstone, ix–xiii. Palgrave Macmillan, 2011.
Sorensen, Eli Park. 'Naturalism and Temporality in Ousmane Sembène's *Xala*'. *Research in African Literatures*, vol. 41, no. 2, 2010, pp. 222–43.
——. 'Postcolonial Literary History and the Concealed Totality of Life'. *Paragraph*, vol. 37, no. 2, 2014, pp. 235–53.
Soyinka, Wole. *Madmen and Specialists*. Methuen, 1971.
——. *The Man Died: Prison Notes*. Rex Collings, 1972.
Spivak, Gayatri Chakravorty. *A Critique of Postcolonial Reason: Toward a History of the Vanishing Present*. Harvard University Press, 1999.
——. 'Nationalism and the Imagination'. *Lectora*, vol. 15, 2009, pp. 75–98.
Srivastava, Ramesh K. 'Limitation of Markandaya in *Nectar in a Sieve*'. *Six Indian Novelists in English*, edited by Srivastava Ramesh. Guru Nanak Dev University, 1987, pp. 145–54.
Stanziani, Alessandro. *Eurocentrism and the Politics of Global History*. Springer International Publishing, 2018.
Stollery, Martin. 'The Question of Third Cinema: African and Middle Eastern Cinemas'. *Journal of Film and Video*, vol. 52, no. 4, 2001, pp. 44–55.
Stolte, Carolien and Su Lin Lewis. *The Lives of Cold War Afro-Asianism*. Amsterdam University Press, 2022.
Stratton, Florence. *Contemporary African Literature and the Politics of Gender*. Routledge, 1994.

Szeman, Imre. *Zones of Instability: Literature, Postcolonialism, and the Nation*. Johns Hopkins University Press, 2003.

Tagore, Rabindranath. [1917]. *Nationalism*. Penguin, 2010.

———. *The Home and the World*. Penguin Classics, 2004.

Tagra, Vinod. *Nehru and the Status of Women in India: An Analytical Study*. Reliance Publishing House, 2006.

Taoua, Phyllis. *African Freedom: How Africa Responded to Independence*. Cambridge University Press, 2018.

Uche, Chibuike. 'Oil, British Interests and the Nigerian Civil War'. *The Journal of African History*, vol. 49, no. 1, 2008, pp. 111–35.

Ukadike, Frank Nwachukwu, ed. *Critical Approaches to African Cinema Discourse*. Lexington Books, 2014.

Upstone, Sara. *Spatial Politics in the Postcolonial Novel*. Ashgate, 2009.

Ureña, Carolyn. 'Fanon's Idealism: Hopeful Resignation, Violence, and Healing'. *Bandung*, vol. 6, no. 2, 2019, pp. 233–51.

Van Schendel, Willem. 'Working Through Partition: Making a Living in the Bengal Borderlands'. *International Review of Social History*, vol. 46, 2001, pp. 393–421.

Vetinde, Lifongo. 'Reels of Conflicting Paradigms: The Black Filmmaker and Africa's Transitional Dilemmas'. *Focus on Nigeria: Literature and Culture*, edited by Gordon Collier. Rodopi, 2012, pp. 457–93.

Vieira, Marco. 'The Decolonial Subject and the Problem of Non-Western Authenticity'. *Postcolonial Studies*, vol. 22, no. 2, 2019, pp. 1–18.

Villet, Charles. 'Hegel and Fanon on the Question of Mutual Recognition: A Comparative Analysis'. *The Journal of Pan African Studies*, vol. 4, no. 7, 2011, pp. 39–51.

Walker, Keith L. 'The Transformational and Enduring Vision of Aimé Césaire'. *PMLA*, vol. 125, no. 3, 2010, pp. 756–63.

Wallerstein, Immanuel. *Geopolitics and Geoculture: Essays on the Changing World-System*. Cambridge University Press, 1992.

Ward, Kathryn B. 'Reconceptualising World System Theory to Include Women'. *Theory On Gender / Feminism On Theory*, edited by Paula England. Aldine De Gruyter, 1993.

Warwick Research Collective. *Combined and Uneven Development: Towards a New Theory of World-Literature*. Liverpool University Press, 2015.

Wayne, Mike. *Political Film: The Dialectics of Third Cinema*. London: Pluto, 2001.

Weigel, Moira. 'Provincializing the Road Movie: Realism, Epic and Mobility in Ritwik Ghatak's *Ajantrik* (1957)'. *The Global Road Movie*, edited by Timothy Corrigan and José Duarte. Intellect Books, 2008.

Werbner, Richard. 'Introduction: Postcolonial Subjectivities: The Personal, the Political and the Moral'. *Postcolonial Subjectivities in Africa*, edited by Richard Werbner. ZED Books, 2002.

Whiteman, Kaye. 'The Man Who Ran Françafrique'. *The National Interest*, 1 September 1997, <https://nationalinterest.org/article/the-man-who-ran-franafrique-1005> (accessed 29 November 2023).

Whyte, Susan Reynolds. 'Subjectivity and Subjunctivity: Hoping for Health in Eastern Uganda'. *Postcolonial Subjectivities in Africa*, edited by Richard Werbner. ZED Books, 2002.

Williams, Raymond. *Marxism and Literature*. Oxford University Press, 1977.

Williams, Susan. *White Malice: The CIA and the Covert Recolonization of Africa*. C Hurst & Co Publishers Ltd., 2021.

Willoquet-Maricondi, Paula. 'African Animism, "Négritude", and the Interdependence of Place and Being in Aimé Césaire's "A Tempest"'. *Interdisciplinary Studies in Literature and Environment*, vol. 3, no. 2, 1996, pp. 47–61.

Wright, Derek. *Ayi Kwei Armah's Africa: The Sources of His Fiction*. Hans Zell, 1989.

——. 'Ayi Kwei Armah and the Significance of his Novels and Histories'. *The International Fiction Review*, vol. 17, no. 1, 1990, pp. 29–40.

Young, Robert J. C. *Postcolonialism: A Very Short Introduction*. Oxford University Press, 2003.

Young, Robert J. C. 'Terror Effects'. *Terror and the Postcolonial: A Concise Companion*, edited by Elleke Boehmer and Stephen Morton. Wiley, 2013.

Zambrana, Rocío. *Colonial Debts: The Case of Puerto Rico*. Duke University Press, 2021.

Zeilig, Leo. *Class Struggle and Resistance in Africa*. Haymarket Books, 2008.

Zeleny, Beth. 'Planting Seeds in Kamala Markandaya's *Nectar in a Sieve*'. *Journal of Cultural Geography*, vol. 17, no. 1, 1997, pp. 21–35.

Zulfiqar, Sadia. *African Women Writers and the Politics of Gender*. Cambridge Scholars Publishing, 2016.

Filmography

Cissé, Souleymane. *Baara [Work]*. Trigon Film, 1978.
Ghatak, Ritwik. *Meghe Dhaka Tara [The Cloud-Capped Star]*. Criterion Collection, 1960.
Ray, Satyajit. *Ghare Baire [Home and the World]*. Criterion Collection, 1984.
Sembène, Ousmane. *Xala*. New Yorker Video, 1975.

Index

Achebe, Chinua, 5, 33, 51, 53, 62, 72, 149
Achebe, Christie, 116, 118, 131
Adalet, Begüm, 15, 139, 140
Adams, Ann Marie, 102, 113
'Africanity', 75, 76–9
Afro-Asianism, 2, 13, 27–8, 30
Afzal-Khan, Fawzia, 128–9, 130
Agathangelou, Anna, 18
Agrawal, Malti, 128–9
Ahmed, Sara, 39, 41, 42
Algeria, 3, 32–3, 43, 109
Althusser, Louis, 34
Ambedkar, B. R., 34
Amuta, Chidi, 102
Anderson, Benedict, 64
Anderson, Warwick, 19, 20
Andrews, Kehinde, 3
Angola, 14, 134n
anti-colonial movements
    African, 1, 8, 10–11, 14, 51–62, 72
    South Asian, 7, 27, 52, 57, 61, 62–72, 107
anti-colonial thought, 14, 18–21, 24–5, 33–5, 45–6, 93, 121, 123–4, 149
anti-colonial violence, 45–6, 53, 61, 148

architecture, 7, 138–41, 145
Armah, Ayi Kwei, *The Beautyful Ones Are Not Yet Born*, 7–8, 15–16, 22, 29, 39, 40, 73–4, 86–96, 150, 151–2, 154
Armes, Roy, 9, 26n, 75, 134
Asokan, Ratik, 103, 104
Ayuk, G. Ojong, 88
Azoulay, Ariella Aïsha, 46, 110

Baara see Work (Cissé)
Bagchi, Amiya Kumar, 62, 103
Balibar, Etienne, 30n, 122, 123, 138
Bandung *see* Afro-Asianism
Banerjee, Prathama, 36, 39
Beautyful Ones Are Not Yet Born, The (Armah), 7–8, 15–16, 22, 29, 39, 40, 73–4, 86–96, 150, 151–2, 154
Bernard, Anna, 36
Bhabha, Homi, 17–18
Bhambra, Gurminder, 14
Biswas, Moinak, 26
body, the *see* embodied experience
Boehmer, Elleke, 16, 30, 53–4, 56, 111, 116, 148
Bose, Anuja, 13, 18

Bose, Sugata, 109
Brass, Paul, 127
Brecht, Bertolt, 108
Brennan, Timothy, 28
Brown, Matthew H., 76
Brown, Nicholas, 22–3
Bruce-Lockhart, Katherine, 61
Buck-Morss, Susan, 38
Butler, Judith, 147

Cabral, Amílcar, 14, 77, 121, 149, 153
Cape Verde, 14, 149
capitalism
　anti-capitalism, 9–10, 102
　colonial, 64–8
　conspicuous consumption, 86–8, 92–3
　continuities with feudalism, 127–31
　exploitation of labour, 106–7, 135–8, 144–6
　exploitation of natural resources, 10, 29, 102, 111–13, 145–6, 152
　industrialisation, 14, 49, 63, 110, 127–31
　urban space and, 9–10, 30, 122–3, 135–8
　see also globalisation; neocolonialism
Casanova, Pascale, 124
Césaire, Aimé, 8, 13, 14, 21, 35, 46, 50, 121, 146, 150, 154
Chabot, Sean, 3, 19, 40, 47
Chakravarti, Sudeshna, 71
Chatterjee, Partha, 71, 104, 107
Chatterji, Joya, 98
Cherki, Alice, 48, 49, 59, 81
Chowdhury, Sayandeb, 105–6

Chrisman, Laura, 13, 18n
cinema
　African, 24–5, 133–4; *see also* Cissé, Souleymane; Sembène, Ousmane
　cinéma engagé, 74–6
　French, 26n, 134
　South Asian, 5, 24, 25–7; *see also* Ghatak, Ritwik; Ray, Satyajit
　Soviet, 24–5, 26, 75, 134
　Third Cinema, 24–6, 134n, 150
　World Cinema, 25–6, 150
Cissé, Souleymane, 24–5
　The Wind, 9, 136n, 143
　Work, 9–10, 13, 25, 30, 44, 122–3, 133–46, 152–3
Clare, Stephanie, 44, 61, 118
class
　African societies, 74n
　cross-class solidarities, 23, 30, 39, 110, 119
　Ghana, 92
　Kenya, 11, 13, 54, 58
　loss of class identity, 101–3, 106
　Mali, 136–7, 143
　Nigeria, 119
　Senegal, 9, 76–86
　South Asian societies, 64–70, 101–3; *see also* India: caste
　Third Cinema, 24
　see also labour; Marxism
clothing, 76–9, 142–3
Cloud-Capped Star, The (Ghatak), 6, 10, 13–14, 16, 24, 27, 29, 43, 98, 100–10, 115, 151, 152
Connerton, Paul, 125, 140
Cooppan, Vilashini, 89
Côte d'Ivoire, 134, 138, 143
Craggs, Ruth, 5, 12

INDEX 185

creative agency, 45–7, 72, 99–100, 116, 148
Cruz, Viriato da, 14

Dasgupta, Chidananda, 27, 101n, 108
Dasgupta, Sanjukta, 62
Dass, Manishita, 105
Davidson, Basil, 14, 149
'decolonising the mind', 3–4, 16, 34, 45–6, 50, 59, 60, 62, 71, 148, 150
Desai, Anita, 63n
Deshpande, Anirudh, 70
Deshpande, Satish, 135
Destination Biafra (Emecheta), 10, 16, 23, 29, 39–40, 98–9, 105, 109–20, 131, 150, 152
dialectic of self and world, 15–21, 36, 38–9, 43, 51–2, 54, 86–9, 124–5, 148
Diawara, Manthia, 9, 74, 134, 140, 141, 143
Diop, Omar Cherif, 84
Dirlik, Arif, 122, 140n, 141
Dovey, Lindiwe, 24n
Dunham, Jarrod, 8, 93

ecocriticism, 121, 146; *see also* feminism: ecofeminism
education
  class, 3, 64, 136
  colonial, 1–3, 18n, 72, 76, 113, 138
  women's, 70, 106–7, 128
Eisenstein, Sergei, 24n, 26, 75
El Alaoui, Khadija, 13
embodied experience, 3–4, 21, 40–5, 87, 90, 109, 123, 127, 129, 137–8, 149–50; *see also* place: embodied placemaking

Emecheta, Buchi, 102, 110, 118
  Destination Biafra, 10, 16, 23, 29, 39–40, 98–9, 105, 109–20, 131, 150, 152
everyday, the, 1, 15n, 21–7, 85, 91–3, 105, 109, 125, 134–5, 150–1
Eze, Emmanuel Chukwudi, 19

Fan, Bonnie, 108
Fanon, Frantz
  African literary responses to, 11, 53
  Black Skin, White Masks, 19, 36–8, 39, 40, 41, 47, 55, 88, 94
  colonial language, 80
  creative agency, 45–7, 72, 99–100, 116, 148
  critique of post-independence states, 13, 75, 76, 77
  decolonisation, 61, 64, 139, 149
  dialectic of self and world, 15, 19–21, 36, 38–9, 43, 51–2, 54, 88, 124–5, 148
  A Dying Colonialism, 3–4, 14, 32
  embodied experience, 40–4, 90, 109, 123, 127, 148
  the everyday, 15n, 21, 125, 134–5
  freedom, 37, 45, 46, 87, 118
  historical materialism, 35, 147
  historicity, 36–40, 99–100, 104, 148
  internationalism, 18
  legacies of colonialism, 2, 12, 13, 18–21, 32–4, 55, 76, 147–9, 153–4
  nation-building, 73
  practical action, 16, 47–50, 91, 96
  temporality of decolonisation, 54–5

Fanon, Frantz (*cont.*)
  Toward the African Revolution, 14, 77, 134–5
  treatment of subjectivities, 28
  The Wretched of the Earth, 38, 45, 46, 73, 91, 109, 113, 134–5, 138
feminism
  African, 118n
  ecofeminism, 125–7; *see also* ecocriticism
  feminist historiography, 107
  postcolonial, 17
  see also gender; women
Flatschart, Elmar, 126n
Foccart, Jacques, 141–2
Fofana, Amadou, 81
Foley, Barbara, 77–8
Fraiture, Pierre-Philippe, 17
Fraser, Robert, 92
Freire, Paulo, 20, 34
Freud, Sigmund, 20; *see also* psychoanalysis

Ganguly, Keya, 27
Gaztambide, Daniel José, 18, 20
gender
  gendered nationalisms, 27, 52–3, 59–62
  gendered space, 52, 62–4, 71, 144–6, 151
  gender relations in West Africa, 116–17
  see also feminism; masculinities; women
George, Rosemary Marangoly, 123–4
Ghana, 7–8, 22, 29, 39, 72, 74, 138
Ghare Baire see Home and the World (Ray)

Ghatak, Ritwik, 6, 27, 102–5, 108
  The Cloud-Capped Star, 6, 10, 13–14, 16, 24, 27, 29, 43, 98, 100–10, 115, 151, 152
  Subarnarekha, 103
globalisation, 2, 5–6, 16, 30, 44, 48, 64, 120, 122n, 131, 140–1, 152–3; *see also* capitalism; world-systems
Gopal, Priyamvada, 71, 124n, 133
Gordon, Lewis, 19, 36–7, 40, 42, 87
Grain of Wheat, A (Ngũgĩ), 1, 11, 15, 28–9, 45–6, 51–62, 64, 72, 150–1
Grosz, Elizabeth, 145
Gugler, Josef, 84
Guha, Ramachandra, 131, 133
Guha, Ranajit, 129
Guinea-Bissau, 14, 134n, 149

Hagan, George, 7
Hammond, Andrew, 53, 54
Harfouch, Ali S., 38, 47, 81
Harlow, Barbara, 40, 119
Harrington, Louise, 100
Harrow, Kenneth, 54
Hartnack, Christine, 98
Hazard, John, 143
Hegel, Georg Wilhelm Friedrich, 37–8, 151
Herbert, Daniel, 27
historicity of subjectivities, 36–40, 54–6, 99–100, 104, 148
history
  collective, 54–6
  cyclical, 88
  feminist historiography, 107
  gendered war historiography, 10, 39–40, 99–100, 110–20

nation-, 52, 98
　relationship with place, 121–3
　relationship with subjectivity, 59, 72, 79, 124, 151
　state-sanctioned historiography, 16, 40, 98–9, 109
　see also mythology; time
Home and the World (Ray), 6–7, 21, 24, 28–9, 51–3, 57, 61, 62–72, 150, 151
home/world dichotomy, 52, 62–72, 151
Hook, Derek, 4n, 148

India
　Bengali culture, 16, 26, 27, 63–9, 101n, 103–4, 108
　caste, 7, 66, 103, 106, 132–3; see also class: South Asian societies
　colonialism in, 2, 3, 18n
　decolonisation, 5–6, 27
　Emergency, 6–7, 64
　feudalism in, 66–8, 124, 127, 133
　industrialisation, 14, 21–2, 102–3, 105, 127–33
　state-sanctioned historiography, 16, 98–9, 109
　Swadeshi nationalism, 7, 52, 57, 61, 62–72
　Western reception of culture, 108, 123–4
　women, 63–4, 68–71, 106–8, 125–9
　see also Partition
Irele, Abiola, 95
Isabella, Brigitta, 30

Jabeen, Neelam, 126
Jain, Jasbir, 107
Jain, Sharda, 129

Jameson, Fredric, 75, 84, 88, 127–8, 131
Jayawardena, Kumari, 69n, 126
Jeyifo, Biodun, 2, 33–4
Juan, E. San, 18

Kakraba, Alexander Dakubo, 89, 90
Keïta, Modibo, 7, 140, 143
Kennedy, Ellen Conroy, 3
Kenya, 1, 10–11, 15, 33, 46, 51–62
Kesteloot, Lilyan, 3
Khanna, Neetu, 40–1
Khanna, Ranjana, 19–20, 21, 150
Kipfer, Stefan, 21, 123, 139
Konaré, Alpha O., 9, 140
Krishnan, Madhu, 10, 115, 138, 144
Kristensen, Lars, 24, 26, 150

labour
　colonial, 3–4, 32, 38
　industrialised/urban, 6, 9–10, 130–3, 135–8, 141–6, 152–3
　traditional/rural, 6, 83–6, 124–33, 141, 152
　see also capitalism; class; Marxism
Lambert, Laurie L., 50
land
　colonial occupation, 32, 58, 61
　constitution of subjectivity, 22, 83–6, 126–9, 131–3, 146, 152
　feudalism, 66–8, 124, 127, 133
　landscape, 22, 100–6
　redistribution, 9, 58
　theft, 8, 83–6
　woman–land association, 58, 125–7
　see also place
Langford, Rachael, 135, 138
language politics, 8, 75, 79–83, 152

Lazarus, Neil, 5–6, 22, 28, 31, 51, 88, 95, 129–30, 151; see also Warwick Research Collective
Lefebvre, Henri, 21, 135
Levich, Jacob, 107
Lugones, Maria, 70
Lukács, György, 9, 23
Lumumba, Patrice, 3
Lutz, John, 88, 92
Lynch, Kevin, 88

Macaulay, Thomas, 2
McCann, Gerard, 28n
Macey, David, 36
McGowan, Abigail, 66
Machiko, Oike, 110
McLuckie, Craig, 99
Maldonado-Torres, Nelson, 19, 72, 87, 91
Maldoror, Sarah, 9, 75
Mali, 7, 9–10, 122, 133, 134, 136, 138–9, 143, 145, 146, 153
Mannoni, Octave, 37
Markandaya, Kamala, 123–4, 146
  Nectar in a Sieve, 5–6, 14, 21–2, 23, 29–30, 48–9, 122–33, 146, 150–1, 152–3
Marks, Laura, 44, 137
Marriott, David, 12, 19, 38, 46, 50
Martín-Baró, Ignacio, 20
Martínez-Alier, Juan, 133
Marx, Karl, 4, 34–5, 84
Marxism, 4, 8, 18, 21, 34–5, 75, 134, 143, 148; see also class; labour
masculinities
  colonial, 46, 69
  Gĩkũyũ, 53–4, 57–8, 61–2
  Indian, 57, 71
  see also gender

'Mau Mau' uprising, 10–11, 52n, 53, 58, 59–61
Mazierska, Ewa, 24, 26, 150
Mbembe, Achille, 90, 94
Mbũgua wa Mũngai, 15n, 55
Meghe Dhaka Tara see *Cloud-Capped Star, The* (Ghatak)
Memmi, Albert, 81
Menon, Jisha, 102
Merleau-Ponty, Maurice, 41
Messier, Vartan, 75
Mills, Charles, 22
Minh-Ha, Trinh T., 83
Misra, Pravati, 128, 129
Mitra, Indrani, 69
Modernist architecture, 138–41
modernity, 77–8, 128–31, 140n
Mohanty, Satya P., 43
Mudimbe, V. Y., 17
Mufti, Aamir, 124
Mukherjee, Ankhi, 20, 37, 147
Mukherjee, Upamanyu Pablo, 122; see also Warwick Research Collective
Mungwini, Pascah, 17
Murphy, David, 8
Mwangi, Evan, 11, 60
Mwikisa, Peter, 54
mythology
  Christian, 53, 54, 55–6
  Gĩkũyũ, 15, 53, 54, 55
  Hindu, 129

Nagib, Lucia, 26
Namboodiripad, E. M. S., 107
Nandy, Ashis, 57, 71
Narayan, R. K., 123, 133
Nayar, Pramod K., 42–3, 90, 149n
Ndlovu-Gatsheni, Sabelo J., 147–8, 154

Nectar in a Sieve (Markandaya), 5–6, 14, 21–2, 23, 29–30, 48–9, 122–33, 146, 150–1, 152–3
Négritude movement, 8–9, 121n
Nehru, Jawaharlal, 6, 7, 30, 98, 99, 106
neocolonialism
    complicity in, 9, 76–9, 84, 89–90
    cultural, 133–4
    debt, 2, 3, 143
    definition, 12n
    land politics, 8–9, 58, 83–6, 127–33
    language, 8, 75, 79–83, 152
    patriarchy, 72, 102, 126, 144–5
    resistance to, 94–6
    resource extraction, 10, 29, 102, 111–13, 152
    time, 89–91
    unfinished decolonisation, 73–6, 95–6
    Western involvement post-independence, 2, 3n, 10, 35, 88, 91, 102, 119, 128
    see also capitalism
Ngũgĩ wa Thiong'o
    anti-colonial nationalisms, 15, 28–9, 72, 151
    collective histories, 54–6
    'decolonising the mind', 3–4, 16, 34, 45–6, 50, 59, 60, 62, 71, 148, 150
    Detained, 33n
    A Grain of Wheat, 1, 11, 15, 28–9, 45–6, 51–62, 64, 72, 150–1
    Homecoming, 14, 46
    language, 75, 83
    men's subjectivities, 46, 53–4, 57–8
    repression by postcolonial Kenyan state, 33
    women's subjectivities, 11, 46, 52–4, 56–62, 72, 151
    Writers in Politics, 83
Nicholls, Brendon, 53, 59, 61
Niemi, Minna, 88
Nigeria
    anti-colonial politics, 149
    Civil War, 5, 10, 16, 29, 39–40, 98–100, 110–20, 152
    neocolonial resource extraction, 10, 29, 102, 111–13, 152
    state-sanctioned historiography, 40, 98
    women, 39–40, 99–100, 110–20, 152
Nixon, Rob, 120, 133
Nkrumah, Kwame, 7–8, 14, 86, 87, 90, 152
Nnolim, Charles, 56

O'Brien, Donal Cruise, 80
Ochieng, W. R., 58
Ogot, Bethwell A., 11, 58, 60
Okuyade, Ogaga, 99
Olaniyan, Tejumola, 2
Opondo, Sam Okoth, 73, 85
Orrells, David, 17

pan-Africanism, 13, 25, 80–1, 139, 152n
Pandey, Gyanendra, 100, 109
Partition
    Bengal (1905), 62–3
    Subcontinent (1947), 6, 13–14, 16, 27, 43, 98–110, 133
place
    displacement, 6, 43, 100–6, 109–10, 116, 132–3

place (*cont.*)
  embodied placemaking, 123, 124–9, 139–40; *see also* embodied experience
  landscape, 26, 100–6, 126
  place memory, 125, 131–3, 140–1
  see also space
Prashad, Vijay, 127
Proctor, Hannah, 100, 119–20
psychoanalysis, 19–21

Quayson, Ato, 30, 42
Quigley, Lakshmi, 64

Radithalo, Sam, 57, 58
Ray, Sandip, 64
Ray, Sangeeta, 17
Ray, Satyajit, 26–7, 108
  Home and the World, 6–7, 21, 24, 28–9, 51–3, 57, 61, 62–72, 150, 151
Raychaudhuri, Anindya, 6, 16, 102, 106, 109
Read, Jason, 4, 34
realism, 21–7, 75, 95, 105, 108
Rosen, Philip, 24–5, 75
Roy, Srila, 61

Said, Edward, 20, 123, 124n
Salamon, Gayle, 41
Samaddar, Ranabir, 93
Sankara, Thomas, 3, 14, 33, 50, 148–9, 154
Sarkar, Sumit, 68–9, 70
Schwarz, Henry, 17
Sekyi-Otu, Ato, 17
Sembène, Ousmane, 8, 24–5, 74–6, 79–82, 85, 134
  Black Girl, 25, 76
  Le Mandat, 8
  Xala, 8–9, 13, 15, 29, 73–86, 87, 96, 113, 142, 151–2
Sen, Arijit, 123, 139–40
Sen, Mrinal, 5
Senegal, 7, 8–9, 15, 29, 133, 138, 139n, 143
Senghor, Léopold Sédar, 3, 8, 9
Sharifi, Majid, 3, 19, 40, 47
Sharma, Devika, 65
Sharma, Govind Narain, 56
Shohat, Ella, 12–13, 154
Silverman, Lisa, 123, 139–40
Simola, Raisa, 98
Smith, Étienne, 80
Sorensen, Eli Park, 22, 75, 150
Soviet cinema, 24–5, 26, 75, 134
space
  gendered space, 52, 62–4, 71, 144–7, 151
  postcolonial space, 121–2, 138–41
  spatial practices of capitalism, 44, 122–3, 130–1, 136, 138
  spatial practices of colonialism, 21–2, 121–3, 135, 138–9
  'worlded' space, 65–9, 142–3
  see also place
Szeman, Imre, 14, 15

Tagore, Rabindranath, 27, 62–3, 69n, 101, 104; *see also Home and the World* (Ray)
temporality
  of decolonisation, 54–5
  multiple, 39, 87, 89–91, 95
  see also time
terror effects, 106–8
textiles, 9, 65–7, 137–8, 141, 143
Third Cinema, 24–6, 150
time, 36–40, 89–91, 141; *see also*

historicity of subjectivities; history; temporality
Traoré, Moussa, 9, 141, 143
Tygstrup, Frederik, 65

Vieira, Marco, 48
violence
  anti-colonial, 45–6, 53, 61, 148
  capitalist, 120, 145
  colonial, 3–4, 46, 59, 100, 148, 152
  gendered, 46, 59, 107–8, 111, 116, 118, 145, 152
  in post-independence states, 10, 29, 98–100, 106, 114–18, 152

Wallerstein, Immanuel, 30n, 122, 123
Ward, Kathryn B., 131
Warwick Research Collective, 137
Wayne, Mike, 9
Weigel, Moira, 108
Werbner, Richard, 57, 58
Whyte, Susan Reynolds, 23n
Williams, Raymond, 65
Williams, Susan, 35n
Wintle, Claire, 12
women
  agency, 72, 110, 111, 116–19, 131–3

education, 70, 106–7, 128
  gendered violence, 46, 59, 107–8, 111, 116, 118, 145, 152
  knowledge of political events, 64, 111–14
  participation in independence movements, 10–11, 60–1, 71–2
  subjectivities unrealised by nationalisms, 7, 10–11, 28–9, 52–4, 56–62, 69–72, 151
  symbolic function, 56–9, 61, 63, 69, 116–19, 126, 129
  war historiography, 10, 39–40, 99–100, 110–20
  woman–land association, 58, 125–7
  see also feminism; gender
Work (Cissé), 9–10, 13, 25, 30, 44, 122–3, 133–46, 152–3
World Cinema, 25–6, 150
world-systems, 112, 122, 131–3, 141–2, 146, 153
Wright, Derek, 87n, 88, 89

Xala (Sembène), 8–9, 13, 15, 29, 73–86, 87, 96, 113, 142, 151–2

Young, Robert J. C., 1, 100, 106

Zeleny, Beth, 126, 129

EU representative:
Easy Access System Europe
Mustamäe tee 50, 10621 Tallinn, Estonia
Gpsr.requests@easproject.com

www.ingramcontent.com/pod-product-compliance
Lightning Source LLC
Chambersburg PA
CBHW051127160426
43195CB00014B/2368